Buster

153-196-EP7

Buster Crabbe

A Biofilmography

JERRY VERMILYE

McFarland & Company, Inc., Publishers

Jefferson, North Carolina

ALSO BY JERRY VERMILYE
Ingmar Bergman: His Life and Films (McFarland, 2002; paperback 2006)

The present work is a reprint of the illustrated casebound edition of Buster Crabbe: A Biofilmography, *first published in 2008 by McFarland.*

Frontispiece: A hawk man's spear barely misses Flash Gordon (Buster Crabbe) who defiles the throne of the sky city king (Universal Pictures, 1936).

LIBRARY OF CONGRESS CATALOGUING-IN-PUBLICATION DATA

Vermilye, Jerry.
    Buster Crabbe : a biofilmography / Jerry Vermilye.
        p.   cm.
    Includes bibliographical references and index.

    ISBN 978-0-7864-9570-2 (softcover : acid free paper) ∞
    ISBN 978-0-7864-5180-7 (ebook)

    1. Crabbe, Buster, 1908– I. Title.
PN2287.C644V47   2014
791.4302'8092—dc22   2008016262
[B]

BRITISH LIBRARY CATALOGUING DATA ARE AVAILABLE

On the cover: Buster Crabbe in a publicity photograph, 1933 (Paramount Pictures)

Printed in the United States of America

McFarland & Company, Inc., Publishers
    Box 611, Jefferson, North Carolina 28640
        www.mcfarlandpub.com

For
Tom Cavanaugh
and
The Bay Street Studio,
where this book
was begun

Acknowledgments

The author wishes to express his gratitude to the following for giving so generously of their time to supply information, research material and pictorial matter—or for offering editorial advice, manuscript assistance, moral support and a conducive environment:

Michael Buckley, Jeff Carrier, Tom Cavanaugh, Priscilla Dibble, Bob Finn, Joe Frazzetta, Barry Gillam, Peter J. Hawke, Mary Huntington, Harry Jackson, Marcia McCreadie, Alvin H. Marill, Terence Murphy, James Robert Parish, Marion Ragsdale, Richard Seff, Dudley Stone, Thom Toney, Allan Turner, Elizabeth Turner-Hall and the archives of *TV Guide*.

And a salute to all of the anonymous news, still and portrait photographers whose artistry illustrate these pages, as well as to the movie companies and releasing corporations who gave us the films of Buster Crabbe: Admiral Pictures, Columbia Pictures, Embassy Pictures, Grand Productions, Majestic Pictures, Mayfair Pictures, Monogram Pictures, Paramount Pictures, Peerless Pictures, Pine-Thomas Productions, Premiere Productions, Principal Distributing Corp., Producers Releasing Corp., RKO Radio Pictures, Rearguard Productions, Republic Pictures, Sol Lesser Productions, 20th Century–Fox Pictures, United Artists, Universal Pictures, Ventura Productions, Vogue Pictures, and Warner Bros. Pictures.

Table of Contents

Preface

Buster Crabbe. Mention his name today, and although you might have to establish that you're not talking about comedian Buster *Keaton*, chances are that there'll be a question like "Buster Crabbe: Didn't he play Tarzan?" Of course, Crabbe *did* portray that celebrated jungle hero, but only *once* (unlike his early swimming rival, Johnny Weissmuller, who made a vine-swinging film career out of that portrayal), and that once was in an obscure 12-chapter 1933 serial that now exists only in a poorly edited feature film, available on DVD and videocassette. At the very least, this volume will clarify Buster Crabbe's minor identification with Tarzan; at most, it will also offer an insight into a lengthy career in areas of show business sometimes considered unworthy of record.

Buster Crabbe's chief claim to fame, aside from his Olympic gold medal (for the 400-meter freestyle event in 1932), rests in the trio of movie serials (1936, 1938 and 1940) in which he brought to screen life the popular science-fiction hero Flash Gordon, as originally created by comic strip artist Alex Raymond in the early thirties. In fact, Crabbe's prolific chapterplay output and identification with the Flash Gordon character crowned his achievements in the motion picture field. No other male actor ever equaled his record of nine starring roles in the genre of talkie serials.

A lifelong swimmer, Crabbe kept himself in admirable physical shape throughout a multi-faceted career that ranged from Hollywood films to water shows to summer camps for young people, and from TV to Wall Street. His lifetime interest in physical fitness led him frequently to travel to lecture on that subject.

Still robust in his sixties, he wrote a book on calisthenics called *Energistics*. And he lent his name to a maker of swimming pools, an affiliation still active at the time of Crabbe's sudden death of a heart attack in 1983.

Buster Crabbe's 75 years took him from teenage swim champ to college student to film actor to TV star to businessman. Initially, the movie money served to finance his law studies—until it became apparent that acting had superseded his intended career as a lawyer. He played action heroes and mustachioed villains, and he rode a lot of horses in B-Westerns. And, when TV became more lucrative for him than movies, Crabbe first hosted a children's show, then starred with his young son Cuffy in a long-running adventure series, *Captain Gallant of the Foreign Legion.*

This is the first book from a mainstream publisher to tell the complete story of this handsome icon of physical culture and action-oriented movies, including casts, credits, and discussions of his 103 feature films and serials.

It is hoped that this volume will inform and entertain those with an interest not only in water sports, but also the motion picture genres of serials and program Westerns. Finally, it will answer the question: Who was the "other" Buster?

The Biography

Late in his half-century film career, Buster Crabbe lamented that he'd never made a grade-A motion picture—which was true. And although he claimed to have filmed over 175 movies (perhaps including episodes of his 1950s TV series *Captain Gallant of the Foreign Legion*), the actual number was 103. Mention his name today, and chances are that the connective factor will be the actor's long association with Flash Gordon, the comic strip hero created by Alex Raymond in 1934, or his short alliance to Tarzan, whom he portrayed in an obscure 1933 serial.

The original 13-episode *Flash Gordon* serial, produced in 1936 by Universal Pictures, proved so popular that it fostered two sequels, produced in 1938 and 1940. These sci-fi chapterplays prolonged Crabbe's fame when they reached nostalgia-minded TV audiences in 1951—and again in 1973. And they served as a reminder that, as the star of no less than nine movie serials, Crabbe was the undisputed king of that long-abandoned black-and-white cinema genre.

Unique to his career is the fact that Crabbe remains the only actor to have portrayed the three most popular pulp fiction heroes of the thirties: Buck Rogers, Flash Gordon and Tarzan.

He was born in Oakland, California, on February 7, 1908, and was named Clarence Linden Crabbe, for his grandfather. His only sibling, a brother who arrived a year later, was christened Edward Clinton Simmons Crabbe, Jr., after their father, who proceeded to dub Clarence "Buster" and Edward "Buddy"—nicknames that would stay with the two boys into adulthood.

Buster always claimed one-sixteenth native Hawaiian heritage, attributable to a seafaring ancestor, Captain John Meek, originally from Massachusetts, who married a "native girl" in the 1820s and settled in the Islands. One of their offspring, a daughter named Elizabeth, grew up to wed an American seaman, one Horace Gates Crabb, who later chose to add a final "e" to his surname "for reasons no one knows," as Buster once told an interviewer.

In 1861, their union produced a son, the first Clarence Linden Crabbe, who would migrate to the States in his early twenties to seek a job in the burgeoning railroad business. Employment opportunities were then slim in Oahu. Clarence Crabbe not only found work in Nevada, but also Emma Rich, whom he married in 1881 before siring Buster's father, Edward, a year later. But four years in desolate Nevada motivated Crabbe to relocate his little family to Hawaii, where he later served in the Senate.

Young Edward grew up and attended schools in the Islands, but eventually left for the mainland and the University of California at Berkeley. However, higher learning failed to hold his interest, and he forsook college to marry Agnes McNamara in 1907 and settle into an initially successful real estate partnership in the San Francisco Bay area. In 1913, Crabbe's business partner unexpectedly cleaned out their corporate bank account and disappeared, leaving the destitute family of four with only one recourse—retreat to Hawaii, where the senior Crabbes could help them start over again. For Edward, it meant going home; for Agnes and her two young sons, it marked the start of an exciting new life as they moved into Buster's grandparents' big house on the island of Oahu. In later years, Buster would always consider the Islands his true home.

With life in Hawaii also came a proximity to outdoor sports, especially swimming. Waikiki in 1913 had not yet become the tourist destination it is today, so it boasted but one hotel, The Moana, and that stretch of sandy beach with its shallow waters became a vast and uncrowded playground for Buster, Buddy and their growing circle of friends. As Buster recalled, "I learned to swim by standing on a shallow sandbar—waist deep, waiting for the waves to lift and carry me a few feet forward. I was too young to think about proper form. I only wanted to be like the others, able to play in deep water and dive through the waves."

Not that their mother and Grandmother Emma weren't solicitous of the boys' beach activities. Recalled Buster, "As we became more comfortable in the water, they became less worried about our well-being and allowed us the freedom to go and come as we pleased. It was a child's paradise."

Edward Crabbe found employment as foreman at the Libby, McNeil & Libby pineapple plantation in Oahu, and moved his family into the small plantation house that went with his new position. Without proximity to the beach, the boys had little chance to practice their water sports. One year later their father left the pineapple business for a return to real estate, and the Crabbe family moved again, this time 200 miles away from Oahu, to the island of Hawaii and its biggest city, Hilo. When their father joined the local yacht club, Buster and Buddy again enjoyed swimming privileges. Their itinerant living patterns had prevented the boys from having a proper schooling, and Agnes Crabbe took steps to change all that. Buster was thus all of eight-and-a-half when he belatedly entered the first grade at Hilo Union School.

Nothing would remain stable for the Crabbe family. With the outbreak of World War I, Edward volunteered for the Army, and after his graduation from officer's candidate school in 1918, he was able to move his wife and sons into officers' quarters at Schofield Barracks in the middle of Oahu. Once again situated far from a beach, Buster and Buddy substituted riding for their beloved swimming, since their father now had charge of the cavalry horses. And they attended Honolulu Military Academy.

With Edward's discharge from service in 1920, the family moved to Honolulu, where the Crabbe marriage, already weakened by Edward's preoccupation with military service, further disintegrated. Unexplained absences on the part of Agnes Crabbe finally culminated in divorce, and it was understood that another man was the cause. Edward was granted custody of his sons, who went to live with their Honolulu grandparents. Emma now became their surrogate mother, remembered by Buster as a "wonderful person, a sweet lady who was rarely without a smile."

When he was 12, Buster's aquatic skills so impressed George "Dad" Center, the swimming coach at Honolulu's Outrigger Canoe Club, that he asked the boy to join his team. But Edward Crabbe refused his permission, deeming Buster too young for such strenuous activity. Three years later, however, the 15-year-old joined his school's ninth-grade swim team and got his first taste of the excitement of competition, placing third in the 100-yard interscholastic event.

In 1923, the boys' father was appointed prohibition administrator for Maui, forcing him to move away to that island in the Hawaiian chain. Buster and Buddy now became even closer to their supportive grandparents. Buster joined the Outrigger Club, and began serious training under the guidance of Coach Center, who corrected some of the faults in the lad's self-taught swimming style. In addition to the usual high-school "ball" sports, Buster swam in as many meets as he could handle.

At 16, the boy landed his first regular job: summer employment with the Oahu firm of C. Brewer & Company, which dealt in island crafts. But what he really wanted was to be a part of the swim team representing Hawaii in Stateside competitions. His big hero was the Islands' super water champion, Duke Kahanamoku. Buster was inspired to reflect upon his own teenage swimming skills, realizing that his best achievements to date were in long-distance events. He now focused on strengthening his endurance in the water, improving his speed and power. Dedicated to the improvement of his style, he filled his non-working summer hours with constant exercise and practice. Hardly a day passed that Buster didn't work out for at least an hour. Buddy too competed in their school's swim meets, but his best efforts were in the short-distance events.

In June of 1926, when Buster was 18, a team from Japan challenged Hawaii in a swimming competition. The Islanders lost to their challengers, with Buster placing third in one of his events. Although the Hawaiians were badly defeated, their Japanese competitors were impressed enough to invite them to Japan for a second match. That competition was held in August, with both Crabbe teenagers participating. Once again, the Islanders were defeated, although not as badly this time. Buster placed second in two events and third in another, with the confident knowledge that he had performed well and with great improvement over his showing earlier that summer. Also, he felt that he had learned much from studying the style and technique of the Japanese team members.

The following year, Buster's final one in high school, he captained the Academy's swim team, graduating with four letters in varsity sports. And, of course, he excelled at swimming. As he later recalled to biographer Karl Whitezel: "Coming into the Hawaiian AAU trials from a strong season made it easy for me to win an invitation to the nationals that were held in Honolulu in 1927. I trained hard, preparing for the middle- and long-distance events ... I was 19 years old, and whatever I was to become as a swimmer, it had to come soon or I'd outgrow the competitive edge that youthfulness gave me."

The nationals were held in June, inaugurating Honolulu's new, state-of-the-art War Memorial Auditorium's 110-yard pool, dedicated to those lost in the Great World War. In the opening event, young Buster Crabbe won the mile in 21 minutes and 52 seconds: "I was less than two seconds away from the national record, held by Arne Borg, of 21.50 and a fraction."

Winning his first national title, he realized that he'd already qualified for the 1928 nationals in San Francisco. "Just knowing I'd won my first title against outstanding competition filled me with uncontrollable joy," he told his biographer. "I fell backward in the water with outstretched arms, as an expression of gratitude."

The following day of competition pitted him for the first time against American swimming champ Johnny Weissmuller, who had already won a trio of gold medals in the 1924 Olympics—an intimidating prospect for Buster. This was the 440-yard freestyle event, which meant four laps in the building's 110-yard pool. In Buster's words, "[Weissmuller] was terrifically strong, and I knew I didn't have much chance of beating him by the time

BC (at left) with unidentified friend, brother Buddy and Johnny Weissmuller in 1928 (Terence Murphy collection).

the race was half over. By the end of the final lap, he had beaten me and the rest of the field by a good 20 yards."

On the following day, Buster came in second to veteran AAU swimmer Walter Spence in the 330-yard individual medley, which consisted of doing 110 yards each in the backstroke, the breast stroke and the freestyle (American crawl). On the final day, once more swimming against Weissmuller, among others, Crabbe scored a close second to that celebrated mainlander in the half mile. His summation: "In my first outdoor national, I'd won a swimming title and came only one point away from tying the great Johnny Weissmuller for the high-point medal. It was enough for a 19-year-old Hawaiian to live on for months."

That August, a third visit to Japan resulted in a narrow victory for the Islanders, with Buddy Crabbe winning his first 50- and 100-meter events and Buster scoring first in his customary longer-distance races.

Buster entered his freshman year at the University of Hawaii, having determined to study law as a career. The youth was inspired by his summer employment at C. Brewer & Company: "I felt comfortable in the framework of discipline." Once he might pass his bar exam, he was promised a job by Brewer's lawyer, Jack Gault. Based on his athletic talents, Buster was offered an academic scholarship by Yale University. Only his tuition would be covered, but he figured he could fill in with odd jobs. After all, Yale was then celebrated for its swim team. A second educational opportunity followed, this time that of an appointment to West Point. Meanwhile, the imminent outdoor nationals in San Francisco required the focus of his attention.

They were held at the gigantic Fleishhacker Pool, west of the Bay City's downtown area, and near the beach. It was an important meet, drawing the bulk of America's Olympic hopefuls, and Buster and his Hawaiian teammates made a point of being there two weeks ahead of time to get accustomed to the pool and the "foreign" climate.

As that competition began, Johnny Weissmuller easily won the 110, while Buster took the mile in just over 58 seconds. Weissmuller was then 24—to Crabbe's 20—and in his athletic prime when the two swam against one another once again in the 440. Buster later recalled a close finish with his competitor winning "by the length of his hand." And, he added, "Had the course been two yards longer, I know I'd have taken him."

Two days later he was to swim against his rival in the 880, and somehow Buster knew that he could win. As they rested in the water at the end of the 440, he quipped to the champ, "You know, John, this race was a little short for me. But I'll see you on Sunday at the 880." Weissmuller's response was as serious-toned as it proved enigmatic: "Kid, I'll never swim

Swimming competitor BC at the 1928 Olympics (Terence Murphy collection).

with you again." And he never did; the two had competed for the last time. The following day, Weissmuller inexplicably left town—and the competition, and Buster took both the high-point medal and two national titles. He also won the 330-yard individual medley, breaking a record in the process.

Having thus qualified for the Olympic tryouts to be held in Detroit, Buster parted company with his brother, whose failure to win had eliminated him from further Olympic possibilities. Buddy returned home to Hawaii, and Buster made a good showing in Detroit, taking both the 400- and 1500-meter events, and became one of six teammates chosen for the 8-meter relays. The Olympic swimmers headed for New York, en route to sailing for Europe and the Amsterdam games. Buster then had an opportunity to visit New Haven and the Yale campus, where his team swam in exhibition, and he got to meet Coach Bob Kiphuth—"A great guy, a real gentleman"—all of which helped him decide on attending Yale over West Point.

The Olympic experience did not turn out well for Buster. First he contracted influenza during the Atlantic crossing, which prevented his working out with the swim team. And by the time his health had improved, the 185-pound six-footer had lost over 10 pounds and much of his normal athletic strength. Regaining that would take time; and when he arrived in Amsterdam, Buster had gained back only 90 percent of his power. At the close of the Olympics he was almost himself again, with his best performance in the 800-meter freestyle, where he captured a bronze medal for third place.

Having now set his academic sights on Yale, Buster joined some of his teammates for a swim tour of European cities before the start of college. Arriving at Yale, he found himself, at 20, two years older than most of his freshman classmates, although he was respected for his Olympic achievements. Two weeks into his first semester, a telegram from his father presented Buster with a major dilemma: His beloved Grandma Emma, who had long been a second mother to him and Buddy, was dying. Indecision gave him pause. Should he make the long journey home to Hawaii, in hopes that he would see her again before it was too late? Or should he honor his commitments to education, athletics and his Yale scholarship? Coach Kiphuth urged him to return home. He was never to return to Yale, for Emma Crabbe lingered on until the following March. Although Buster had attended the University of Hawaii in an attempt to keep up with his college education, Yale now informed him that he could return to resume with his scholarship there only if he were to begin over again as a freshman. It appeared that there were different standards between Yale and lesser institutions of higher learning. Their condition was one that Buster (at 21) found unacceptable, and so he tried to enroll at Stanford, another scholarship-offering university with a respected law school—only to be faced with the same stipulation as Yale. While he mulled his future possibilities, Buster and Buddy passed the summer of 1929 at Waikiki, working as lifeguards and swimming teachers, but mostly just enjoying the beach.

That summer, a chance meeting with a vacationing Southern Californian named Adah Virginia Held led to a few movie dates for Buster and an exchange of addresses. Buster surely couldn't have known then what an important role Virginia (as she was called) would have in his future.

In midsummer a letter from the University of Southern California miraculously arrived when Buster Crabbe most needed it. On the basis of his Olympic swimming, he was offered a scholarship that would pay for his tuition and, most importantly, they'd accept him as an advanced sophomore. At USC, he wouldn't have to face four *more* years of college.

Buster and Buddy sailed in late July for San Francisco and the outdoor nationals with their Outrigger Canoe Club, at that city's now-familiar Fleishhacker Pool. Once again in top shape at 21, Buster took first place in four events, setting two national records and winning the high-point gold medal. In fact, of the 23 points won by the Hawaiian team, he alone was responsible for 21! Buddy and their fellow swimmers returned home, where Buddy planned to study agriculture at the University of Hawaii, while Buster headed to USC. To help support himself, he found part-time work at Silverwood's in downtown Los Angeles, "pushing cartons around in the basement for eight dollars a week." With little time to enjoy its benefits, he also joined the Sigma Chi fraternity. Buster's spare time, such as it was, was occupied with water sports under the guidance of Coach Fred Cady, who made him an integral part of USC's first swimming team. His non-academic objective: to stay in shape for the indoor and outdoor nationals, as well as the AAU and the NCAA championships, all scheduled for the spring and summer of 1930.

Despite his busy academic and athletic schedules, Buster lost no time in contacting Virginia Held and renewed their friendship with weekend trips to the beach.

The star athlete was initially introduced to movie acting when Metro-Goldwyn-Mayer sent out a casting call to USC in search of young men to perform as extras in the college-set "all-singing, all-dancing" musical *Good News*, in which one must look hard to find him as a pipe-smoking student.

Athletically, 1930 proved a winning year for Crabbe. In Chicago's late-winter indoor nationals, he earned a trio of first-place medals and set as many records. He continued his winner's streak that summer at California's Long Beach outdoor nationals, where he broke existing records in the mile, half-mile and medley events, taking home the meet's high-point medal.

Buster found additional movie work in Columbia's 1931 football picture, *The Maker of Men*. An assistant director on the film offered him valuable advice when he urged: "Get in close to the people starring in the scenes. That way, if they have a callback to re-shoot the scene, they'll have to call you back, too." The tip paid off for the novice extra when his several days of prom-ised employment developed into a 16-day paycheck of $160. In addition, Buster had his first speaking role with the enigmatic line, "It's tough, coach." Uncertain how to deliver those three words, he sought out the picture's star, Jack Holt, who played the coach. Holt's advice: "Don't make a big thing of it. Just say the words." Buster remembers enjoying the experience, while congratulating himself that he didn't have to do this for a living!

He continued to set swimming records with the USC team, receiving his Bachelor of Science degree in June of 1931; that done, he focused his thoughts on the next year's Olympic Games, for which he'd need funding. To help him out, Virginia's Aunt Adah Dolson offered Buster a spare bedroom in her Los Angeles home, while a friend got him a top salesman's job at the Pacific Mutual Insurance Company. Also, he managed to obtain several bit parts at Columbia and Paramount. Buster branched into stunt work when he doubled for Joel McCrea in *The Most Dangerous Game* at RKO in 1931. He was offered $30 to dive, dressed as the star, from the upper deck of a yacht just as it exploded, and to swim ashore. Because of the explosive device, timing was obviously vital to the safety of those involved, and everything went off successfully.

A casting call went out from MGM to the USC student union seeking a dozen college boys for the football movie *Huddle*. Ramon Novarro starred as a gridiron hero being cheered on by his classmates amid a pregame torchlight parade. Buster's assignment was to shout and wave at Novarro, along with the assemblage of other "student" extras. In the acting novice's recollections: "Since we were being paid $7.50 for a few hours of fun, it seemed like highway robbery to me when compared to Silverwood's paying me almost the same amount for a full week's work." In addition to that afternoon's scenes, the USC lads were promised more work the following day, and the notion of getting the equivalent of nearly two *weeks'* pay for two *days'* work thrilled Buster. Unfortunately, during rehearsals a fellow extra convinced him to shout a few derogatory words in Spanish to Novarro as he passed, immediately inflaming the star's Latin temperament. Unaware of the insulting English translation, Buster was summarily fired from the movie.

Despite the Novarro blunder at MGM, where Virginia's father was a film editor, his luck appeared to be improving. The studio was then preparing to produce its first Tarzan movie, and Tom Held urged Buster to test for the title role—one for which a number of well-known actors were already being considered. Frank Merrill, the screen's then-most-recent portrayer of the legendary jungle hero, had retired from the part and Metro was now inclined to cast an athletic newcomer, rather than a familiar screen face. As a law student without motion picture ambitions, who had only spoken a few words on screen heretofore, Buster had very mixed feelings about pursuing a major movie role like Tarzan. Nevertheless, because Virginia's father had gone to bat for him with the studio, he submitted to a succession of photographic tests and readings. Hollywood scuttlebutt indicated that the part would likely go to Johnny Weissmuller, which it did. But even if Tarzan had been offered to him at that time, Buster doubted that he would have accepted. Not if it had meant pre-empting his Olympic prospects and a possible gold medal. Also, he still had his sights on a career in law, not the performing arts.

April, 1932 found him back in New Haven, Connecticut, where he took three titles in the AAU swimming championships, including the 440-

Swim champ BC at Yale's Carnegie Pool in March 1932 (author's collection).

yard free-style, the mile and the medley. As a top prospect for Olympic triumphs, Buster Crabbe couldn't have felt better prepared.

August brought the Los Angeles Olympic trials and he experienced some concern about his competition, especially those from Japan, whose swimmers were then considered the world's finest. Buster studied closely the leading contenders' styles, noting their strong and weak points. Those present to root him on included Virginia, his USC pals, and Crabbe senior from Hawaii. In the 400-meter freestyle, Buster was the sole American entrant in that event, with three of Japan's best swimmers his most serious competition. The Japanese were also favorites with many of the spectators, who nevertheless remained supportive of their lone native son—especially when Crabbe scored a 4:48:40 win to take the gold in the 400-meter freestyle. His closest runner-up: none of the Japanese contenders, but rather France's Jean Taris, who scored a close 4:48:50. Buster won by a mere tenth of a second, setting a new world record! Spectator Johnny Weissmuller came by to congratulate him, but the new champ's fondest memory was that of his father leaning over the pool's edge to kiss him on the cheek. And, he recalled, "I wore a faceful of smiles for the newsreel cameras that recorded my comments for Movietone News."

To please his coach, who needed a swimmer for the 1500-meter freestyle, Buster agreed to compete, although at 24 he felt ill-equipped to score. And sure enough, he came in fifth, with the Japanese taking both first and second place. In fact, Buster Crabbe's gold medal was the only one taken by a male swimmer in the 1932 Olympics. It identified him as a sports celebrity of international renown. However, the swimmer was now ready to put that sport behind him to concentrate on completing his studies and establishing a career—in law.

Along with Buster's Olympic triumph, the summer of 1932 also brought new fame to Johnny Weissmuller as the star of MGM's adventure picture, *Tarzan the Ape Man.* It wasn't his film debut; that had occurred three years earlier with Paramount's *Glorifying the American Girl,* a musical extravaganza which also briefly glorified Weissmuller's swimmer's physique. As Edgar Rice Burroughs' fictional jungle hero, the former swim champ would achieve an immortal association with that one character, affording him a succession of Tarzan sequels spanning the next 16 years. Buster Crabbe would eventually achieve a sort of parallel identification with one mythological superhero, but with a far more varied screen future.

As a folk hero, Tarzan's cultural popularity dated back to his initial appearance in Burroughs' 1912 pulp fiction novel and a 1918 silent film starring barrel-chested Elmo Lincoln. The original movie's success had inspired two silent serials and such obvious publishing imitations as Charles Stone-

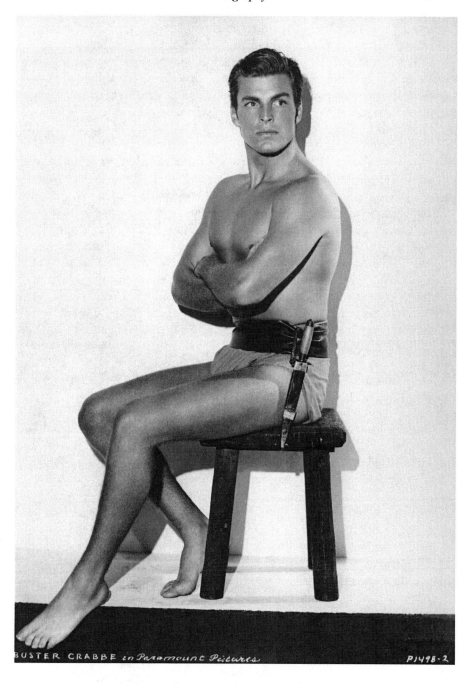

BC in a publicity pose for *King of the Jungle* (Paramount Pictures, 1933).

ham's novel *The Lion's Way*, which Paramount now adapted for the screen in a blatant bid to attract the audiences that had readily embraced Metro's recent Weissmuller vehicle. Amid his Olympic preparations, Buster had tested for the Kaspa role at Paramount several times. With the knowledge that they were also auditioning other candidates, as well as his constant pre-occupation with the 1932 Games, he had deliberately stifled any great expec-tations about the film—especially after losing out to Weissmuller in the Tarzan sweepstakes.

That October he received an unexpected call from Paramount still photographer John Engstead, requesting his presence at a sitting. In this roundabout fashion, Buster learned that he'd won the part of Kaspa, the Lion Man in the film to be called *King of the Jungle*. But thoughts of movie stardom failed to excite the fledgling actor; what did please him was the idea that this job would pay well enough to finance his post-graduate law stud-ies. And as for his theatrical inexperience in a major role, Buster reasoned that Paramount coaches would help him achieve professionalism. After all, the studio must know its business in assigning him the part.

Actually, Crabbe now had an agent: Morris Small of the Edward Small Agency, who had first taken an interest in him when word got out that this star swimmer was in the running for MGM's Tarzan. Consequently, Buster signed with Paramount for a year, with options to renew, should they be satisfied with his work. His salary was $100 a week, a sum he couldn't imag-ine making elsewhere in Depression-strapped 1932. Master lensman Eng-stead—later to be celebrated for his flattering soft-focus portraits of mature film actresses—shot a succession of pictures of Buster that fully captured his athletic good looks. Rumor had it that a group of Paramount secretaries had secured the Kaspa role for Crabbe by choosing his photo over those of the four other finalists.

While suitably flattered, Buster never quite believed that story: "I'm sure the primary reason I got the part was the Olympic gold medal I won. The fact that I was the only American swimmer to win gave me a lot of publicity around the country, and movie moguls were always masters of expediency."

Interestingly, it was decided that Buster's voice recorded at too high a pitch to match his hunky, macho image, so Paramount engaged a vocal coach to help him suitably deepen his speech.

Aside from being on-camera for most of *King of the Jungle*, Buster was required to perform opposite a trained lion named "Jackie" and handle a couple of love scenes—his first—with co-star Frances Dee, an experienced professional who taught him to relax and approach such challenging moments with ease. Most of the film was shot in four months on the studio lot, with location scenes filmed in Mexico and at El Monte, California, where its climactic circus fire sequence was created. Of its kind, the 1933 release was an entertaining programmer, and Buster Crabbe's performance, under the joint direction of H. Bruce Humberstone and Max Marcin, looked thoroughly professional. Had Buster wanted a full-fledged movie career, *King of the Jungle* seemed like an auspicious introduction to the Hollywood "big time." Helped by publicity, including trumped-up stories about an unfriendly rivalry between Crabbe and Weissmuller, *King of the Jungle* was a box-office success for Paramount. But the film would never be a serious challenge to the über-successful franchise that Metro had established with its Tarzan adventures and which that studio would successfully continue to churn out with Weissmuller for another decade.

Analyzing this experience in a mid–1960s *Kaleidoscope* magazine interview with editors Don Shay and Ray Cabana, Jr., Buster reflected: "It's a funny thing, you know—everybody would think that doing a Tarzan-type picture like *King of the Jungle* would be a good start in the picture business,

The cast of a studio theater stock company production of *Double Door* (Paramount Pictures) with (left to right) Julian Madison, Lona Andre, Alfred Delcambre, BC, Barbara Fritchie, John Engstead, Ida Lupino, Gwenllian Gill, Colin Tapley, Eldred Tidbury and Clara Lou (later renamed Ann) Sheridan.

but actually, it wasn't at all. They looked basically for a guy who looked well with very little on and was fairly athletic and handled himself well physically. There were a few words of dialogue—'Me Tarzan, you Jane' sort of thing. That's fine. So you go ahead and make the film. Then, all of a sudden, you're through. The film goes out. It does well. You're established as an actor—so-called. But the parts are few and far between. If you have more than three or four words to say at one time, they look at you in a different light. What they don't go into is your background. I was a college guy—fairly intelligent—but that didn't make any difference at all. If they needed a guy to sit around a swimming pool in a pair of swimming trunks and to look good, but not talk too much, fine; I did the part."

With his new-found financial stability, Buster now felt confident enough to take on marriage, and he and Virginia were wed on April 13, 1933. Following a two-week honeymoon, he reported to Paramount for his first follow-up assignment, a Western to be directed by Henry Hathaway. *Man of the Forest* starred Randolph Scott, and this time Buster's status as a mere contract player was confirmed by his brief supporting role as a cow-

BC grins for the Paramount portrait photographer in 1933.

boy henchman with no lines to speak. The completed film's publicity made no mention of Crabbe—until its producer requested retakes from director Hathaway. To cash in on his chesty appearance in *King of the Jungle*, a brief and farcical scene was added in a wintry cabin setting in which Buster, unaccountably stripped to the waist, shared conversation with actor Barton MacLane, with the latter directing him to "Throw more wood on the fire." Buster now had the single line, "Okay, boss"—one word less than he'd had in his *Maker of Men* bit two years earlier. And yet, Buster recalled,

At the Santa Monica Canyon home of producer Sol Lesser in 1933: Actor George O'Brien and his actress-wife Marguerite Churchill with BC and Virginia Crabbe (author's collection).

Paramount's revised ad campaign for *Man of the Forest* now featured the sidebar slogan, "also starring the *King of the Jungle* star, Buster Crabbe."

The novice movie star now found himself required to attend acting classes, along with Paramount's other young contract players, coached by Phyllis Loughton. "It was more like an actors' workshop, where we could practice reading lines or ask questions. We could study different techniques, play different characters in little skits and learn how to play our best sides to the camera—anything that would ease us out of our amateurism into passable professionals."

Buster also remembered learning by studying the acting styles and techniques of such fellow Paramount pros as Fredric March, Akim Tamiroff and J. Carrol Naish. He also enjoyed the invaluable experience of performing in fully rehearsed and costumed stage plays in the studio's own little theatre.

On the heels of *Man of the Forest* came yet another Zane Grey B-Western, *To the Last Man*, reuniting the star-director team of Randolph Scott and Henry Hathaway. It was the first major studio feature to employ five-year-old Shirley Temple a year before her big break in 1934's Fox musical, *Stand Up and Cheer*. Buster's role was bigger than in the earlier film, though equally unimportant to this story about a post–Civil War feud. It didn't take him long to realize that this was Paramount's method of keeping his face before the public, rather than challenging him as an actor. By way of "grooming" him, the studio afforded contract players like Buster the opportunity of reading for bigger parts in upcoming Paramount productions—most of which he didn't get. But Buster knew when he'd read well, and it strengthened his confidence in his potential thespian talents.

Independent film producer Sol Lesser, who had earlier acquired the rights to Tarzan from author Edgar Rice Burroughs, delayed production of his Principal Pictures project because MGM had reached the screen earlier with its 1932 Weissmuller vehicle. Additionally, Lesser had to contend with the stipulation that he star Burroughs' son-in-law, James Pierce, an actor who had portrayed the legendary ape-man in a 1927 silent feature, *Tarzan and the Golden Lion*, and more recently on radio, but whom Lesser now considered too out-of-shape for the role. By offering Pierce the sum of $5,000 and a screen test for another picture, Lesser got the actor to waive all rights to recreate Tarzan for the planned movie. Lesser had tried unsuccessfully to pry Weissmuller loose from MGM; failing that, and cognizant of Paramount's Tarzan-like *King of the Jungle*, he reached an agreement with that studio to borrow Buster for his own production, which would be titled *Tarzan the Fearless*.

Lesser's idea was to distribute the project as a 12-chapter serial. Eventually, he decided on a unique release plan: re-edit the first four episodes into feature-length, and create a trailer promoting the remainder of the story, to be shown serially over the following eight weeks. The industry's *Film Daily* hailed this as an "innovation in the presentation of serials." However, not all theatres elected to show the promotional trailer, nor did they screen the subsequent serial episodes. Buster readily agreed to visit a number of key cities to help publicize *Tarzan the Fearless*, but its corner-cutting production values worked against its success, and Principal Pictures could do little to disguise that fact. *Tarzan the Fearless* marked Crabbe's first visit to Hollywood's so-called "Poverty Row" breeding ground of low-budget features. It wouldn't be his last.

Buster was also loaned to minor-league Monogram Pictures that year as the athletic male lead opposite blonde Mary Carlisle in the college-sports drama, *Sweetheart of Sigma Chi*, inspired by a popular song of the day.

Amid the Depression, Crabbe was at least gainfully employed, although he still considered Hollywood moviemaking a temporary diversion to his goal of a legal career. As he later recalled: "I made six films in 1933, and managed to save $3,700 from my salary. Whatever happened to my film career as my option expired, I was ready for law school."

As the year neared its end, Buster was called in to a conference with Paramount's head honcho Adolph Zukor, who announced plans to pick up the actor's contract for a second year, adding, "We're boosting your weekly salary to $150, and you should be making a lot more before long." They would be words to reflect on later.

Buster recalled signing that contract with a mixture of surprise and relief: "While a lot of my movie work wasn't what you'd call outstanding, I did make three movies where I was the leading man and three where I played bit parts under Randolph Scott. I thought that maybe if I put greater effort into my acting during the upcoming year, there might be something to this motion picture business, after all. It wasn't that I didn't work hard on the lot, but I still had it in my mind that, win or lose, I was going to be a lawyer, not an actor."

Zukor also brought up a question as to the actor's professional name, suggesting that "Buster" was suitable for a boy, but not for a leading man. He suggested that they try "Larry Crabbe," testing it on a few of his 1934 movies. So as not to lose his former identity altogether, Buster advocated going with "Larry 'Buster' Crabbe" as a compromise. Zukor agreed.

During this period, Buster kept up his swimming by working out with the water polo team at the Los Angeles Athletic Club. At 26, he could compete in a medley race on an amateur basis, but the distance races—as he once had swum them—were now beyond him, due to a lapse in his speed and buoyancy.

In 1934, the actor appeared in six more movies, although only two were for Paramount: *Search for Beauty*, in which he had the male lead opposite a platinum-blonde Ida Lupino in her first American picture; and *You're Telling Me*, a W. C. Fields vehicle with Buster cast as the love interest for Fields' on-screen daughter, Joan Marsh. The studio toyed with the idea of teaming Buster again with Lupino in *Come On Marines!* before casting Richard Arlen instead. He fared only slightly better on loan to RKO (*We're Rich Again*); to Majestic (*She Had to Choose*); and to Mayfair (*Badge of Honor* and *The Oil Raider*). While Paramount now billed him as "Larry 'Buster' Crabbe," the other studios chose to stick with his Olympics—*King of the Jungle*—*Tarzan the Fearless* identity of simply "Buster Crabbe."

He spent most of 1935 studying scripts and watching other actors' work, in an effort to justify the studio's continued faith in his talents. Paramount renewed his contract for a third year, raising his salary to $300 a week while casting him in only three of that year's studio releases: another pair of Zane Grey programmers, *Nevada* and *The Wanderer of the Waste-land,* and the college-football comedy *Hold 'Em Yale.* There were no further loan-outs to lesser studios.

With few filming assignments, Buster took advantage of the opportunity to swim and get back into tiptop condition. With the 1936 Olympics

BC poses for *Flash Gordon* publicity (Universal Pictures, 1936).

on his horizon, he reasoned that he'd surely be a candidate for the American water polo team. By mistake, he cancelled those hopes by accepting $250 to pose in bathing trunks beside a pool for a Camel cigarettes ad that bore the slogan "Cigarettes don't affect my wind!" It seemed that the Amateur Athletic Union had rules against an athlete taking payment tied in with his/her athletic accomplishments. Because this was several years after his Olympic gold medal, Buster had, in his mind, only connected the ad with his screen career. But the AAU's disqualification had a domino effect, and the Olympic Committee ruled similarly. As an amateur athlete, Buster Crabbe's future lay behind him.

Buster had been encouraged by praise from Adolph Zukor and the promise that Paramount finally intended to cast him in an A-picture. He may have dreamt of appearing in a Carole Lombard, Mae West or Marlene Dietrich vehicle at the studio—or working with Cecil B. DeMille, Paramount's most celebrated director—but all he got was continued assignments to B-films and program Westerns. At 27, with his ideas about a law career now fading, Buster at least had money in the bank and a happy home life. On July 13, 1936, Virginia gave birth to their first child, a daughter they named Caren Lynn Crabbe, but soon to be known simply as "Sande."

In mid–1936, Buster read in a trade paper that Universal Pictures was in the process of preparing a multi-chaptered serial based on Alex Raymond's popular science-fiction strip, *Flash Gordon*, and were testing candidates for the title role. Because he was a Raymond fan and not then involved in any filmmaking, Buster contrived to get onto the Universal lot to watch the screen tests, whose best bets appeared to be two athletic small-part players named George Bergman and Jon Hall (soon to be cast in his breakthrough role in *The Hurricane*). Immediately recognized by the serial's producer, Henry MacRae, Buster was asked if he were there to audition. When he claimed to be merely an interested onlooker, he was instantly offered the role of Flash. Unable to visualize *Flash Gordon* as any kind of successful movie enterprise, Buster explained that he was under contract to Paramount, adding, "I don't know what plans they have for me."

MacRae's response was immediate: "We'll arrange to borrow you. The part is yours if you want it. Alex Raymond and I discussed the qualities to look for in casting the lead, and from what I've seen of your work, you fit the bill."

Buster allowed that the decision would be up to Paramount, but if they'd sanction the loan to Universal, he'd be happy to portray Flash. Years later, the actor recalled hoping that his studio would refuse the deal on the grounds that they had bigger things planned for him. But Paramount was agreeable to the loan; an arrangement, as it turned out, that would grant Buster Crabbe movie immortality.

In an era without the benefits of today's digital special effects, and automation, the serial's sets and fantastic visuals were considered state-of-the-art, especially for Universal, Hollywood's then-leading studio for horror and science fiction. This super-serial is variously reported to have cost as little as $350,000—and as much as $750,000. But it looks even better than that modest budget thanks to the ingenuity of writer-director Frederick Stephani, who cleverly recycled sets from Lon Chaney's silent *Hunchback of Notre Dame* and *Phantom of the Opera* and the studio's two *Frankenstein* films.

Buster reports that they had only six weeks to film the entire 13-chapter serial, which was shot as if it were one marathon-length feature. His sole complaint about the whole experience was that fidelity to Raymond's comic strip required the actor to have his naturally straight, dark-brown hair bleached and waved. In retrospect, "It was as if someone had lifted the roof—everything looked suddenly brighter. Having always looked out at the world from under a dark brow, it was an unusual experience being a blond." Embarrassed by his startling new appearance, Buster took to wearing a hat when away from the *Flash Gordon* set.

He also remembered a grueling production schedule that began at seven every morning but Sundays, halted for a brief half-hour lunch break, then went on to five or six o'clock. There would be an hour-long dinner break, followed by a return to the set for another bout of filming, finally quitting for the night at ten "or whenever it was convenient to quit." Buster would usually be home in bed by eleven, then up again at six—with Sundays off only "if we were on schedule." Needless to say, his family saw little of Buster during those six hectic weeks. And when did he learn his lines? Well, since this was an action picture, there wasn't that much to memorize, and, fortunately, the man was a "fast study." In his own words: "It never took me more than a few minutes to commit my sentences to memory. Plotting out the action sequence was usually more difficult than doing the dialogue." As the actor later remembered, "We didn't use many stunt men in the filming of *Flash Gordon*. Most actors who were involved in the dialogue did their own fight scenes, unless something especially dangerous came up." Actually, stunt man Eddie Parker doubled for Buster in some scenes.

Despite his serial stardom at Universal, Buster felt the frustration of a would-be "serious" actor: "I'd done six movies in 1936—all class-B fare—and I still yearned to get into a class-A picture. Action was fun and the pay was good, but for all the acting practice I was getting, I wanted to see how good I could really be."

Paramount once again renewed his contract in 1937, with an attendant salary raise which, however, failed to compensate Buster's dissatisfaction with his studio casting. It's interesting to speculate on the direction his career might have taken had they given him roles opposite such top Paramount luminaries as Lombard, Dietrich or West. Instead, he got Gertrude Michael, Mary Carlisle, Marsha Hunt and a not-yet-a-star Betty Grable. And more often than not, Buster wasn't even the male lead, but the "heavy," in programmers like *Murder Goes to College, King of Gamblers* and *Sophie Lang Goes West*. There were also more Zane Grey Westerns, although no longer did he support Randolph Scott, who had progressed to more important Paramount productions.

When *Flash Gordon* reached movie theatres in 1936, Universal realized a success second only to their Deanna Durbin blockbuster *One Hundred Men and a Girl*, featuring the teenage soprano in her first starring vehicle. To a degree, Buster enjoyed the increased visibility afforded him by the serial's popularity, while, at the same time, deploring his position as a secondary player at Paramount. When the following year brought him a raise to $600, Buster took satisfaction in the fact that at least he had regular employment—and at a good salary for 1938.

There was little variation in his assignment to crime programmers like *Tip-Off Girls* and *Hunted Men*, but some consolation in Universal's borrowing him once again, this time for *Flash Gordon's Trip to Mars*. The 1938 sequel united Buster with the original serial's principals, Jean Rogers, Charles Middleton and Frank Shannon, under the co-direction of genre veterans Ford Beebe and Robert Hill, the latter having guided Buster's first serial, *Tarzan the Fearless*. Despite his continued dissatisfaction

BC smiles for the *Buck Rogers* portrait photographer.

with the steady pattern of grade-B acting assignments, at least his ongoing identification with the role of Flash gave the actor a certain cachet. Again, Buster had to submit to a hair-bleaching, while Jean Rogers was allowed to retain her brown locks, because she was then shooting a feature which required her natural coloring.

Buster was aware that the second *Flash* serial was produced more cheaply than the original, with Universal encouraging the re-use of footage from the earlier adventure, presuming that the average moviegoer would be none the wiser. Universal continued to bill him as Larry "Buster" Crabbe, and they borrowed him again later that year for another serial, *Red Barry*. Like *Flash Gordon*, this one was also derived from a popular comic strip, this one created by Will Gould; Buster played the detective of its title, caught up in the Tong wars of San Francisco's Chinatown. Action-film veteran Ford Beebe, who had co-directed the second Flash Gordon serial, now teamed with Alan James. Buster was happy to let his brown hair grow back for this change-of-pace chapterplay.

A lobby card heralding the third (and final) *Flash Gordon* (Universal Pictures) serial.

Lest their contract player now harbor any false delusions of stardom at Paramount, the studio assigned Buster to also-ran roles in *Unmarried* and *Million Dollar Legs*, both filmed in 1938 for 1939 release, and he was then freed from his contract altogether. In his six years with them, he had been featured in 26 Paramount pictures. But where they really profited was in loaning Buster out to other studios for nine outside features and serials, which brought Paramount several thousand dollars for each week that the actor was employed elsewhere. Observed Buster, "By computing my salary and fees, I confirmed that my six years cost them absolutely noth-

Publicity for *Billy Rose's Aquacade* in a 1940 photo by Al Aumuller of *The New York World-Telegram* (author's collection).

ing. It didn't cost them a cent to keep me, because of the big returns I brought them on loan-outs. I felt cheated. I was only an expediency to them."

After the initial shock of Paramount's dumping him, Buster realized that it was time for a major decision. At 31, did he still want to become a lawyer? Or was he now in the acting business to stay? Still convinced that he had it in him to be a better actor than he'd yet had a chance to demonstrate, Buster felt that he wasn't ready to give it all up for law school. After all, there were *other* Hollywood studios. Maybe there was still a film future for him.

At 20th Century–Fox, he obtained third billing, after Jon Hall and Nancy Kelly, in a 66-minute programmer called *Sailor's Lady*. And although that studio gave him a screen test, utilizing a dramatic scene from *A Bill of Divorcement*, nothing substantial resulted. After viewing Buster's test, Fox chief Darryl F. Zanuck had commented (as the actor later learned), "He's a character actor. We can hire all of them we need."

Eleanor Holm and BC publicize their 1940 appearance as stars of *Billy Rose's Aqua-cade*. Photograph by Hale Haberman (author's collection).

At that time, Buster chose to part company with his long-time agent, Morris Small, and sign on with Lou Snitzer, who had shown interest in representing him. Under Snitzer's aegis the actor returned to work at Universal in *Buck Rogers*, based on the original sci-fi comic strip hero, in his fourth serial for them. As a result, Crabbe now commanded a highly respectable 1939 salary of $1,000 per week. Once more, he had the expert directorial guidance of Ford Beebe, in collaboration with Saul Goodkind.

Faced with the popularity of their previous sci-fi serials, Universal had to decide between producing a *Buck Rogers* sequel or continuing with their lucrative *Flash Gordon* franchise. Financial considerations moved them to offer Buster another chance to recreate the popular superhero in *Flash Gordon Conquers the Universe* (1940) directed by Ford Beebe and Ray Taylor. Charles Middleton and Frank Shannon returned as, respectively, Ming the Merciless and Dr. Zarkov, but Carol Hughes replaced Jean Rogers as Dale Arden, and Roland Drew took over from Richard Alexander as Prince Barin. For the first time, Buster could realize a serial star's full pay, without the bulk of his salary going to Paramount. For *Flash Gordon Conquers the Universe*, he got a flat $25,000. Life was definitely better away from the studio system. Also, he was beginning to appreciate a new position of Hollywood importance with no serious competition: king of the serials!

Buster realized that it was considered second-rate stardom in movie land to be merely a *serials* headliner. Yet, what had he to lose? His marquee value as a "name" owed little to Paramount and everything to his five Universal serials. Perhaps he had found his niche—even if most of his films never got reviewed in the major newspapers.

Flash Gordon Conquers the Universe, as it turned out, marked the end of the series. Buster held little liking for it, due to Universal's cost-cutting use of recycled footage from the previous *Flash* adventures. Nor did he care for the script, which veered away from Alex Raymond's original comic strip concept. In Buster's estimation, "I thought it was a poor product that was nothing more than a doctored-up script from earlier days. Being a perfectionist, I regretted that we couldn't remain true to either the creator's intentions or the prototype series that had been so successful."

Public indifference supported Buster. *Flash Gordon Conquers the Universe* failed to conquer the box-office, marking the end of his serial career at Universal. In fact, seven years would pass before he would shoot another multi-chapter adventure yarn and that one would be for Columbia Pictures.

Buster then took a welcome hiatus from moviemaking by replacing Johnny Weissmuller in the "live" New York production of *Billy Rose's Aquacade*, in which he teamed with another, prettier swimming champ, Eleanor Holm. Following a suitable rehearsal period, they opened in May 1940, performing four 90-minute shows a day in an open-air pool, rain or shine, utilizing facilities built for the 1939 World's Fair and designed for a seating capacity of 8,026. The Aquacade ran through the summer and into autumn, closing in late October. By that time, Billy Rose had whittled away so much of the novelty and song-and-dance material that Buster recalled its running time was now closer to a mere hour. It was a serious challenge for the swimmers to continue performing in the cold outdoor arena, While entertaining thoughts of eventually producing his own water show, Buster left New York for Milwaukee, lending his famous name to a smaller-scale production called *Sam Snyder's Water Follies.*

By Christmas, he was back in California with his family, which now included a second daughter, Susan, born in 1938. The place they now called home was a mountain lodge at Lake Arrowhead, some 80 miles east of L.A.

Not only was Buster back in his element, swimming again, but as a freelance actor he discovered he could make more money than his former contract with Paramount ever permitted.

Producers Releasing Corporation (better known as PRC) now supplanted the far more prestigious Paramount Pictures in Buster's movie career when he accepted an offer from veteran low-budget producer Sigmund Neufeld, who had turned out Tim McCoy Westerns in the '30s. And so, for the next five years (1941–46), Buster would star in a series of minor Westerns, initially centering on a crime-fighting cowboy named "Billy the Kid." There was no real connection in these B-Westerns to the infamous 19th-century American outlaw; all were directed by the producer's brother Sam Newfield, who had Anglicized the family name and occasionally used the pseudonyms "Sherman Scott" or "Peter Stewart." However, the pay was good, and when Buster signed on with Neufeld, it was initially for only two pictures. Who knew how popular they would soon become?

In this outdoor series, Buster was teamed with 57-year-old character actor Al "Fuzzy" St. John, who had started out in support of his famed uncle, Roscoe "Fatty" Arbuckle, in the silent comedy shorts produced by Mack Sennett.

Designed to fill half of a double-bill, these "Billy the Kid" Westerns were churned out in an average 10 to 12 days of shooting time and at an approximate cost of $25,000 per feature (running anywhere from 55 to 60 minutes in length). Between 1941 and 1946, Buster usually starred in about eight mini-budget PRC features annually, with one or two per year allowing him to forsake his saddle for an occasional grade-B adventure melodrama. In 1942, Paramount hired him back to team with action hero Richard Arlen in the oil-field drama *Wildcat,* but his other non–Westerns (*Jungle Siren, Queen of Broadway, Nabonga*) were all made for PRC.

As Buster would reflect in 1975, "The accent in formula Westerns was on good versus evil, expressed in absolute terms of black versus white. The plots were simple ones, usually passed from one studio to another, from one movie to another and from one cowboy to another. Basically, there were four standard formats: cattle rustlers, land grabbers, outlaws stealing money or gold, or outlaws terrorizing a community."

Buster was outfitted with a basic, serviceable Western wardrobe and allowed to select a steed from those available to filmmakers at a San Fernando Valley horse ranch. He chose a Palomino named Falcon, and spent several hours riding the animal about the ranch prior to the start of filming *Billy the Kid Wanted*. It was Buster's first leading role in an outdoor picture since 1937's *Forlorn River* at Paramount.

"Ninety percent of these formula Westerns were filmed at the same location," recalled Buster, citing a hilly area between Chatsworth and the Simi Valley, known as the Santa Susanna Mountains. "Given several movable Western-town fronts, boulders, scrubby oak trees and a plethora of dusty trails, the B-Western mills ground out an endless chain of action cheapies, of which I starred in over 45."

Buster and Al "Fuzzy" St. John worked well together, and the first two Billy the Kid Westerns scored well enough with the public to prompt Sigmund Neufeld to sign them on to continue the series. But, with a wartime rise in production costs, PRC countered by cutting the hours allotted to filmmaking. Thus, their B-Westerns, that had earlier taken a maximum of 12 days to shoot, were now brought in in as few as seven or eight! Buster remembered one of his PRC oaters that was completed in a mere *four* days. "We started on a Monday and wrapped up the 60-minute feature on Thursday night. It was done under the rationale that B-Western fans didn't expect epics like *Ben-Hur* or *Stagecoach*, so no one would care. God, what a horrible thing that turned out to be!"

As for the inevitable goofs and flubs, there was no time to waste, and Buster recalled no retakes: "Stumbles and missed lines were just passed over; sloppy fight scenes were just cut and patched into useful footage. One hurried chase scene showed my double leaping from his galloping horse to drag an escaping crook from his mount. But the stuntman missed the villain completely and fell over the other horse's rump onto the ground—alone. The badman, noticing the miss, took it upon himself to lean over and fall from his horse in order to try and save the take. The director yelled 'cut,' I took the stuntman's place, ran over to the villain, the action resumed, and we began the fight scene as if nothing had happened."

With the need for escapist movie fare amid World War II, Buster realized his busiest year yet with the 1942 release of *eight* starring vehicles, five of them Billy the Kid pictures. Draft-wise, he was deferrable as a 34-year-old family man, but Buster joined Fuzzy in contributing to the war effort by making training films for the Field Artillery. These were shot at Oklahoma's Fort Sill, where for several months the two actors mingled and chatted with soldiers, many of whom were movie fans. While regretting his inability to entertain with songs, dances or joke-telling, Buster "tried to visit with the men and let them know how much everybody appreciated the sacrifice they were making."

Back in Hollywood, Buster made seven more Billy the Kid Westerns in 1943. The following year, with the belated realization that "Billy the Kid" was not an appropriate name for a bonafide American film hero, PRC changed that name—if not the character—to "Billy Carson." Buster continued to play this role through 1944, with no improvement in the production quality of any of his films. Save for *The Contender*, a prizefight yarn, and the jungle melodrama *Nabonga*, all were Westerns teaming Crabbe and St. John,

For Buster, the only highlight in a routine year of low-budget moviemaking was the birth, on September 4, 1944, of his son Cullen, thereafter to be known as "Cuffy." When a Hollywood trade paper hailed the event with the banner line "Flash Gordon Has a Son," Buster realized the probable future of his status as a star: The motion picture industry, like the public, would forever identify him with that comic strip hero.

In the midst of the numbing sameness of shooting those repetitious Billy Carson Westerns, Buster enjoyed a welcome respite with the 1946 bayou melodrama *Swamp Fire*, opposite Johnny Weissmuller. Not only did he get to switch from sagebrush hero to mustachioed villain with a Cajun accent, but Buster also performed a climactic underwater fight-to-the-death with his old swimming rival. At 42, Weissmuller was no longer in top physical form, and the retakes required to accommodate the screen's famed Tarzan challenged even Buster's endurance—especially since the water was ice cold, in order to keep the alligators lethargic. Nevertheless, this was one of his favorite moviemaking experiences, mainly because it afforded him a genuine acting opportunity. Although a B-picture, this 89-minute Pine-Thomas production was quite a few notches above Buster's routine PRC pictures, and the prestige of a Paramount release brought *Swamp Fire* to a wider audience than had his Billy Carson Westerns.

With the conclusion of his PRC contract in late 1946, Buster finally bade goodbye to that series of low-budget Westerns. In five years, he had made 36 of them—as he later put it, "probably 35 more than were worth remembering." PRC promptly replaced him with Al "Lash" LaRue.

During the summer months, when the hot weather brought a hiatus to outdoor California film-making, Buster had remained active in water shows. Now, having carefully saved a substantial amount of his $1,500 weekly PRC salary, he felt secure enough to invest in his own "live" aquatic production. As such, he could not only double as producer and star, but could also exercise control over the show's quality—"a condition denied me in my movies."

Inspired by *Billy Rose's Aquacade* of 1940, Buster called his production *The Aqua Parade*, expressing no embarrassment at the number of ideas and details he openly borrowed from his predecessors. One slight

BC sits for a Paramount portrait photographer in 1948.

innovation was in having his bathing beauties smile and express enthusiasm in their water-ballet movements. Buster had never liked the automaton-like coldness of Rose's women swimmers, and he was determined that *The Aqua Parade* would be a more entertaining experience for his audiences.

Buster was smart enough to work out the kinks by testing his show in smaller locales for several months before playing major cities. His swimmers, ranging from top athletes to performing clowns, were recruited from many of the aquatic achievers Buster had encountered during his years of association with water sports. He later recalled it as a "labor of love, as well as a profitable occupation for me." And never for a minute did he regret breaking his bondage to the world of low-budget Westerns.

In 1947, *The Aqua Parade* performed a five-month season at state fairs from San Diego to Detroit. Buster was encouraged by favorable reviews and enthusiastic audiences, and he invested in a large portable swimming pool, which gave the production freedom to perform where he wished, no longer dependent on any existing pool. By 1948, *The Aqua Parade* was sufficiently seasoned to get bookings in most of the big cities that they targeted.

Between engagements, Buster found time to appear in an adaptation of James Fenimore Cooper's classic *Last of the Mohicans*, which was released by Columbia in 1947 as *Last of the Redmen*. In this outdoor drama, his first experience with color filmmaking, the fifth-billed Buster would portray Magua, a villainous renegade Indian, in a cast headed by Jon Hall, Michael O'Shea and Buster's *Tarzan the Fearless* leading lady of 14 years earlier, Jacqueline Wells, now known as Julie Bishop.

He remained at that studio for *The Sea Hound*, a 15-chapter adventure melodrama, produced by Sam Katzman and based on characters from a comic book and radio program. It would be the first of three serials that the actor would headline for Columbia over a span of six years. Secondary as he frequently was in feature films, Crabbe was never less than the top-starred main attraction in any of his nine serials. In that genre, he remained king.

Before *The Aqua Parade* resumed touring in 1948, Buster returned to Paramount to play another heavy, this time a murderous circus clown named Smiley, in the Pine-Thomas production *Caged Fury*. The 60-minute B-picture once again pitted him against Jackie the Lion, the animal he had "killed" in *King of the Jungle*—only this time Jackie got to polish off Buster.

Years later, questioned about his attitude toward playing villains versus heroes, the actor acknowledged that he had achieved his screen fame in the latter capacity. However, he admitted, it was as a "heavy" that he had had the most satisfaction as an artist. "It's much more interesting work. You don't have to worry about what the audience's reaction to your performance is going to be. The nastier you are, the better it is. So I really had a lot of fun doing the heavies. I did a lot of them while working in the pictures, and I've done some on television, too. It's more fun for me, and I must say I work a little harder at it, because I'm enjoying what I'm doing."

But it was largely hero-worship of the Buster Crabbe they admired as Flash Gordon and Billy Carson that attracted audiences to his *Aqua Parade*, and he appeared to thrive in his double role of producer and swimming star. For its 1948 edition, the production boasted 20 synchronized swimmers and almost as many musical performers, in addition to featured divers and swimmers. And, of course, there was also a behind-the-scenes staff of people responsible for the show's set construction, and its music, choreography and scheduling. Buster's public contribution to the two-hour show consisted of a solo turn in which he demonstrated "The Evolution of Swimming" and a synchronized performance with swim star Patricia Robinson to the music of Eddie Bush and his Hawaiian Trio. They, in turn, were supported by six Aqua Maids in a water ballet, "which utilized romantic music, lights and flowing motions to create an atmosphere of aquatic beauty." The show opened that April and closed near the end of the year in Los Angeles, having successfully played such U.S. cities as Cleveland, Chicago, Boston and Philadelphia, as well as Montreal and Toronto.

With *The Aqua Parade*'s tour keeping him away from his family for many months at a time, Buster tried to compensate by staying close to their Pacific Palisades home that winter, playing golf and getting better acquainted with 12-year-old Sande, 10-year-old Susan, and Cuffy, age four. Virginia had frequently managed to join Buster on tour for brief reunions, while her parents looked after the children. Nevertheless, his prolonged absences severely tested the Crabbe family. Buster was generous in his praise of Virginia, later commenting, "The strain of producing *The Aqua Parade* would have been intolerable if she hadn't been such a wonderful companion."

He began 1949 by filming a Jungle Jim feature called *Captive Girl*, in which he played the villain opposite Johnny Weissmuller, and then continued his serials career with *Pirates of the High Seas*. Both were released the following year by Columbia, and showed Crabbe, at 41, to be in far better shape than his 45-year-old former swimming rival.

That year, Buster toured the country again with his profitable *Aqua Parade*, and was encouraged by a show business friend to branch out and try European cities the following year. The tour kicked off that spring with a two-week engagement in Hawaii, beginning at Honolulu's Mailili Park. Buster took advantage of the occasion to arrange a rare family reunion, bringing Virginia and their three children over from California; they were joined by his father, mother and stepfather, as well as his brother Buddy— now the manager of a pineapple plantation—and his family. The Islands' engagement concluded an equally successful week on Maui, where the show's South Seas motif made it seem like a well-planned native tourist attraction. In retrospect, Buster might have cause to regret not remaining indefinitely in Hawaii with *The Aqua Parade*, rather than proceed, as he did, to the capitals of Europe.

Opening in Zurich in May of 1950, the show attracted satisfactory audiences and played into June. Then, three weeks before they were scheduled to open in Paris, their French booking agent, having attended a performance, informed Buster that their product would not go over well in his country, that it needed sophisticated re-styling in every aspect, from its costumes to its dance routines to its music. Buster's protest met with a threat of cancellation—and the problems attendant on a possible month-long European layover before their next scheduled locale, Rome. The additional costs of at least $25,000 gave Buster serious pause. They could skip Paris, close down and return home. Or they could proceed to revamp the show, which would necessitate a suspension of salaries until their efforts again became profitable. The company voted to meet the demands for a Parisian makeover, and the re-tuning immediately began.

"On opening night in Paris," according to Buster, "the costumes and scenery got a standing ovation." Unfortunately, performing in June meant bucking the traditional holiday season when most Parisians leave for the seashore and countryside. Without full theatres, and now in debt to the tune of some $60,000, Buster took desperate measures to find food and housing for his company, and shore up their fast-dwindling morale. While Virginia Crabbe returned home to seek financial aid for the show, Buster and company moved on to a far more successful engagement in Rome, followed by London, where a planned month-long stay extended profitably into six weeks. But in Milan, the next stop on their tour, mounting expenses and local mismanagement reached a boiling point, and Buster despaired of ever climbing out of debt. Sensing his desperation, one of the show's managers wired Virginia, "Buster needs you badly. Suggest you come at once." And she did, staying on through a relatively successful Milanese engagement and a potentially disastrous opening in Turin, where the game but unfortunate swimmers were obliged to carry out their routines in icy water, because there hadn't been time to warm it. When the troubled tour finally ended, there was barely enough money to send the company home from Turin on the liner *Vulcanian*. With Virginia's invaluable moral support, Buster put the show's collapsible pool, sets and costumes into Italian storage, because he couldn't afford to ship them home.

Now in debt to the tune of more than $100,000, the Crabbes headed back to the U.S. to pick up the pieces of their lives. At 42, Buster would need to find new avenues of enterprise and financial survival. And so he moved from the big screen to the small screen: television.

In 1950, before major Hollywood studios had come to terms with selling or leasing their rich backlog of star-studded pictures to this competitive new medium, TV stations had found a source of low-priced programming in the wealth of independently made—and now available—movies of the thirties and forties. Among such products were the films of PRC, including Buster Crabbe's 36 program Westerns. At the outset of 1951, the actor had an offer from New York's WOR-TV to host a daily children's entertainment to be called *The Buster Crabbe Show*. This would center on the actor's old Billy Carson—Billy the Kid flicks, as well as his *Flash Gordon* serials, edited into 15-minute segments and commercially sponsored, with a studio audience of children who'd be members of a nationwide society known as "Buster's Buddies." For this live, half-hour weekday show, the actor was initially paid $1,250 a week, a salary that enabled the now-bankrupt Californian to relocate East. As host, his duties encompassed introducing the film segments with footnotes and anecdotes, as well as reading viewer letters, handling commercials and bestowing prizes on his contest entrants such as weekend vacations in Florida. With such exciting come-ons, "Buddy" membership understandably swelled to over 35,000, necessitating the hiring of two secretaries to handle mail.

BC and son Cuffy in the TV series *Captain Gallant of the Foreign Legion* (NBC, 1955).

Buster took a conscientious approach to this unusual job: "Because the medium was new to me, I didn't just do it off the top of my head. I put in a few hours each afternoon going over the plans for each day's show, ran over the list of prizes to be given away, read the mail, worked out my pep talk for the closing spot and generally paced the show." And because he still faced major debts stemming from his disastrous *Aqua Parade*, Buster continued to look around for other avenues of income. Fortunately, *The Buster Crabbe Show* didn't require all of his time.

By lending his name to help promote New York's Shelton Hotel Health Club, he became a silent partner in a profit-sharing enterprise whose membership would grow to some 900 men, each of whom would shell out $150 a year for the use of the club's facilities. This soon led to a women's morning TV exercise show, *Figure Fashioning*, on which Buster advised his viewers and participants in matters of calorie counting and physical fitness. Finally, the Crabbe family's mountain of debt began to diminish.

In the summer of 1951, Buster moved Virginia and the children out of California and into a small rented ranch in Somerville, N.J., and began to spread his talents even thinner by teaching swimming at the popular Palisades Amusement Park in Fort Lee. On Saturdays, he was Director of Water Sports at the renowned Concord Hotel on Kiamesha Lake in New York's upstate Catskill Mountains. This was the beginning of a part-time, name-lending alliance that would last, amazingly, for 18 years.

In May of 1952, Buster Crabbe made his "live" dramatic TV debut in a family-oriented play called "A Cowboy for Chris" on NBC's *Philco Playhouse*. With his prior experience in live television, and with no studio audience present to intimidate him, Buster handled this drama involving a range rider and youngster much as he'd have done while making a feature film. Although faced with performing a complete script from start to finish, as would an actor in a stage play, he did it with ease. His early training in Paramount's little theatre productions had proved invaluable.

Later that year, Buster starred in his ninth and last serial, Columbia's 14-chapter *King of the Congo*. Once again he was required to bare his chest and portray a jungle character—this time named "Thunda." Like his two previous Columbia serials, *The Sea Hound* and *Pirates of the High Seas*, this one is seldom seen and nearly forgotten half a century later. In fact, only four years later, Columbia would kill off that waning genre altogether with their lackluster multi-part Western *Blazing the Overland Trail* (1956).

As Crabbe later observed, "My last serial had to compete, literally, with my *Flash Gordon* serials of 15 years earlier, which I was showing on my television show daily. And my show, if watched by no one but the 35,000 members of 'Buster's Buddies,' pulled in more viewers in a day than any

BC displays great middle-aged form as Director of Water Sports for the Concord Hotel in upstate New York, circa 1956 (author's collection).

theatre could hope to attract in a month." With movie palaces folding at an alarming rate, Hollywood realized that it could no longer take TV lightly.

Buster now joined in partnership with his agent Bob Bundy and a fellow named Bob Higgins, who owned an expanse of property in upstate Onchiota, New York, that had once been an exclusive boys' school. With its boat dock, swimming facilities, kitchen and dormitory accommodations, the 16-building Adirondacks spread lent itself to becoming a co-educational summer camp to which the actor could bring his name. As Buster Crabbe's Camp Meenahga, the eight-week summer operation at Saranac Lake would feature his occasional on-site presence as counselor on swimming and boating when his TV schedule allowed. And of course, *The Buster Crabbe Show* was an ideal means of spreading the word about Camp Meenahga. For its first three summers, the operation built a steady co-educational clientele until, in its fourth season, growing problems with keeping the sometimes-unruly boys and girls in line caused Buster to switch to a boys-only policy. After the summer of 1953, Crabbe and Bundy bought out Higgins and acquired a new partner in Charles Izzo. As a boys' camp, Meenahga's enrollment swelled from 37 to 50, although Buster's increasingly busy television career now kept him occupied elsewhere.

Beginning in 1951, the actor's resurgence as a celebrity resulted in the publication of *Buster Crabbe* comic books from Famous Funnies (12 issues between 1951 and 1953) and, less successfully, *The Amazing Adventures of Buster Crabbe, The All-American Hero* (four issues in 1953–54).

In 1953, he accepted an offer from producer Harry Saltzman to star in a TV adventure series to be called *Captain Gallant of the Foreign Legion*. It was set in the contemporary Moroccan desert where Capt. Gallant, in charge of a Legion outpost, had to contend with assorted villains, including smugglers, treasure-seekers and potentially hostile Arab tribes. He also had the responsibility of an orphaned lad whose officer-father had died in action.

Buster convinced TV packagers that his nine-year-old son Cuffy would be ideal for this role, and the pair initially signed for three half-hour films. Saltzman reasoned that, should the project not sell as a series, he could edit those episodes into a 90-minute feature for movie theatres. The three-part pilot was shot in Paris, where Buster's risky gamble with Cuffy paid off; though inexperienced as an actor, the neophyte proved a natural under his father's tutelage.

Eventually, the H. J. Heinz Company picked up the series' sponsorship, and *Captain Gallant* was contracted for 36 additional 30-minute segments in 1954, paying its star $1,000 an episode, with father and son sharing in the profits. The show's location filming was set in Africa, so something had to go from Buster's busy schedule—in this case, *The Buster Crabbe Show*. The actor would trade in local, late-afternoon TV stardom in New York for prime-time evening exposure that the NBC network would beam throughout the country. Formerly identified as a serial star and B-Western hero, Buster Crabbe now became known to a whole new audience.

Beginning production in April of 1954, *Captain Gallant* used North Africa for exterior locations, and studios in Paris and Rome for interiors. With the addition of character actor Fuzzy Knight, with whom Buster had worked 20 years earlier in *To the Last Man* and *She Had to Choose*, the requisite 39 episodes were completed that October, and the Crabbes returned to the U.S. Before *Captain Gallant* began its successful NBC run, Buster appeared in a *Pond's Theatre* drama, "The Cornered Man," which aired January 27, 1955 on ABC.

Captain Gallant first reached American homes on February 13, 1955, and immediately found its target audience of youngsters, as well as older Buster Crabbe fans. The show's popularity soon resulted in a fan club for Cuffy Crabbe and a comic book reflecting their TV adventures: Charlton Comics' *Captain Gallant of the Foreign Legion* enjoyed a four-issue run in the 1955–56 season.

While Buster and Cuffy were filming abroad, an unforeseen problem was developing back home. "Anorexia nervosa" was a little-known medical term in mid-fifties America, and yet young Sande Crabbe's persistent concern with dieting became a source of worry for her parents. She was an attractive 20-year-old student at the University of Southern California, boarding with her Held grandparents in Santa Monica. Buster believed that his slim, 5'7" daughter's determination to lose weight was only a passing phase, caused by influence from her peer group. Her stubborn determination, in addition to Buster's preoccupation with a busy career, made it difficult for him and Virginia to intercede. They could make their observations known only when she was home between semesters, while trusting that she'd outgrow this strange obsession.

Early in 1956, Buster returned to Hollywood to star in the independent, low-budget Western *Gun Brothers*, which Sidney Salkow directed for release by United Artists. It was the actor's first feature film in six years, and undoubtedly resulted from his TV fame. There followed a return abroad to shoot a second season of *Captain Gallant*, which had been renewed by NBC, and Buster asked Sande to spend part of her vacation visiting him and Cuffy in Italy, where they'd be working on the series throughout that summer and fall. Aside from all this theatrical activity, Buster still had his Adirondacks summer camp, as well as his nominal alliances with Manhattan's Shelton Hotel Health Club and the Concord Hotel in the Catskills.

And, to compound his business affiliations, he now lent his name and promotional powers to New Jersey's Cascade Industries, the manufacturers of a line of built-in vinyl-lined swimming pools.

Sande flew to Rome that summer of 1956 to spend two weeks of her vacation time with Cuffy and Buster, who noticed that she appeared even thinner than when they had visited during the shooting of *Gun Brothers*. When she came East to join her family for Thanksgiving, Sande alarmed them with her appearance. She ate very little, maintaining that being thinner made her more attractive to boys, as well as being good for her heart. She now weighed in at 100 pounds. By Christmas, she had dropped to 95 and looked emaciated. Finally, her alarmed parents sought professional help at a Westchester hospital, incurring her resentment when she was kept there for treatment of anorexia and malnutrition. There followed psychiatric visits, which failed to establish any basis for her problem, nor any solution.

Sande began psychoanalysis, and was advised by her New York doctors that she could return to continue her studies at USC at the start of 1957. In a little more than three months, Buster and Virginia would be devastated to receive news of Sande's death on April 10. The cause: malnutrition. Her final weight: 60 pounds.

Amid family tragedy, with Buster indulging in much soul-searching, *Captain Gallant* remained a popular TV staple. Had he been too much the absent father, neglecting family for career? Susan Crabbe helped compensate for the loss of her older sister by attempting to give Buster the affection of *two* daughters. As he later stated, "I think, partly because of Susan's love, I was able to put Sande's death back into perspective."

Captain Gallant ran through February 1957 on the NBC network, and was brought back for a cycle of repeat airings from 1960 to 1963. There was a total of 65 black-and-white half-hour shows.

After *Captain Gallant*'s initial run, Cuffy Crabbe retired from acting to complete his education at Arizona State University, before going into real estate. Later, he would join his father in the business of Buster Crabbe Pools. Cuffy reflected on his brief acting experience in a 1970s interview: "The only reason I was on the show to begin with was that the producers couldn't find the right boy to play it ... at least, not one whose parents would allow him to go to North Africa for all that time."

Settled briefly in the town of Larchmont, in New York's Westchester County, the Crabbe clan later relocated to the nearby community of Rye, where they would remain for over a decade. It was easy commuting distance for Buster's commitments in New York City, and equally convenient to airports connecting with the West Coast. Over the next eight years, the

BC and series star Gil Gerard in the "Planet of the Slave Girls" episode of the TV series *Buck Rogers in the 25th Century* (NBC, 1979).

BC as the senior member of a stunt team plagued by deadly accidents in the "S.T.U.N.T." episode of the TV series *BJ and the Bear* (NBC, 1981).

actor would continue as a big-screen cowboy in such minor-league outdoor pictures as *The Lawless Eighties* (1957), *Badman's Country* (1958), *Gunfighters of Abilene* (1960), *The Bounty Killer* and *Arizona Raiders* (both 1965). None were considered even minor classics.

In June 1959, Buster enjoyed a change of pace with his guest appearance on an episode of NBC's *Ellery Queen* series, entitled "The Murder Comes to You Live." And in April 1961, he and singer Rosemary Clooney co-hosted an NBC-TV Easter special called *Marineland Circus*, in which Buster took part in a water ballet with Mary Ann Hollingsworth and the Marine Maids. However, at 53, observed *Variety*, "The years seem to be catching up with him, for he was puffing during his lead-in to the Minute Maid juice plug."

On December 27, 1965, the CBS network telecast the formal opening and installation ceremonies from Fort Lauderdale, Florida, of the Swimming Hall of Fame. Its dozen past and present champion swimmers named as original members included Buster Crabbe, a tribute that may have meant more to him than all of his Hollywood fame.

The following year, Buster tested new waters when he passed a tough exam to become a New York City stockbroker with the Wall Street firm of Lieberbaum, Richter & Co. Not that he had completely forsaken show business: he was then concurrently seen in a TV commercial for a pharmaceutical firm in which, clad in "a phony leopard skin," he appeared once again as Tarzan, this time using the company's chemical product to shoo away mosquitoes!

By now, Buster was also serving his home community by conducting the annual Red Cross swimming sessions at Rye's Durland Scout Center. In July of 1969, now a very fit 56, he maintained his physique with a daily swim, while continuing as Director of Water Activities at the Concord Hotel. In the Adirondacks, Buster now operated two summer camps: one for boys ages six to 15 and the other a co-educational water camp for teenagers. And he continued his association with Cascade Pools.

In 1970, Buster wrote a physical-fitness book for seniors that he called *Energistics*. That fall, he was offered the part of an over-the-hill cowboy star who returns to filmmaking in *The Comeback Trail*, an independent comedy–Western shot in New York and Santa Fe, New Mexico. It was the 62-year-old actor's first movie role in five years, and was completed in five weeks. It would be five years before the picture was briefly released. In a 1977 interview with writer John C. Tibbetts, Buster would term *The Comeback Trail* "the best thing I ever did." Conjecturing on the movie's obscurity, he said, "Few people saw it in theatres. Some scenes were pretty strong—too sexy for family viewing. All the producer had to do was take out three scenes and it would have been a good B-Western. But he was adamant about not cutting anything. They ran it in Atlanta, and the thing lasted only two days. Without that family viewing audience, you're dead."

Buster would complete his filmography with a pair of low-budget, independently made obscurities, *Swim Team* (1979; released on video in 1987) and the sci-fi horror flick *The Alien Dead* (1981; released on video in 1985). Neither film won sufficient notice to dim fans' memories of—or affection for—the motion picture serials of which Crabbe remains unchallenged king.

Reflecting objectively on his talent, Buster told an interviewer: "Some say my acting rose to the level of incompetence and then leveled off. I was a lot better actor than people gave me credit for. I didn't have any training, but I feel if I had been given the chance, I could have become a really good, top-rate actor. I didn't make it like a Gable or Boyer. But I wonder what would have happened if things had been different."

As he continued to operate his summer camps and work out with the Boy Scouts, he commented on his continuing zest for living: "Winning and keeping the respect of the young helps you keep young yourself. Maybe that's really my secret, eh?"

In August 1972, Buster was once again in the news for his athletic skills when he competed in the National AAU Masters Long Course Swimming Championships at the University of Indiana in Bloomington. At 64, he added to his 1932 Olympics laurels with two more gold medals: one for the 1500-meter freestyle in 25:57:82; the other on the following day taking the 200-meter freestyle, at 2:53:50. Both races were in the 60–65 age group.

The following year witnessed a penchant for American nostalgia, frequently in the guise of "camp," that renewed public interest in the *Flash Gordon* serials. In campus polls conducted at the University of Maryland, that comic strip hero placed a close third on the nostalgia chart, after W.C. Fields and the Marx Brothers. There followed a demand for campus screening of the *Flash Gordon* serials, as well as renewed airings by nationwide television stations. In New York City, the local Public Broadcasting channel leased the films to compete with the network newscasts that aired during the same 7 P.M. half-hour.

The *Flash Gordon* revival quite naturally led to new public appearances by Buster. During one such engagement in Bridgeport, Connecticut, (June 1974), he was reported hospitalized with "a virus," although no further details were later revealed. However, Buster's workaholic lifestyle was well-known and, despite his fondness for physical fitness, interviewers sometimes commented on his chain-smoking.

By the mid-seventies, when Buster and Virginia Crabbe left New York's Westchester suburbs to relocate in the drier climate of affluent Scottsdale, Arizona, Susan was married, living in northern California, and the mother of several children.

Life in Arizona did not mean "retirement" for Buster. Nostalgia-based conventions would continue to be a magnet for his presence in locales like New Orleans (dedicating a Tarzan memorial at the Morgan City Swamp Gardens, where Elmo Lincoln's *Tarzan of the Apes* was shot in 1918), Nashville (the annual Western Film Festival) and New York's Nostalgia Convention, saluting Buster's portrayal of comic book heroes. He was also a popular lecturer on college campuses, where he gladly answered student questions about *Flash Gordon*, and revealed such screen secrets as how the Clay People emerged from the walls ("just double exposure") and the light bridge that people walked across on the planet Mongo ("They just scratched the film—scratched it frame by frame"). Nor was he averse to sharing his career disappointments: "I always wished I could have been in one really good film. But they decide you're a guy who can fall off a horse and take a breakaway table over your head, and there's nothing you can do about it."

In 1975, Buster reflected on his screen image and its possible influence on impressionable young minds: "Many fans have told me they saw in my portrayals a moralistic mien, something they could identify with or fantasize about as children. There's a place for hero worship in any society. It gives people something to look up to, even if no real hero can ever live up to the image people have of them."

Buster continued to promote swimming and physical fitness into his late sixties and early seventies. In 1979, he returned to Hollywood, well publicized as "the original Buck Rogers," to film two episodes of the NBC-TV series *Buck Rogers in the 25th Century*, which featured Gil Gerard in the title role. Buster was cunningly cast as "Brigadier Gordon," a character the network's press material extravagantly identified as "a fighter pilot called out of retirement to save Earth from a massive attack directed by a powerful sorcerer who deals in slave-trading on an agricultural planet!" Starting off with a feature-length two-hour episode entitled "Planet of the Slave Girls" that aired on September 27, Buster appeared to be enjoying himself as he guest-starred along with such movie names as Jack Palance, Roddy McDowall and Macdonald Carey. The following January 17 he was back in a 60-minute segment, "A Blast for Buck." And on March 11, 1981, he appeared in the "S.T.U.N.T." episode of the series *B.J. and the Bear*, playing a character NBC-TV publicity described as "an old-time stunt man with a terrifying secret."

Near the end of his life, Buster had some final thoughts: "I was never one to think that because you are in the picture business, because you're an actor, you're a special person. Not at all, and I have little regard for any people who act that way. If you're lucky, you bring a little excitement to the world. If you're really lucky, you lend your fame to worthwhile causes—as I was recently privileged to do, raising money for the 1984 Olympics. Apart from that, you're just another human being, trying to make a living, doing it the best way you possibly can. That's the way I've always operated, and I will continue to do so, just doing the best I can."

His favorite co-stars remained Jean Rogers (of the first two *Flash Gordon* serials) and Frances Dee (*King of the Jungle*), his first leading lady.

The week before his death, Buster and Virginia celebrated their fiftieth wedding anniversary, as he made plans to attend an arthritis telethon in Tennessee.

Buster Crabbe died following a heart attack, at the age of 75, at his Scottsdale home on the morning of April 23, 1983. He is buried in Scottsdale's Green Acres Cemetery. Surviving family members included Virginia, his wife of 50 years, his daughter Susan, son Cuffy and seven grandchildren.

The Films

(in order of release)

Good News

A Metro-Goldwyn-Mayer Picture: 1930

Credits—Directors: Nick Grinde and Edgar J. MacGregor; Screenwriters: Frances Marion and Joe Farnham; Cinematographer: Percy Hilburn; Editor: William Le Vanway; Art Director: Cedric Gibbons; Songs: "He's a Lady's Man," "The Best Things in Life Are Free," "Varsity Drag," "Good News," "Tait Song" and "Students Are We" by Buddy De Sylva, Lew Brown and Ray Henderson; "If You're Not Kissing Me" and "Football" by Arthur Freed and Nacio Herb Brown; "I Feel Pessimistic" by J. Russell Robinson and George Waggner; "I'd Like to Make You Happy" by Reggie Montgomery; Musical Interpolations: Nacio Herb Brown, Arthur Freed, Felix Feist, Jr. and Reggie Montgomery; Dance Director: Sammy Lee; Costumes: David Cox; Running Time: 90 minutes.

Cast—Mary Lawler (*Connie*); Stanley Smith (*Tom Marlowe*); Bessie Love (*Babe*); Cliff Edwards (*Kearney*); Gus Shy (*Bobby*); Lola Lane (*Pat*);Thomas Jackson (*Coach*); Delmer Daves (*Beef*); Billy Taft (*Freshman*); Frank McGlynn (*Professor Kenyon*); Dorothy McNulty [Penny Singleton] (*Flo*); Helen Virgil, Vera Marshe and Ann Dvorak (*Girls*); Buster Crabbe (*Student with Pipe*); Abe Lyman and His Band.

Broadway's 1927 collegiate musical first reached the screen amid the early talkie vogue for song-and-dance movies. Its large cast included future stars Ann Dvorak and Dorothy McNulty (later famous as Penny Singleton, star of Columbia's long-running "Blondie" series). But it takes an eagle eye to locate Buster among the film's student population. *Good News* is best known for its 1947 MGM remake starring June Allyson and Peter Lawford.

The setting is fictitious Tait College, where football star Tom Marlowe (Stanley Smith) has been neglecting his studies, thus jeopardizing the school team. Smart-aleck freshman Bobby (Gus Shy) pursues school vamp Babe (Bessie Love), while fellow student Connie (Mary Lawlor) falls for

49

Tom. Not surprisingly, Tait students put singing and dancing before studying, with the "Varsity Drag" their main preoccupation. Professor Kenyon (Frank McGlynn) is eventually able to help Tom balance his scholastic achievements with success on the football field. Finally, Connie wins the love of Tom.

The Maker of Men (*Yellow*)

A Columbia Picture: 1931

Credits—Director: Edward Sedgwick; Assistant Director: David Selman; Screenwriter: Howard J. Green. Original Story: Howard J. Green and Edward Sedgwick; Cinematography: L. William O'Connell; Editor: Gene Milford; Running Time: 67 minutes.

Cast—Jack Holt (*Coach "Uncle" Dudley*); Richard Cromwell (*Bob Dudley*); Joan Marsh (*Dorothy*); Robert Alden (*Chick*); John Wayne (*Dusty*); Walter Catlett (*McNeill*); Natalie Moorhead (*Mrs. Rhodes*); Richard Tucker (*Mr. Rhodes*); Ethel Wales (*Aunt Martha*).

Buster was hired as an athletic extra for this college gridiron drama about the contention between a reluctant student-athlete (Richard Cromwell) and his father (Jack Holt), the gung-ho football coach at fictitious Western University.

Huddle

A Metro-Goldwyn-Mayer Picture: 1932

Credits—Director: Sam Wood; Assistant Director: John Waters; Screenwriters: Walton Hall Smith, C. Gardner Sullivan, Robert Lee Johnson and Arthur S. Hyman; Based on the novel by Francis Wallace; Cinematographer: Harold Wenstron; Art Director: Cedric Gibbons; Editor: Hugh Wynn; Costumes: Adrian; Song: "The Whiffenpoof Song" by Meade Minnigeroode, George S. Pomeroy and Tod B. Galloway; Running Time: 104 minutes.

Cast—Ramon Novarro (*Tony Amatto*); Madge Evans (*Rosalie Stone*); Una Merkel (*Thelma*); Ralph Graves (*Coach Malcolm Gale*); John Arledge (*Jim "Pidge" Pidgeon*); Frank Albertson (*Larry Wilson*); Kane Richmond (*Tom Stone*); Martha Sleeper (*Barbara Winston*); Henry Armetta (*Mr. Amatto*); Ferike Boros (*Mrs. Amatto*); Rockliffe Fellows (*Mr. Stone*); Joe Sauers [Sawyer] (*Slater*); Charley Grapewin (*Doctor*); Tom Kennedy (*Moving Man*)

In this college football drama starring Ramon Novarro, Buster again served as an atmospheric extra in several scenes, one of which included cheering on Novarro the night before the big game. (Buster was fired from the film for his inadvertent rudeness to the star during rehearsals.)

The Most Dangerous Game (*The Hounds of Zaroff*)

An RKO Radio Picture: 1932

Credits—Directors: Ernest B. Schoedsack and Irving Pichel; Executive Producer: David O. Selznick; Associate Producer: Merian C. Cooper; Screenwriter: James Ashmore Creelman; Based on the short story by Richard Connell in *Golden Book Magazine*; Cinematographer: Henry Gerrard; Art Director: Carroll Clark; Editor: Archie F. Marshek; Costumes: Walter Plunkett; Special Effects: Harry Redmond, Jr.; Music: Max Steiner; Running Time: 63 minutes.

Cast—Joel McCrea (*Bob Rainsford*); Fay Wray (*Eve Trowbridge*); Robert Armstrong (*Martin Trowbridge*); Leslie Banks (*Count Zaroff*); Noble Johnson (*Ivan*); Steve Clemento (*Tartar*), William Davidson (*Captain*); Dutch Hendrian, Hale Hamilton.

Buster Crabbe served as stunt double for Joel McCrea in this cat-and-mouse adventure thriller, which was remade in 1945 as *A Game of Death* with John Loder and Audrey Long, and in 1956 as *Run for the Sun* with Richard Widmark, Jane Greer and Trevor Howard. Crabbe's assignment: to dive off the top deck of an exploding boat and swim ashore. Because of the requisite timing, a one-take performance was mandatory.

That's My Boy

A Columbia Picture, 1932

Credits—Director: Roy William Neill; Assistant Director: Jay Marcant; Screenwriter: Norman Krasna; Based on a novel by Francis Wallace; Running Time: 71 minutes.

Cast—Richard Cromwell (*Thomas Jefferson Scott*); Dorothy Jordan (*Dorothy Whitney*); Mae Marsh (*"Mom" Scott*); Arthur Stone (*Pop*); Douglas Dumbrille (*Coach Daisy Adams*); Lucien Littlefield (*Uncle Louie*); Leon Waycoff [Ames] (*Al Williams*); Russell Saunders (*Pinkie*); Sumner Getchell (*Carl*); Otis Harlan (*Mayor*); Dutch Hendrian (*Hap*); Elbridge Anderson, Crilly Butler (*Students*); Douglas Haig (*Tommy as a Boy*).

Buster reported to have been one of many extras in this college football drama, which utilized championship-winning members of the University of Southern California's 1931 football team. As in *The Maker of Men*, again Richard Cromwell starred, this time as an undersized player whose running and tackling talents make him an unexpected hero, and whose gridiron success interferes with his plans to study medicine.

King of the Jungle

A Paramount Picture: 1933

Credits—Directors: H. Bruce Humberstone and Max Marcin; Associate Producer: E. Lloyd Sheldon; Screenwriters: Philip Wylie and Fred Niblo, Jr.; Based on the novel *The Lion's Way: A Story of Men and Lions* by Charles Thurley Stoneham; Cinematographer: Ernest Haller; Running Time: 73 minutes.

    Cast—Buster Crabbe (*Kaspa the Lion Man*); Frances Dee (*Ann Rogers*); Sidney Toler (*Neil Forbes*); Nydia Westman (*Sue*); Robert Barrat (*Joe Nolan*); Irving Pichel (*Corey*); Douglas Dumbrille (*Ed Peters*); Sam Baker (*Gwana*); Patricia Farley (*Kitty*); Ronnie Cosbey (*Kaspa, aged 3*); Florence Britton (*Mrs. Edith Knolls*); Leonard Carey (*Clerk*); Warner Richmond (*Gus*); William J. Kelly (*Government Inspector*); Mabel Stark, Thomas Amos, William Dunn, Harold Farley, George Turner, Sam Farrell, F. M. Pitts.

After a sort of apprenticeship in stunt-work and extra parts, Buster Crabbe experienced his nominal movie debut starring in what he'd later refer to as "the only A-film I ever made." Recalling *King of the Jungle* in a 1979 TV interview, he added, "If I hadn't won the [Olympics] gold medal, Paramount would never have taken me for it."

    Buster had tested at MGM for the role that his former swimming colleague, Johnny Weissmuller, had famously won in 1932's *Tarzan the Ape Man*. The immediate popularity of that champion athlete's jungle hero inspired Paramount to purchase the rights to Charles Thurley Stoneham's 1931 novel *The Lion's Way* and join the bandwagon. Perhaps to avoid protests by Metro, Paramount retained the book's original title. When the similarly themed film was completed, Paramount cannily switched to the obviously derivative *King of the Jungle*. Only *this* jungle-bred Caucasian was a *lion* man, orphaned as a toddler when his explorer-parents were killed by wild animals during an African photographic

King of the Jungle. BC plays Kaspa the Lion Man in his first starring role (Paramount Pictures, 1933).

expedition. The child had been reared to manhood by lions, as if he were one of their own cubs, and he had communicated with them by roaring.

During a lion raid on a cattle ranch, the young man is captured and sold to an American circus, along with his lion family. The circus manager (Sidney Toler) names him Kaspa, and sends him to San Francisco, where the jungle lad jumps ship and escapes ashore, clad only in a leopard skin. He then takes refuge in a private house, where he's discovered by school-teacher Ann Rogers (Frances Dee) and her friend, Sue (Nydia Westman).

Policemen escort Kaspa back to the circus in the company of Ann, who agrees to stay on to help educate the inarticulate youth, since he obviously responds to her. Love inevitably follows as Kaspa learns English. But all is not serene with the circus, one of whose workers (Warner Richmond) taunts a lion and loses his arm, embarking on a path of vengeance that involves Kaspa and a blazing circus fire. In the film's idealistic finale, Kaspa returns to Africa with Ann to set free his lion friends.

The movie neglects to explain how that orphaned little boy, armed with only his father's hunting knife, survived jungle perils to grow into the

King of the Jungle. BC and co-star Frances Dee (Paramount Pictures, 1933).

healthy, well-muscled "lion man," nor how he so readily masters the white man's language in the company of Ann. But realism has little relationship to *King of the Jungle*, an obviously escapist entertainment concocted with tongue-in-check humor by screenwriters Philip Wylie and Fred Niblo, Jr., and directed for the apparent fun of it by the fledging team of H. Bruce Humberstone and Max Marcin.

Paramount's handsome production values incorporated location shooting (September–November 1932) that ranged from San Francisco and Santa Catalina Island to Mexico, and featured a pair of exciting action sequences that showed wild animals in mortal combat, leading to the spectacular, realistic-looking circus fire that highlights the picture's climax.

King of the Jungle's success also owes much to Buster Crabbe. For an untrained movie actor, he carries off with skill and dignity what must have been a very challenging assignment. He hasn't a lot of dialogue, but his role more than compensates in its vigorous physical demands, including much body contact with the big cats.

In its review of *King of the Jungle*, *Time* magazine compared Buster's physical appearance favorably with Weissmuller's, opining: "From the neck up he is a vast improvement." *Variety*'s critic concluded "Minus any help from the marquee it will have to attract on merit alone, and on merit it rates fair business."

Man of the Forest (*Challenge of the Frontier*)

A Paramount Picture: 1933

Credits—Director: Henry Hathaway; Associate Producer: Harold Hurley; Screenwriters: Jack Cunningham and Harold Shumate; Based on the novel *The Man of the Forest* by Zane Grey; Cinematographer: Ben Reynolds; Running Time: 63 minutes.

Cast—Randolph Scott (*Brett Dale*); Verna Hillie (*Alice Gayner*); Harry Carey (*Jim Gayner*); Noah Beery (*Clint Beasley*); Barton MacLane (*Mulvey*); Buster Crabbe (*Yegg*); Guinn Williams (*Big Casino*); Vince Barnett (*Little Casino*); Blanche Friderici (*Mrs. Forney*); Tempe Pigott (*Madame*); Tom Kennedy (*Sheriff Blake*); Frank McGlynn, Jr. (*Pegg*); Duke Lee (*Jake*); Lew Kelly, Matt Hawkins.

Zane Grey's 1920 novel was first filmed by Paramount in 1926, when John Waters directed a silent version starring Jack Holt and Georgia Hale in the roles here assigned to studio contract players Randolph Scott and Verna Hillie. Scott plays mountain trapper Brett Dale, whose pal Jim Gayner (Harry Carey) reports problems over water rights with neighboring landowner Clint Beasley (Noah Beery). Gayner sends for his niece Alice (Verna Hillie) to help sustain rights to the property, while Beasley plans to kidnap the young woman. Brett foils their plot and takes Alice to his cabin for safety; but she misunderstands his intentions and attempts to leave—until his pet mountain lion persuades her to remain there. Gayner heads for Brett's cabin to get Alice, but Beasley and his cohorts arrive in time to kill Gayner, buying off the sheriff to implicate Brett in the crime. Beasley tricks Alice into remaining there with his housekeeper, Mrs. Forney (Blanche Friderici), while he falsifies a deed to the water rights to file with the sheriff. Later, Beasley attempts to force his attentions on Alice, but the housekeeper puts him in his place.

Brett's pet lion then sneaks into the jail and mauls the sheriff into confessing his knowledge of the real murderer, and Brett is freed to get back the deed, while his pals (Guinn Williams, Vince Barnett) aid Alice in escaping from Beasley. Finally, there's a shoot-out between the Beasley gang and Brett in a burning barn. When the landowner grabs Alice, Mrs. Forney shoots him, leaving Brett and Alice to anticipate a more peaceful future.

Buster wordless role, as one of Beasley's henchmen, was so insignificant—considering his sixth-place billing—that he was called back to shoot an additional scene, shirtless, despite the wintry setting! Someone in the Paramount production office had suddenly gotten wise to the film's promotional possibilities, for *Man of the Forest*'s revised advertising posters now proclaimed: "Also starring the *King of the Jungle* star, Buster Crabbe."

To the Last Man (*Law of Vengeance*)

A Paramount Picture: 1933

Credits—Director: Henry Hathaway; Screenwriter: Jack Cunningham; Based on the novel by Zane Grey; Cinematographer: Ben Reynolds; Running Time: 60 minutes.

Cast—Randolph Scott (*Lynn Hayden*); Esther Ralston (*Ellen Colby*); Noah Beery (*Jed Colby*); Jack La Rue (*Jim Daggs*); Buster Crabbe (*Bill Hayden*); Fuzzy Knight (*Jeff Morley*); Barton MacLane (*Neil Stanley*); Gail Patrick (*Ann Hayden Stanley*); Muriel Kirkland (*Molly Hay-*

To the Last Man. BC as Bill Hayden (Paramount Pictures, 1933).

den); Egon Brecher (*Mark Hayden*); James Eagles (*Eli Bruce*); Eugenie Besserer (*Granny Spelvin*); Harlan Knight (*Grandpa Spelvin*); Shirley Temple (*Mary Stanley*); John Peter Richmond [John Carradine] (*Pete Garon*); Harry Cording (*Harry Malone*); Erville Alderson (*Judge*); James Burke (*Sheriff*); Cullen Johnston (*Bill Hayden as a child*); Jay Ward (*Lynn Hayden as a child*); Rosita Butler (*Ann Hayden as a child*); Russ Powell (*Greaves*).

Shot on location at California's Bear Valley and Pine Knot, this historical Western begins in the post–Civil War era as widowed soldier Mark Hayden (Egon Brecher) heads homeward with the intent of moving his family West. But before he can get there, his father-in-law (Harlan Knight) is murdered by Jed Colby (Noah Beery), who has long been feuding with the Spelvin clan. Fed up with warring of any kind, Mark heads West to stake a claim, accompanied by children Ann and Bill (Rosita Butler, Cullen Johnston) and leaving son Lynn (Jay Ward) to look after their newly widowed Granny Spelvin (Eugenie Besserer).

Fifteen years pass, and the imprisoned Colby is released, but bent on vengeance as he heads West to find Mark, in the company of daughter Ellen (Esther Ralston) and crony Jim Daggs (Jack La Rue). While the lawbreakers stage raids on Hayden's ranch, the now-grown Ann (Gail Patrick) marries Neil Stanley (Barton MacLane), and the adult Bill (Buster Crabbe) weds Molly (Muriel Kirkland). As the Colbys continue to plunder Mark's herd, Neil kills one of the raiders, but is himself wounded.

Now grown to manhood, Lynn (Randolph Scott) appears on the scene, and is immediately attracted to Ellen. When hostilities lead to a gun battle, Bill is killed, inciting the pacifist Mark to action. But he is shot by Jed, and the infuriated Haydens pursue the Colby gang into a canyon that Daggs has booby-trapped with explosives. In the ensuing explosion, everyone but Daggs and Lynn are wiped out by a landslide. The injured Lynn heads for Ellen, who's also coveted by Daggs. The two men engage in a fight and Daggs is killed, leaving Lynn to wed Ellen.

Paramount's lengthy history of filming Zane Grey's popular Western novels included a silent version of this story, shot in 1923 with Richard Dix, Lois Wilson and—originating his villainous Jed Colby—Noah Beery, here repeating that casting a decade later. Little Shirley Temple, who would be seen to far better advantage the following year in Paramount's *Now and Forever* and *Little Miss Marker*, is billed fourteenth in the cast of *To the Last Man*, for her fleeting appearance as the child of Gail Patrick and Barton MacLane. Henry Hathaway, this film's director, saw Temple's potential and recommended that Paramount sign her to a contract. But apparently, that studio's executives failed to share his enthusiasm, while the powers at Fox (yet to become 20th Century–Fox) were more prescient; Temple's major career as Hollywood's most successful child star would soon take flight at the rival studio.

Crabbe's fifth-billed supporting role, as the grown-up Bill Hayden, reflected Paramount's obvious indecision over the direction of his post–*King of the Jungle* career; his natural ease with the requirements of riding horses and handling action scenes would only pave the way for future Western assignments at his home studio. And who could forget the harsh but pivotal scene in which Buster's murdered corpse is propped up on his horse and sent back to a devastated Muriel Kirkland?

In its brief review of *To the Last Man*, the trade weekly *Variety* opined that the names of Buster Crabbe and Jack La Rue "might help it at the box office."

Tarzan the Fearless

A Sol Lesser Production of a serial in 12 episodes (also released as a feature film in various edited versions running, respectively, 61, 68 and 85 minutes).

Tarzan the Fearless. BC with co-star Jacqueline Wells (later Julie Bishop) in his first serial (Principal Distributing, 1933).

Released by Principal Distributing Corp.: 1933

Chapter Titles: 1—"The Dive of Death"; 2—"The Storm God Strikes"; 3—"Thundering Death"; 4—"The Pit of Peril"; 5—"Blood Money"; 6—"Voodoo Vengeance"; 7—"Caught by Cannibals"; 8—"The Creeping Terror"; 9—"Eyes of Evil"; 10—"The Death Plunge"; 11—"Harvest of Hate"; 12—"Jungle Justice."

Credit—Director: Robert F. Hill; Assistant Director: Doc Joos; Screenwriters: Basil Dickey, George Plympton and Walter Anthony; Based on characters created by Edgar Rice Burroughs; Cinematographers: Harry Neumann and Joseph Brotherton; Editor: Carl Himm; Music: Abe Meyer.

Cast—Buster Crabbe (*Tarzan*); Jacqueline Wells [Julie Bishop] (*Mary Brooks*); Edward Woods (*Bob Hall*); Philo McCullough (*Jeff Herbert*); E. Alyn Warren (*Dr. Brooks*); Mischa Auer (*High Priest*); Matthew Betz (*Nick*); Frank Lackteen (*Abdul*); Carlotta Monti (*Priestess of Zar*); Symona Boniface (*Arab Woman*); Darby Jones (*Head Bearer*).

Considering Buster's predominant Flash Gordon fame, it's surprising how many people continue to identify him with the character of Tarzan, for this serial (his first of nine), and concomitant 1933 feature entitled *Tarzan the Fearless* have now become quite obscure. Deservedly so, for relatively few ever saw the complete original serial, which has yet to be available for home viewing. And even its feature-film version only exists in seldom-seen public-domain videocassettes or DVDs of inferior quality.

In this independently made Sol Lesser production, publicized as "a new Edgar Rice Burroughs story," ape-man Tarzan prevents a lion from killing Jeff Herbert (Philo McCullough), the jungle guide hired by Mary Brooks (Jacqueline Wells), who is searching for her missing scientist-father Dr. Brooks, while accompanied by fiancé Bob Hall (Edward Woods). Jeff shows Tarzan a London solicitor's letter offering £10,000 for proof that the illiterate Tarzan (in reality, a titled British landowner's heir) is dead, as has been rumored. The search party locates Dr. Brooks' hut, where they find a treasure map that Jeff's sidekick Nick (Matthew Betz) attempts to steal. While Bob contends with Nick, Mary is abducted for sale to the high priest of an idol-worshipping native tribe, but Tarzan rescues her and takes her to his lair. Meanwhile, Nick is done in by a marauding lion, and Bob and Jeff are captured and taken to a cave where Dr. Brooks (E. Alyn Warren) is about to be sacrificed to an evil god.

Tarzan swings to their collective rescue, but Jeff later turns traitor, steals an emerald from the tribe's idol, and threatens to kill the jungle hero for the reward money unless Mary promises to marry him. Tarzan falls into a pit where he's threatened by a lion, but is saved by an elephant and an ape. The tribesmen take Mary captive and retrieve the jewel, while Bob secures their freedom in exchange for the treasure map. Jeff tries to kill Tarzan but, in a struggle over his gun, is himself killed. At the conclusion, Mary's busy teaching Tarzan English, while the jungle animals dance to music from her phonograph.

Original distribution plans called for showings of the first four episodes, edited into a feature-length movie, to be accompanied by a promotional trailer heralding further two-reel chapters, to be shown serially over the following eight weeks. At the time, this plan was lauded as "an innovation in the presentation of serials." But it seems that some theatres neglected to show the promotional short at all, thus upsetting patrons who were confounded by the picture's abrupt and inconclusive ending. Other exhibitors, perhaps discouraged by the feature's inferior quality, never screened those remaining eight episodes at all. Some 70 years after the work's 1933 release, it seems difficult to ascertain just how many venues actually showed *Tarzan the Fearless* in its entirety. Judging from the existing picture's sloppy editing and hard-to-watch prints, the entire enterprise appears to have been something of a fiasco. Certainly, there was no comparison with MGM's handsomely produced Johnny Weissmuller film of 1932, nor its many sequels.

Contemporary reviewers, while finding *Tarzan the Fearless* poorly written and weakly acted, nevertheless singled out Buster for being—as one critic put it—"physically very well fitted for the popular fictional character."

Through the complex skein of legalities, producer Sol Lesser continued to hold rights to make Tarzan pictures at the same time as MGM's ongoing Tarzan franchise proliferated. And, while Lesser would turn out further low-budget films—albeit without the services of Buster Crabbe—based on the Edgar Rice Burroughs character (*Tarzan and the Green Goddess, Tarzan's Revenge*), none would sabotage Weissmuller's permanent identification with Tarzan.

This was the first of Buster's many loan-outs from Paramount, whose consequent profits (as the actor later figured) more than compensated for all the salaries paid him during his years at that studio.

Sweetheart of Sigma Chi (*Girl of My Dreams*)

A Monogram Picture: 1933

Credits—Director: Edwin L. Marin; Producer: W.T. Lackey; Screenwriters: Luther Reed and Albert E. De Mond; Story: George Waggner, suggested by the song "Sweetheart of Sigma Chi"; Cinematographer: Gil Warrenton; Editor: J. Edwin Robbins; Dance Director: Eddie Prinz; Songs: "Sweetheart of Sigma Chi" by Byron D.

Sweetheart of Sigma Chi. BC and Mary Carlisle (Monogram Pictures, 1933).

Stokes and F. Dudleigh Vernor; "It's Spring Again" and "Fraternity Walk" by Ted Fio Rito, Edward Ward and George Waggner; Running Time: 76 minutes.

Cast—Mary Carlisle (*Vivian*); Buster Crabbe (*Bob North*); Charles Starrett (*Morley*); Florence Lake (*Dizzy*); Eddie Tamblyn (*Coxswain*); Sally Starr (*Madge*); Mary Blackford (*Bunny*); Tom Dugan (*Trainer*); Burr MacIntosh (*Professor*); Major Goodsell (*Coach*); Ted Fio Rito and his Orchestra, Glenn Erikson [Leif Erickson], Bill Carey, Betty Grable, Muzzy Marcellene, The Three Midshipmen, The Three Blue Keys.

Buster Crabbe's second loanout during his first contract year at Paramount again resulted in the lead in an independent film company's low-budget production—this time at Monogram, a so-called Poverty Row studio. *Sweetheart of Sigma Chi*'s bit players included a young blonde destined to play Buster's love interest but a few years later at Paramount: Betty Grable. Monogram remade the film in 1946 with Elyse Knox and Phil Regan.

Edwin L. Marin smoothly directed this rather conventional collegiate comedy-drama, which nevertheless sidesteps such standard campus-movie clichés as fraternity hazing and jealousy-based fisticuffs, while sprinkling its screenplay with tuneful song numbers like "It's Spring Again." The song which gave title to the film was earlier popularized by crooner Rudy Vallee. Introducing some suspense, the film's highlight is a well-shot varsity crew race.

Mary Carlisle has the title role of blonde, flirtatious Vivian, whose romantic interest centers on husky Bob North (played by Buster), a fellow Rawley College student. Unlike his more susceptible fellow crew members, Bob is too focused on the university rowing competition to notice Vivian. When she stages a phony "drowning," he swims to her rescue before realizing that he has been tricked. Since her previous attentions appear to have been lavished on another collegian, Morley (Charles Starrett), Bob suspects that Vivian may simply be using him to toy with Morley's feelings, and his athletic performance suffers a sharp decline. When he's replaced on the team by Morley, Bob reclaims the fraternity pin he had given Vivian, who retaliates by informing him that she's engaged to Morley.

On the occasion of the big homecoming crew race, Morley suffers a fractured arm, and Bob is reinstated on the team, although he continues to row poorly, so distracted is he by Vivian's "betrayal." When he's informed that she has broken off with Morley, and will be rooting for *him* at the finish line, Bob is inspired to row his crew to victory. He further solidifies himself with Vivian by saving the coxswain (Eddie Tamblyn) and his girlfriend Dizzy (Florence Lake) from drowning.

Variety's critic "Waly" termed *Sweetheart of Sigma Chi* "an excellent indie which should be able to stand alone ... on its appeal to adolescent patronage." As for Buster, he was judged "slightly uncomfortable in the college atmosphere," although the reviewer allowed, "evidently, that is intended."

Originally, John Wayne, who was then under contract to Warner Bros., was announced to star in this movie. However, his home studio apparently had second thoughts about loaning even their minor-league cowboy star to lowly Monogram, thus opening the way for Buster.

The Thundering Herd (*Buffalo Stampede*)

A Paramount Picture: 1933

Credits—Director: Henry Hathaway; Assistant Director: Neil Wheeler; Executive Producer: Emanuel Cohen; Producer: Harold Hurley; Screenwriter: Jack Cunningham; Based on the novel by Zane Grey; Cinematographer: Ben Reynolds; Art Director: Earl Hedrick; Running Time: 58 minutes.

Cast—Randolph Scott (*Tom Doane*); Judith Allen (*Milly Fayre*); Buster Crabbe (*Bill Hatch*); Noah Beery (*Randall Jett*); Raymond Hatton (*Jude Pilchuck*); Blanche

The Thundering Herd. Randolph Scott, Judith Allen and BC (Paramount Pictures, 1933).

Friderici (*Mrs. Jane Jett*); Harry Carey (*Clark Sprague*); Monte Blue (*Joe Billings*); Barton MacLane (*Pruitt*); Al Bridge (*Catlee*); Dick Rush (*Middlewest*); Frank Rice (*Blacksmith*); Buck Connors (*Buffalo Hunter*); Charles McMurphy (*Andrews*); Francis Ford, Tom London, Marie Elliott.

This was yet another of the many Zane Grey stories that Paramount had filmed in the silent '20s and recycled a decade later, frequently with a re-use of action footage from its earlier incarnation. *The Thundering Herd* was originally brought to the screen in 1925 (the same year Grey's novel was published), starring Jack Holt and Lois Wilson. Raymond Hatton played the role of Jude Pilchuck in both versions.

It's set in the West of 1874, where Tom Doane and Bill Hatch (Randolph Scott, Buster Crabbe) are employed by trader Clark Sprague (Harry Carey), whose main line is the sale of buffalo hides. Tom's fiancée Milly Fayre (Judith Allen) is forced to cope with a stepfather, Randall Jett (Noah Beery), who lusts after her, and who leads a gang of white men masquerading as Indians to rob traders of their buffalo hides. Among those victimized is Tom's friend Jude Pilchuck (Raymond Hatton), who's attacked by these predators but rescued by Tom. Jude later finds a clue that implicates Jett in the robbery attempt.

Just as Tom and Milly are about to wed, Jett kidnaps her and holds her hostage among his wagon train. In an effort to rescue her, Tom is savagely beaten by Jett, who ties his unconscious body to his horse and sends him back to Sprague.

While still intent on getting Milly back, a recovered Tom joins Sprague in skinning many buffalo. One of their men is robbed of the hides and murdered by the Jett gang at the same time that the local Indian tribe, disgusted by the decimation of buffalo herds, declares war on their killers. Tom and Sprague are warned of an impending Indian attack, as well as a threatening blizzard, and they retreat to town.

Jett's jealous wife Jane (Blanche Friderici) nevertheless rescues Milly from Jett's advances, and in the ensuing battle, both Jetts are killed. Tom saves Milly from perishing in a buffalo stampede, but they are caught up in an Indian attack against Sprague's wagon train. Finally, the Indians are defeated, leaving Tom and Milly safely free to marry.

Once again, Henry Hathaway directed a B-Western notable for its rousing action scenes and rugged outdoor melodrama, with Randolph Scott well-cast as the virile hero was Noah Beery in his now-patented villain role. And again, Buster was wasted as the hero's little-seen sidekick.

In the movie's re-release version, re-titled *Buffalo Stampede*, its introductory credits inexplicably contain no mention of either long-forgotten leading lady Judith Allen or character actress Blanche Friderici, allowing uninformed viewers to mistakenly anticipate an all-male cast.

Search for Beauty

A Paramount Picture: 1934

Credits—Director: Erle C. Kenton; Producer: E. Lloyd Sheldon; Executive Producer: Emanuel Cohen; Screenwriters: Frank Butler, Claude Binyon and Sam Hellman; Story: David Boehm and Maurine Watkins; Based on the play *Love Your Body* by Schuyler E. Grey and Paul R. Milton; Cinematographer: Harry Fischbeck; Editor: James Smith; Art Directors: Hans Dreier and John Goodman; Music: Ralph Rainger and Leo Robin; Dance Director: LeRoy Prinz; Running Time: 77 minutes.

Cast—Larry "Buster" Crabbe (*Don Jackson*); Ida Lupino (*Barbara Hilton*); Robert Armstrong (*Larry Williams*); James Gleason (*Dan Healy*); Toby Wing (*Sally*); Gertrude Michael (*Jean Strange*); Bradley Page (*Joe*); Frank McGlynn (*Reverend Rankin*); Nora Cecil (*Miss Pettigrew*); Virginia Hammond (*Mrs. Archibald Henderson-James*); Eddie Gribbon (*Adolph Knockler*); James B. "Pop" Kenton (*Caretaker*); Roscoe Karns

Search for Beauty. BC and Ida Lupino in her first American movie (Paramount Pictures, 1934).

(*Newspaper Reporter*); Verna Hillie (*Susie*); Del Henderson (*Mac*); Phil Dunham (*Heinie*); Harry Stubbs (*Fat Man in Bed*); Ara Haswell (*Blonde in Bed*); Tammany Young (*Formation Director*); Vigne, Manya Andre and Arthur Rankin (*Authors*); Charles Williams (*Cameraman*); William Norton Bailey (*Cement Form Foreman*); Earl Pingree (*Prison Clerk*); with the 30 winners of the International Beauty Contest, chosen from England, Scotland, Ireland, Australia, New Zealand, South Africa, Canada and the U.S.

Buster's next picture gave him some occasion for optimism as to his status at Paramount: He was given the male lead opposite teen-aged, platinum-haired, British newcomer Ida Lupino in this 77-minute comedy-drama. Now billed as Larry "Buster" Crabbe, the actor was cast as Olympic swimmer Don Jackson, who's recruited, along with his fellow-champ girlfriend Barbara Hilton (Lupino), to co-edit a resuscitated health-and-fitness magazine. The brains behind the operation are Larry Williams and Jean Strange (Robert Armstrong, Gertrude Michael), ex-con victims of an oil-stock scam whose former accomplice, Don Healy (James Gleason), the magazine's publisher, profited from the alliance.

In conjunction with their purchase of the magazine, Larry and Jean find they're also the owners of a gone-to-seed farm-resort named Health Acres, and they devise a plan to stimulate circulation by taking ads from health quacks and featuring photos of scantily clad females. In an effort to keep the publication legitimate, Don sponsors a tie-in health-and-beauty contest, while Barbara makes an unsuccessful attempt to foil management's efforts to sensationalize the periodical with scandalous stories. Not unexpectedly, their circulation triples, and Don persuades Healy to give him a controlling interest in Health Acres as a trade-off to Don's stock in the publication.

Don and Barbara play host to the contest winners at the now-refurbished resort, and invite them to take part in the opening bathing-suit pageant, as well as serve as fitness instructors for the guests. Attempting to sabotage the resort, Jean circulates pictures of well-built men to the female guests, while Healy and Williams titillate the men with enticing girly photos. When the pageant leads to uninhibited parties in the various rooms, Don rallies some of the contest winners to help break them up. He and Barbara suffer a rift in their relationship over her suspicions about Don's friendship with Jean, but he manages to reinstate himself with Barbara. With the aid of their friend Reverend Rankin (Frank McGlynn), Don and Barbara are found to be the enterprise's chief stockholders, with Jean controlling a mere ten percent of the health farm. As the movie concludes, a defeated Jean, Healy and Williams are obliged to participate in a calisthenics session.

In conjunction with this film, Paramount gained added publicity by staging a bona fide, international "Search for Beauty" contest that assured winners of a free trip to Hollywood, as well as a movie role. Perhaps the luckiest such participant was a Texas redhead named Clara Lou Sheridan, who can be briefly glimpsed in *Search for Beauty*'s poolside pageant sequence. For her, fame and fortune would lie ahead, once the "Clara Lou" was changed to "Ann."

Variety, while noting that Buster gave "a few flashes of the lily white in a bathing suit and later under a shower in the locker room," observed "a big improvement in his facial makeup and appearance." The show-business weekly also reported, "Crabbe gives a much better performance than in his first start, indicating he doesn't necessarily have to confine himself to playing Tarzan, but can venture into broader histrionic fields."

Unfortunately, none of the Paramount brass seemed to be paying attention. Aside from supplying juvenile love-interest in the W.C. Fields comedy *You're Telling Me*, Buster would spend the remainder of 1934 on loan-outs to other studios.

You're Telling Me

A Paramount Picture: 1934

Credits—Director: Erle C. Kenton; Producer: William Le Baron; Screenwriters: Walter De Leon, Paul M. Jones and J.P. McEvoy; Based on the story "Mr. Bisbee's Princess" by Julian Leonard Street in *Red Book Magazine*; Cinematographer: Alfred Gilks; Editor: Otho Lovering; Art Directors: Hans Dreier and Robert Odell; Music: Arthur Johnston and Sam Coslow; Running Time: 67 minutes.

Cast—W.C. Fields (*Sam Bisbee*); Larry "Buster" Crabbe (*Bob Murchison*); Joan Marsh (*Pauline Bisbee*); Adrienne Ames (*Princess Marie Lescaboura*); Louise Carter (*Mrs. Bessie Bisbee*); Kathleen Howard (*Mrs. Edward Quimby Murchison*); Tammany Young (*Caddy*); Del Henderson (*Major Brown*); James B. "Pop" Kenton (*Doc Beebe*); Robert McKenzie (*Charles Bogle*); Nora Cecil (*Mrs. Price*); George Irving (*Mr. Robbins, President of the National Tire Co.*); Alfred Delcambre (*Phil Cummings*); Fred Sullivan (*Mr. Murchison*); Jerry Stewart (*Frobisher*); George MacQuarrie (*Crabbe*); John M. Sullivan (*Gray*); William Robyns (*Postman*); Vernon Dent (*Fat Man*); Harold Berquist (*Doorman*); Lee Phelps (*First Cop*); Frank O'Connor (*Second Cop*); Florence Enright (*Mrs. Kelly*); Isabelle La Mal (*Rosita*); Edward Le Saint (*Conductor*); James C. Morton (*George Smith*); Elise Cavanna (*Mrs. Smith*); Billy Engle (*First Lounger*); George Ovey (*Second Lounger*); Albert Hart (*Third Lounger*); Hal Craig (*Motor Cop*); Dorothy Bay (*Mrs. Kendall*).

As with its Zane Grey Westerns, Paramount continued its resourceful streak by remaking silent films of the '20s, in this case showcasing the unique comedy star W.C. Fields in a talkie makeover of his 1926 vehicle *So's Your Old Man.*

Set in the mythical hamlet of Crystal Springs, this Fields-tailored farce stars the comedian as bibulous Sam Bisbee, a career optician and failed inventor whose daughter Pauline (Joan Marsh) hopes to wed Bob Murchison (Buster Crabbe), the son of an upper-crust local family. Bob's snobbish mother (Kathleen Howard) does her best to sabotage the union until she learns that Mrs. Bisbee (Louise Carter) is descended from a prominent Virginia clan. However, Sam's behavior gives the Murchisons pause, as he goes about trying to promote his inventions, foremost of which is a punctureproof tire. Needless to report, there's a succession of slapstick complications—including the appearance of a visiting Russian princess (Adrienne Ames), who eventually helps Sam get a fortune for his invention—before Bob and Pauline leave town on their honeymoon.

Although *Variety* credited Buster with giving "a negligible performance," the actor managed to present an attractive appearance in a neat wardrobe, as well as turn in a professional-looking acting job. In the mid-'30s, a W. C. Fields film seldom allowed his supporting cast any opportunity for being more than a foil for the master comedian.

You're Telling Me. Joan Marsh and BC (Paramount Pictures, 1934).

Badge of Honor

A Mayfair Picture: 1934

Credits—Director: Spencer Gordon Bennet; Producer: Lester F. Scott, Jr.; Screenwriters: Robert Emmett, Roger Tansy and George Morgan; Cinematographer: James S. Brown, Jr.; Editor: Fred Bain; Art Director: Paul Palmentola; Running Time: 62 minutes.

Cast—Buster Crabbe (*Bob Gordon*); Ruth Hall (*Helen Brewster*); Ralph Lewis (*Randall Brewster*); Betty Blythe (*Mrs. Van Alstyne*); John Trent (*Harvey Larkin*); Ernie Adams (*Tip Crane*); Alan Cavan, Charles McAvoy, William Arnold, Broderick O'Farrell.

For some reason, Paramount found it easier to loan Buster out to other movie companies than to find suitable roles for him in that studio's own 1934 productions. And thus the actor found himself at low-budget Mayfair Pictures, one of Hollywood's many Depression-era "Poverty Row" corporations. There he was the top-featured star in a pair of minor-league action melodramas, both directed by the serials veteran Spencer Gordon Bennet. Both films billed their visiting leading man as simply "Buster Crabbe."

Badge of Honor, the first of his two Mayfair programmers, was a newspaper yarn, casting him as Bob Gordon. (This was Buster's third recent assignment as "Bob," a frequently employed character name that appeared to suit him.)

An out-of-work reporter, Bob rescues damsel-in-distress Helen Brewster (Ruth Hall) from her runaway horse. As luck would have it, she's the daughter of financially troubled newspaper publisher Randall Brewster (Ralph Lewis), whose best reporters have been lured away from *The Record* by a rival publication, thus conveniently providing an opening for Bob. To prove himself capable, Bob helps settle several libel suits against *The Record* before he is assigned to interview Trim Fuller, a notorious gangster who has just been acquitted of murder. When Bob uncovers a connection between Fuller and rival newspaperman Howard Kent, it leads to a succession of dangerous escapades that finally brings the culprits to justice and romantically unites Bob with Helen.

As the movie's nominal action hero, Buster not only enjoyed the novelty of top-star billing, but was kept busier than in any role he'd had since *Tarzan the Fearless*.

We're Rich Again

An RKO Radio Picture: 1934

Credits—Director: William A. Seiter; Assistant Director: Doran Cox; Executive Producer: Pandro S. Berman; Associate Producer: Glendon Allvine; Screenwriter: Ray Harris; Based on the play *And Let Who Will Be Clever* by Alden Nash; Cinematographer: Nick Musuraca; Editor: George Crone; Art Director: Van Nest Polglase; Costumes: Walter Plunkett; Music: Max Steiner; Song: "Senorita," words and music by Albert Hay Malotte; Running Time: 72 minutes.

Cast—Edna May Oliver (*Maude Standing*); Billie Burke (*Linda Page*); Marion Nixon (*Arabella*); Reginald Denny (*Bookington "Bookie" Wells*); Joan Marsh (*Carolyn Page*); Larry "Buster" Crabbe (*Erasmus "Erp" Rockwell Pennington*); Grant Mitchell (*Wilbur Page*); Gloria Shea (*Victoria "Vic" Page*); Edgar Kennedy (*Healy*); Otto Yamaoka (*Fugi*); Lenita Lane (*Charmion*); Dick Elliott (*Mr. Green*); Andreas de Segurola (*José*); Nellie Wilson Baldwin (*Mrs. Green*).

Loaned to the more prestigious RKO Radio Pictures, which followed Paramount's current tendency to list him as "Larry 'Buster' Crabbe," the sixth-billed Buster was chiefly employed in this wacky society-comedy to display his impressive physique in a bathing suit and to serve as the mostly silent butt of jokes.

Known as "Erp" (for Erasmus Rockwell Pennington, if you please!), he's a backstroke swim champ whose semi-unclad presence decorates the Santa Barbara residence of the well-to-do families of Wilbur and Linda

We're Rich Again. Joan Marsh, BC, Gloria Shea (seated), Billie Burke and Marion Nixon (RKO Radio Pictures, 1934).

Page (Grant Mitchell, Billie Burke), who are on the verge of bankruptcy. On the eve of their daughter Carolyn's (Joan Marsh) marriage to wealthy Bookington "Bookie" Wells (Reginald Denny), the family is further burdened by the unexpected appearance of their tiresomely garrulous country-bumpkin cousin Arabella (Marion Nixon), who manages to disrupt the planned nuptials. At the same time, she encourages the younger Page daughter, Victoria (Gloria Shea), to elope with Erp, whom Arabella discovers is actually the rich and titled Lord Pennington.

By the picture's conclusion, Carolyn has broken off with the divorced Bookie to go to New York and become a novelist, leaving her ex-fiancé to marry Arabella, who has miraculously solved the family's financial crisis.

Having little to do with all this in any integral fashion is the top-billed Edna May Oliver, whose inimitable way with a tart line of dialogue provides a running commentary on the nutty proceedings. *Variety*'s critic was generally unimpressed, simply crediting the movie's "moderate laughs" to the presence of "experienced farceurs in the cast."

The Oil Raider

A Mayfair Picture: 1934

Credits—Director: Spencer Gordon Bennet; Assistant Director: Harry Knight; Producer: Lester F. Scott, Jr.; Screenwriters: Rex Taylor, George Morgan and Homer King Gordon; Cinematographer: Edward Snyder; Editor: Fred Bain; Art Director: Paul Palmentola; Running Time: 59 minutes.

Cast—Buster Crabbe (*Dave Warren*); Gloria Shea (*Alice Varley*); George Irving (*J.T. Varley*); Max Wagner (*Simmons*); Emmett Vogan (*Jim Walker*); Harold Minjir (*Morrison*).

Produced by substantially the same team as his previous Mayfair loan-out, *The Oil Raider* reunited Buster romantically with his *We're Rich Again* co-star Gloria Shea. This time he was cast as Dave Walker, an oil prospector contending with a problematic employee named Simmons (Max Wagner), whom he fires. At the office of J.T. Varley (George Irving), his financial backer, Dave takes a shine to Alice (Shea), whom he mistakes for the switchboard operator, but who's actually Varley's niece. After agreeing to invest in Dave's well and to loan him an additional sum, Varley learns that

The Oil Raider. BC and Gloria Shea (Mayfair Pictures, 1934).

a stock market dive has left him near bankruptcy. On a visit to Dave's well, Varley interrogates foreman Jim Walker (Emmett Vogan) about both the operation's prospects and Dave's falling out with Simmons. Informed that Dave is about to strike oil, Varley, who has secretly added a damaging clause to Dave's loan contract, makes a deal with Simmons to wreck the well and thus prevent the realization of oil before the three-month loan period is up.

The vengeful Simmons nearly succeeds in killing Dave by tampering with the brakes on his truck. Learning the extent of Varley's underhanded tactics, Dave so informs Alice, who accompanies him to confront her uncle in Simmons' hotel room. Varley turns remorseful, but an angry Simmons hurries to sabotage the well before it strikes oil. Dave manages to stop him, embracing Alice as they're showered with gushing oil.

The Oil Raider offers little more than routine supporting-bill melodramatics, modestly produced and easily forgotten. But once again Buster was topping the cast as an action hero and gaining valuable experience for the career opportunities that lay ahead. In the similar *Wildcat* (1942), Richard Arlen handled the heroics and Buster provided the villainy.

She Had to Choose

A Majestic Picture: 1934

Credits—Director: Ralph Ceder; Assistant Director: J.A. Duffy; Producer: Larry Darmour; Screenwriters: Mann Page, Izola Forrester and Houston Branch; Cinematographer: James D. Brown, Jr.; Editor: Charles Harris; Art Director: Frank H. Dexter; Songs: "A Cup of Coffee, a Sandwich and You" by Billy Rose, Al Dubin and Joseph Meyer; and "There's a Tavern in the Town" (traditional); Running Time: 65 minutes.

Cast—Larry "Buster" Crabbe (*Bill Cutler*); Isabel Jewell (*Sally Bates*); Sally Blane (*Clara Berry*); Regis Toomey (*Jack Berry*); Maidel Turner (*Mrs. Cutler*); Fuzzy Knight (*Wally*); Arthur Stone (*Pop*); Edward Gargan (*Higgins*); Huntley Gordon (*Attorney*); Wallis Clark (*District Attorney*); Kenneth Howell (*Announcer*); Eddie Fetherstone, Max Wagner (*Hold-up Men*).

For his fourth and final loan-out movie of 1934, Buster had the male lead in this reasonably entertaining little "Poverty Row" drama, teaming him with blonde Isabel Jewell, who was usually cast in supporting character roles in major-studio pictures. In this, her first starring part, Jewell plays Sally Bates, an out-of-work Texas tomboy looking for a job in Los Angeles. Stopping for coffee at a drive-in stand, she meets proprietor Bill Cutler (the actor once again billed as "Larry 'Buster' Crabbe"), a former college-football hero. Later, Bill and his waiter-friend Wally (Fuzzy Knight) find Sally asleep in her car and buy her dinner. When two hold-up men invade the restaurant, Bill puts up a struggle while Sally produces a six-shooter and wounds one of the bandits, saving Bill's life. In gratitude, he offers her a waitress job, insisting that she board with his mother (Maidel Turner).

Now secretly in love with Bill, Sally believes his real affections are for the sophisticated Clara Berry (Sally Blane), a rich girl whom his mother wants him to marry. And, while Bill dates Clara, Sally spends time with her ne'er-do-well brother Jack (Regis Toomey). It's a situation of which Bill disapproves and one that turns unpleasant when Jack takes Sally (dressed in one of Clara's borrowed frocks) to a nightclub where the other couple is dining. Clara recognizes her dress and humiliates Sally in front of Bill, after which Sally rips off the dress and goes off with Jack.

Bill concerned about Sally, tracks her to Jack's apartment, where he fights for her honor, accidentally killing Jack in the struggle. Charged with murder, he asserts he was only trying to protect an innocent young lady. When Sally's story is undermined by a blackmailer who knows that she and Jack had recently wed in Mexico, she borrows the blackmail money for Clara to save Bill.

During the subsequent trial, Bill learns about the blackmail loan and turns against Sally, whom he brands a traitor. Once he's acquitted, Sally leaves L.A. Later, Bill discovers how much he misunderstood everything, and he pursues her to express his gratitude for all she's done for him. Eventually, Bill catches up with Sally at a gas station, where they're reconciled. Finally, he proposes marriage.

In reviewing *She Had to Choose*, weekly *Variety* thought Isabel Jewell "miscast" as Sally, while allowing that "Buster Crabbe is not bad." As for the movie itself, it was dismissed as "too unreal and implausible to hold even passing attention."

Considering the brief production schedule allotted for most such low-budget independent productions, Buster may have been grateful that prestigious Paramount kept him employed on their studio lot for all three of his 1935 films.

Hold 'Em Yale (Uniform Lovers)

A Paramount Picture: 1935

Credits—Director: Sidney Lanfield; Producer: Charles R. Rogers; Screenwriters: Paul Gerard Smith and Eddie Welch; Based on the short story by Damon Runyon in *Colliers* magazine; Cinematographer: Milton Krasner; Editor: Jack Dennis; Running Time: 65 minutes.

Cast—Patricia Ellis (*Clarice Van Cleve*); Cesar Romero (*Georgie the Chaser*); Larry "Buster" Crabbe (*Hector Wilmot*); William Frawley (*Sunshine Joe*); Andy Devine (*Liverlips*); George Barbier (*Mr. Van Cleve*); Warren Hymer (*Sam the Gonoph*); George E.

Stone (*Benny South Street*); Hale Hamilton (*Mr. Wilmot*); Guy Usher (*Coach Jennings*); Grant Withers (*Cleary*); Leonard Carey (*Langdon*); Garry Owen (*Laverty*); Ethel Griffies (*Mrs. Peavey*); Kendall Evans (*Train Conductor*); Theodore Lorch (*Pullman Conductor*); Oscar Smith (*Porter*); Stanley Andrews (*Judge*); Reed Howes, Phillips Smalley, Edward Gargan, Arthur Housman.

In this Damon Runyon adaptation, Buster has the secondary role of Hector Wilmot, a studious Yale football player whose romantic interest in spoiled heiress Clarice Van Cleve (Patricia Ellis) goes unreciprocated. Her unusual problem: She's only interested in men in uniform. In fact, Clarice has a history of rash elopements with three inappropriate but uniformed men, the disposal of whom has cost her father (George Barbier) thousands of dollars in payoffs.

Now, it seems, a racketeer named Sunshine Joe (William Frawley) has read about Clarice's weakness, and has plans of his own to get some of that Van Cleve fortune. His ploy: dress Casanova con artist Georgie the Chaser (Cesar Romero) in a uniform and send him to Lonesome Pines, New Jersey, where Clarice is enjoying a "rest cure" in the joint company of her protective father, his friend Wilmot (Hale Hamilton) and Wilmot's son Hector.

Hold 'Em Yale. Patricia Ellis and BC (Paramount Pictures, 1935).

Posing as Captain Mario Valdez of the Foreign Flying Corps, Georgie manages to meet and make a play for susceptible Clarice, who's smitten enough to accept his marriage proposal. However, Hector intercedes just in time to prevent their elopement, after which Van Cleve installs her in a girls' school for safe-keeping.

The wacky screenplay then has Clarice running away from school to marry Georgie, regardless of being disinherited by her father. When Georgie discovers that development, he abandons her to pursue another girl, while his shady colleague Benny (George E. Stone), hopeful of a reward, informs Van Cleve of her whereabouts. Van Cleve employs Benny and his cohorts Joe, Liverlips (Andy Devine) and Sam (Warren Hymer) to convince Clarice to marry Hector, who's playing in a Yale-Harvard game. The gang escorts Clarice to the game, pressuring the coach at gunpoint to put the incompetent Hector onto the playing field. Hector surprises everyone by miraculously scoring the goal Yale needs to win. Suddenly, Clarice sees him in a romantic new light, and they are wed.

Variety's reviewer found some amusement in the movie's dialogue, while calling the story "a daffy dilly." As for Buster, he was thought to display "some histrionic improvement, but still has mostly his appearance to recommend him." *Variety* also knocked the film's lack of box-office names in the cast, for whose female lead both Bette Davis and Frances Dee had been mentioned before Paramount borrowed the blonde and bland Patricia Ellis from Warner Bros.

The Wanderer of the Wasteland

A Paramount Picture: 1935

Credits—Director: Otho Lovering; Executive Producer: Henry Herzbrun; Producer: Harold Hurley; Associate Producer: William T. Lackey; Screenwriter: Stuart Anthony; Based on the novel by Zane Grey; Cinematographer: Ben Reynolds; Editor: Everett Douglas; Art Directors: Hans Dreier and David Garber; Running Time: 66 minutes.

Cast—Dean Jagger (*Adam Larey*); Gail Patrick (*Ruth Virey*); Edward Ellis (*Dismukes*); Larry "Buster" Crabbe (*Big Ben*); Trixie Friganza (*Big Jo*); Monte Blue (*Guerd Larey*); Raymond Hatton (*G. August Merryvale*); Charles Waldron, Sr. (*Mr. Virey*); Anna Q. Nilsson (*Mrs. Virey*); Glenn Erikson [Leif Erickson] (*Lawrence*); Tammany Young (*Paducah*); Kenneth Harlan (*Bob*); Fuzzy Knight (*Deputy Scott*); Benny Baker (*Piano Player*); Stanley Andrews (*Sheriff Collishaw*); Jim Thorpe (*Charlie Jim*); Alfred Delcambre (*Deputy Hines*); Marina Schubert [Marina Koshetz] (*Blonde Dance Hall Girl*); Al St. John (*Tattooer*); Chester Gan (*Ling*); Pat O'Malley (*Jed*); Hal Price (*Bartender*); William Welsh (*First Man*); Jules Cowles (*Second Man*); Lew Kelly (*Guide*); Eddie Sturgis (*Dealer*); Brady Kline (*Dealer at Dice Game*); Marian Mansfield (*Lady at Card Game*); Maxine Rainer (*Second Girl*); Philo McCullough (*Squid*); Irving Bacon

(*First Bartender*); Clarence L. Sherwood (*Second Bartender*); Frank Lackteen (*Half-Breed Indian*); Bruce Mitchell (*Dealer in Big Joe's Place*).

After his loan-out leading roles in three independent productions, it was almost as though Paramount sought to underscore Buster's contract-player status by assigning him to a villainous supporting part in this, another of their routine Zane Grey remakes. The studio had first filmed this tale in a silent 1924 version with Jack Holt, Billie Dove and Noah Beery. In 1945, RKO would shoot a third adaptation starring James Warren, Audrey Long and Richard Martin.

The story centers on Adam Larey (Dean Jagger), who's heading for California's Death Valley in search of gold, accompanied by his fiancée Ruth Virey (Gail Patrick) and her parents (Anna Q. Nilsson, Charles Waldron, Sr.). Adam's treacherous brother Guerd (Monte Blue) plots to victimize him to pay off a gambling debt Guerd owes Sheriff Collishaw (Stanley Andrews), and they manage to cheat Adam out of $4,000 in a drunken poker game. But Adam discovers Guerd's cheating and refuses to pay up, leading to a fight in which Guerd is seriously wounded.

Collishaw threatens Adam, who informs Ruth of what transpired before taking off into the desert, where he's given refuge by a gold prospector named Dismukes (Edward Ellis). The old-timer saves Adam from arrest, and then sends him away to pass the winter with Dismukes' Indian friends.

En route, Adam's mule runs away, and he's robbed by the outlaw Big Ben (played by Buster), who keeps him prisoner. Adam manages to escape, only to find that Dismukes has gone away with Ruth to bury her now-deceased parents, and he succeeds in saving them from the predatory Ben, who is trampled to death.

Adam returns to surrender to Collishaw, only to find him replaced by a new sheriff, G. August Merryvale (Raymond Hatton), who reveals that Guerd had merely been wounded by Adam, but was later killed by Collishaw, following Adam's disappearance. Merryvale has seen Collishaw hanged for Guerd's murder. Finally, Dismukes leaves Death Valley to retire, and Adam is reunited with Ruth.

Variety ambiguously reported, "Buster Crabbe is a pretty bad villain." Whether this was intended as a critique of his acting skills wasn't explained.

Nevada

A Paramount Picture: 1935

Credits—Director: Charles Barton; Assistant Director: Lonnie F. D'Orsa; Executive Producer: Henry Herzbrun; Producer: Harold Hurley; Associate Producer: William T. Lackey; Screenwriters: Garnett Weston, Stuart Anthony and Virginia

Van Upp; Based on the novel *Nevada, A Romance of the West* by Zane Grey; Cinematographer: Archie Stout; Editor: Jack Dennis; Art Directors: Hans Dreier and David Garber; Set Decorator: A.E. Freudeman; Running Time: 58 minutes.

Cast—Larry "Buster" Crabbe (*Jim "Nevada" Lacey*); Kathleen Burke (*Hettie Ide*); Sid Saylor (*Cash Burridge*); Monte Blue (*Clem Dillon*); William Duncan (*Ben Ide*); Richard Carle (*Judge John Franklidge*); Stanley Andrews (*Cawthorne*); Frank Sheridan (*Tom Blaine*); Raymond Hatton (*Sheriff Frank*); Glenn Erikson [Leif Erickson] (*Bill Ide*); Jack Kennedy (*Mac Turk*); Albert Taylor (*Hodge*); Murdock MacQuarrie (*Watson*); Robert E. Homans (*Carver*); Henry Roquemore (*Bartender*); William L. Thorne and Henry Dunkinson (*Card Players*); Barney M. Furey (*Bartender at Card Game*); William Desmond (*Wilson*); Frank Rice (*Shorty*); Dutch Hendrian (*Cawthorne's Henchman*).

Apparently, Paramount had come to appreciate Buster's supporting-player contributions to so many of their programmers of the two preceding years, for he was now accorded his first starring role in the studio's ongoing Zane Grey series. *Variety* called *Nevada* "[a] shade above the average," praising its photography and production values, and citing Buster for performing "with some amount of dash."

The plot is set in the 1900 West, where lawbreakers Jim "Nevada" Lacey (Buster) and his pal Cash Burridge (Sid Saylor), on the run from the authorities, save lady-in-distress Hettie Ide (Kathleen Burke), whose horse team has bolted with her. Later on, Nevada unexpectedly becomes a rancher when he tries to help a victimized landowner win back his property in a card game—and finds himself a suicide's beneficiary.

Nevada joins with his neighbors, including Hettie and her father Ben (William Duncan), on a cattle drive during which some of the cowboys are ambushed and killed by rustlers. All except the Ides suspect Nevada, forcing him to leave the drive, and arranging with Ben to sell his herd. Nevada and Cash learn that two other ranchers, Dillon and Cawthorne (Monte Blue, Stanley Andrews), are plotting to massacre everyone else and make off to nearby Mexico with the cattle, and they return to inform Ben. When the rustlers strike, the ranchers are prepared for battle. In the subsequent shootout, a wounded Nevada takes Clem hostage while the other culprits surrender. Nevada passes out while Clem gets away, only to be shot by the sheriff (Raymond Hatton). In the story's wrap-up, Nevada recovers to see his name cleared, anticipating a wedded future with Hettie.

This was a remake of Paramount's 1927 film starring a fledgling Gary Cooper and Thelma Todd. As usual with the Zane Grey series, Paramount cut financial corners by recycling footage from the silent version. The giveaway: stepped-up action, as both cattle and cowboys suddenly move in double time, with laughably mismatched results. In 1944, RKO would again remake the Zane Grey story with Robert Mitchum and Anne Jeffreys.

Drift Fence (Texas Desperadoes)

A Paramount Picture: 1936

Credits—Director: Otho Lovering; Executive Producer: Henry Herzbrun; Producer: Harold Hurley; Associate Producer: William T. Lackey; Screenwriters: Robert Yost and Stuart Anthony; Based on the novel by Zane Grey; Cinematographer: Virgil Miller; Editor: Everett Douglas; Art Directors: Hans Dreier and David Garber; Set Decorator: A.E Freudeman; Running Time: 56 minutes.

Cast—Larry "Buster" Crabbe (*Slinger "Buddy" Dunn*); Katherine De Mille (*Molly Dunn*); Tom Keene (*Jim Travis*); Benny Baker (*Jim Traft*); Glenn Erikson [Leif Erickson] (*Curley Prentiss*); Stanley Andrews (*Clay Jackson*); Richard Carle (*Sheriff Bingham*); Irving Bacon (*Windy Watkins*); Effie Ellsler (*Grandma Dunn*); Walter Long (*Bev Wilson*); Jan Duggan (*Carrie Bingham*); Chester Gan (*Clarence*); Richard Alexander (*Seth Haverly*); Bud Fine (*Sam Haverly*); Jack Pennick (*Weary*); Henry Roquemore (*Judge*); Jack Clifford (*Rodeo Announcer*); Frank O'Connor (*Bartender*); Don Roberts (*Man Behind Counter*).

For a change, this Zane Grey Western *wasn't* a remake of any silent picture, for Grey's novel was a 1932 publication. Buster Crabbe's top billing is misleading; actually, his is a supporting, somewhat "heavy" role. The movie's real lead is Tom Keene, a veteran star of numerous RKO Westerns of the early-sound years, and at this time under contract to Paramount, which inexplicably accorded him *third*-place billing.

And, while Buster's Paramount career now seemed to have taken a step backward, one critic observed that his acting was "considerably improved."

The story opens at a rodeo, where cowboy Jim Travis (played by Keene) replaces intimidated New Yorker Jim Traft (Benny Baker) as the rider of a bucking bronco. Traft has come West to learn cattle ranching from his uncle, who has orders to build a drift fence to foil rustler Clay Jackson (Stanley Andrews). Tenderfoot Traft then cleverly arranges to have Travis pinch-hit for him again, this time as a fence-builder. It's a plan that goes well—until Travis is threatened by Jackson's confidante Slinger Dunn (played by Buster). In fact, the Dunn family has good reason to sabotage that drift fence, for its presence will curtail their resources; indeed, Slinger's father and grandfather died attempting to prevent the building of an earlier fence. His sister Molly and grandmother (Katherine De Mille, Effie Ellsler) are equally determined to stop the fence-builders, although Molly is attracted to Travis at a local dance.

Discovering that Slinger has injured one of his ranch hands, Travis sets out for a confrontation that's complicated by the intervening Molly. While Travis is off mending the fence, the real Jim Traft turns up incognito and Slinger teams up with Jackson to steal a thousand of Traft's prime cattle.

Drift Fence. BC and Katherine De Mille (Paramount Pictures, 1936).

But Slinger has a change of conscience, refusing Jackson's compensating cash and even warning Travis of Jackson's planned trap.

There follows a shootout, during which Travis reveals to Slinger that he's actually a Texas Ranger who's after Jackson for killing his best friend. Tracking Jackson to the Dunn ranch, Travis rescues Molly from the villain's clutches. Jackson is killed in the ensuing fight, and Traft inherits his uncle's ranch. Travis and Molly anticipate a future together.

Desert Gold

A Paramount Picture: 1936

Credits—Director: James Hogan; Producer: Harold Hurley; Associate Producer: William T. Lackey; Screenwriters: Stuart Anthony and Robert Yost; Based on the novel by Zane Grey; Cinematographer: George Clemens; Editor: Chandler House; Art Directors: Hans Dreier and David Garber; Set Decorator: A.E. Freudeman; Running Time: 58 minutes.

Cast—Larry "Buster" Crabbe (*Moya*); Robert Cummings (*Fordyce "Ford" Mortimer*); Marsha Hunt (*Judith Belding*); Tom Keene (*Randolph "Randy" Gale*); Glenn Erikson [Leif Erickson] (*Glenn Kasedon*); Monte Blue (*Chetley Kasedon*); Raymond Hatton (*Doc Belding*); Walter Miller (*Hank Lade*); Frank Mayo (*Bert Lash*); John Merkyl and Anders Van Haden (*Elders*); Si Jenks (*Driver*); James P. Burtis (*Sleeping Passenger*); Ed Thorpe (*Indian*); Philip Morris (*Sentry*); Willis Marks (*J.T. Winters*); Gertrude Simpson (*Guest*); Billy Bletcher, Robert McKenzie.

Desert Gold. Robert Cummings, Tom Keene and BC (Paramount Pictures, 1936).

This Zane Grey story had been twice brought to the screen in the silent era: a 1919 adaptation starred E.K. Lincoln (not to be confused with the movies' first Tarzan, Elmo Lincoln) and Margery Wilson; and a 1926 remake featured Neil Hamilton, Shirley Mason and William Powell. This 1936 sound version marked Buster Crabbe's first portrayal of a Native American. It would not be his last. Aside from Buster in dark make up, there wasn't anything remarkable about this 58-minute supporting feature. And, once again, his top billing failed to reflect the ensemble nature of his role.

It's set in contemporary Arizona, where the educated Indian Moya (Buster) becomes his tribe's chief upon the death of his father. Quick to take advantage of the situation is enterprising Chetley Kasedon (Monte Blue), who attempts to set up a partnership with Moya to mine the tribe's hidden gold. When Moya disdains any such arrangement, Kasedon's henchmen track him down and take him hostage, with the intent of forcing him to take them to the mine, which lies in the Superstition Mountains.

Meanwhile, a stagecoach bound for that locale carries a mixed group of passengers, among them Eastern mining engineer Randolph "Randy" Gale (Tom Keene) and his bumbling sidekick Fordyce "Ford" Mortimer (Robert Cummings), along with Doc Belding (Raymond Hatton) and his pretty daughter Judith (Marsha Hunt), who's engaged to marry Chet. Randy meets with Chet, who informs him of the legendary mine, predicting that it will belong to the first white man who locates it, leading the two Easterners to start their search. In the mountains, they discover Chet beating the kidnapped Moya, who refuses to tell what he knows of the mine. That night, Randy rescues the bloodied Moya, whom he takes to Doc for medical attention.

At the Belding home, Randy again meets Judith, to whom he's attracted. He's encouraged to find that she's no longer wearing Chet's ring, despite their announced engagement. When Moya recovers, he expresses his gratitude to Randy by making him an honorary tribal member, enlisting his expertise to make the mine profitable.

Chet proceeds with his wedding plans, ordering his men to put a stop to Randy's operations by kidnapping him and Fordyce. But Randy foils that plot and moves to prevent the marriage from taking place. Abducting Judith in her wedding gown, he takes her to the mining camp, where it becomes clear that she reciprocates Randy's affections. Chet, who has tracked them down with his followers, wages an armed attack on the camp, but it is stopped by Randy, who fights him atop a cliff. Moya comes to his rescue by shooting Chet, who falls to his death. Judith is now free to wed Randy.

As with *Drift Fence*, Tom Keene is the real hero here, while Buster continued to prove his worth as a supporting character actor. Robert Cummings, in his second year as a Paramount contract player, displays a flair for the comedy roles with which he'd later be most frequently identified, although his toothsome, over-energetic presence tends to become irritating.

Variety called *Desert Gold* "just another Western, made up of the usual ingredients."

Flash Gordon

A Universal serial: 1936

(Later re-edited into the feature films *Spaceship to the Unknown, Perils from the Planet Mongo* and *Atomic Rocketship*)

Chapter Titles: 1—"The Planet of Peril"; 2—"The Tunnel of Terror"; 3—"Captured by Shark Men"; 4—"Battling the Sea Beast"; 5—"The Destroying Ray"; 6—"Flaming Torture"; 7—"Shattering Doom"; 8—"Tournament of Death"; 9—"Fighting the Fire Dragon"; 10—"The Unseen Peril"; 11—"In the Claws of the Tigron"; 12—"Trapped in the Turret"; 13—"Rocketing to Earth."

Credits—Director: Frederick Stephani; Producer: Henry MacRae; Screenwriters: Frederick Stephani, George Plympton, Basil Dickey and Ella O'Neill; Based on the comic strip by Alex Raymond; Cinematographers: Jerry Ash and Richard Fryer; Editors: Saul A. Goodkind, Edwan Todd, Alvin Todd and Louis Sackin; Special Effects: Norman Dewes and Elmer A. Johnson; Art Director: Ralph Berger; Music: Franz Waxman (from *Bride of Frankenstein*); Shown in 13 chapters running approximately 20 minutes each.

Cast—Larry "Buster" Crabbe (*Flash Gordon*); Jean Rogers (*Dale Arden*); Charles Middleton (*Emperor Ming*); Priscilla Lawson (*Princess Aura*); John Lipson (*King Vultan*); Richard Alexander (*Prince Barin*); Frank Shannon (*Dr. Zarkov*); Duke York, Jr. (*King Kala*); Earl Askam (*Officer Torch*); George Cleveland (*Professor Hensley*); Theodore Lorch (*High Priest*); House Peters, Jr. (*Shark Man*); James Pierce (*Prince Thun*); Muriel Goodspeed (*Zona*); Richard Tucker (*Flash Gordon, Sr.*); Fred Kohler, Jr., Lane Chandler, Al Ferguson and Glenn Strange (*Soldiers*).

Of all the many "chapterplays" released to movie theatres in the thirties, *Flash Gordon* was by far the most popular. Based on the King Features comic-strip characters created in 1934 by Alex Raymond, its space-oriented action offered something fresh and innovational to mid–thirties Depression-era moviegoers: science fiction. And although Universal economized by utilizing existing studio sets, props and costumes from 1931's *Frankenstein*, 1932's *The Mummy* and 1935's *Bride of Frankenstein*, (as well as Franz Waxman's original music from the latter score), they nevertheless allotted a record budget reported to have been $350,000. In fact, experts claim that this original *Flash Gordon* was the top-budgeted serial of all time.

Director Frederick Stephani, who collaborated on the action-packed script, evidenced an appropriate flair for this sort of extravagant adventure yarn, and the serial was well cast.

Flash Gordon. Jean Rogers, BC and Frank Shannon (Universal Pictures, 1936).

Buster Crabbe wasn't Universal's first choice to portray the futuristic hero. Many actors were tested, among them Jon Hall (then acting under his original name of Charles Locher), before Crabbe was offered the role, necessitating another loanout arrangement with Paramount. For him, the one drawback was the condition that he bleach his brown hair blond to more closely resemble the comic-strip Flash. The already-blonde Jean Rogers, with her hair further lightened, was engaged to portray female lead Dale Arden, with character actor Charles Middleton a perfect choice for the film's evil super-villain, bald-pated Ming the Merciless.

The world is put into a state of panic when it's learned that the planet Mongo is on a collision course with Earth. In the hope of altering the situation, Flash and girlfriend Dale set off for Mongo in an experimental rocket ship built by the eccentric scientist Dr. Zarkov (Frank Shannon). On Mongo, with Earth temporarily diverted from disaster, the three are taken prisoner by the minions of Ming the Merciless, who aims to become Emperor of the Universe. Providing what might now be termed "sexual tension" is the assertive presence of Ming's curvaceous daughter Princess

Flash Gordon. Earl Askam, Frank Shannon, BC, Richard Alexander and Jean Rogers (Universal Pictures, 1936).

Aura (Priscilla Lawson), who expresses a keen interest in Flash, while her father is sufficiently distracted by Dale's beauty to want Flash eliminated. But that's only Chapter One.

Twelve subsequent episodes permit script and direction to invent a succession of exciting and mind-boggling events, as the indomitable Flash battles and defeats incredible opponents (i.e., Tigrons, Lion Men, Shark Men and Octasacs, as well as Mongo's Sacred Dragon and Orangopoid), and always manages to evade Ming's insidious traps. Not unexpectedly, however, the megalomaniacal dictator is defeated in Chapter 13, just in time for Flash, Dale and Dr. Zarkov to return to Earth, having saved the world from destruction.

Flash Gordon won great popularity among the Saturday-matinee crowd, as well as comic-strip fans, encouraging Universal to think "sequel." Two years later there would be *Flash Gordon's Trip to Mars* and, in 1940, *Flash Gordon Conquers the Universe*—after which, where else was there to take the sci-fi series, especially amid World War II?

In 1980, Universal released an updated *Flash Gordon* feature, which was more notable for its costly and spectacular production design than for its decorative but lackluster stars, Sam Jones and Melody Anderson.

The Arizona Raiders (Bad Men of Arizona)

A Paramount Picture: 1936

Credits—Director: James Hogan; Assistant Director: Harry Scott; Producer: A.M. Botsford; Associate Producer: Dan Keefe; Screenwriters: Robert Yost and John Krafft; Based on the Zane Grey story *Raiders of the Spanish Peaks*; Cinematographer: Leo Tover; Editor: Chandler House; Art Directors: Hans Dreier and Robert Odell; Set Decorator: A.E. Freudeman; Running Time: 57 minutes

Cast—Larry Crabbe (*Laramie Nelson*); Raymond Hatton (*Tracks Williams*); Marsha Hunt (*Harriett Lindsay*); Jane Rhodes (*Lenta Lindsay*); Johnny Downs ("*Lonesome*" *Alonzo Q. Mulhall*); Grant Withers (*Monroe Adams*); Don Rowan (*Luke Arledge*); Arthur Aylesworth (*Andy Winthrop*); Richard Carle (*Sheriff Boswell Albernathy*); Petra Silva (*Tiny*); Augie Gomez, Ken Cooper and Spike Spackman (*Cowboys*); Herbert Heywoord (*Sheriff*).

The Arizona Raiders. Marsha Hunt, BC and Raymond Hatton (Paramount Pictures, 1936).

As he continued to headline Paramount's seemingly endless succession of Zane Grey Westerns, Buster was now simply billed as "Larry Crabbe." It would continue thusly throughout his remaining years at that studio.

In contemporary New Mexico, innocent cowboy Laramie Nelson (Buster) befriends outlaw Tracks Williams (Raymond Hatton) and they both evade the hangman's noose of lawless Sheriff Albernathy (Richard Carle), who'd have executed them without a trial. Subsequently, Laramie encounters Harriett Lindsay (Marsha Hunt), a strong-minded rancher who is in town with her lawyer Monroe Adams (Grant Withers) to prevent her under-age sister Lenta (Jane Rhodes) from eloping with mild-mannered "Lonesome" Alonzo Q. Mulhall (Johnny Downs), who is jailed for running off with a minor. Laramie engineers their escape from incarceration, and all three head out for Harriett's Spanish Peaks ranch. Adams, who had conspired with ranch foreman Andy Winthrop (Arthur Aylesworth) to steal the Lindsay horses, savagely beats Winthrop and blames him for the bungled theft. Harriett hires Tracks and Laramie as ranch hands, but when Adams realizes that Tracks knows of his horse-thieving past, he plots unsuccessfully to have them killed.

Meanwhile, wouldbe-bridegroom Alonzo secretly hides out at the ranch to resume his courtship of Lenta. Adams now tries to get Laramie killed by ordering the ranch hand to saddle a dangerous horse named "Honey Boy." In a misunderstanding, Harriett fires Laramie, but not before he kisses her. Learning that Adams has a plan to rob the ranch of its entire cattle herd, Laramie, Tracks and Alonzo rally to Harriett's aid, convincing her of Adams' duplicity and devising a counter-plan to save the ranch. Alonzo proves himself a man of action to Lenta as Adams' rustlers wage open warfare with Harriett's loyal ranch hands. Laramie saves her from being trampled in a fall from her horse, and Adams and his men are apprehended. Finally, a double wedding unites Laramie with Harriett and Alonzo with Lenta.

Variety called *The Arizona Raiders* "a very compact horse and cow-country contribution," citing it for featuring "a lot of good comedy" in between obligatory action scenes.

For a change, *The Arizona Raiders* afforded Crabbe not only top billing, but a leading role calling for a lot of on-screen footage with plenty of action. It was a shaky sort of stardom that would not last, for his home studio would soon have the actor back in supporting parts. His true stardom would remain with Universal Pictures and its adventure serials.

Lady Be Careful (Sailor, Beware)

A Paramount Picture: 1936

Credits—Director: Theodore Reed; Associate Director: Sidney Salkow; Assistant Directors: Edgar Anderson and Ray Lissner; Executive Producer: William Le Baron; Producer: Benjamin Glazer; Screenwriters; Dorothy Parker, Alan Campbell and Harry Ruskin; Contributors to Special Sequences: Eddie Welch, Patterson McNutt, Ralph Spence and Dale Van Every; Based on the play *Sailor, Beware!* by Kenyon Nicholson and Charles Robinson; Cinematographer: Henry Sharp; Editor: Hugh Bennett; Art Directors: Hans Dreier and Roland Anderson; Set Decorator: A. E. Freudeman; Music Director: Boris Morros; Running Time: 71 minutes.

Cast—Lew Ayres (*Dud "Dynamite" Jones*); Mary Carlisle (*Billie "Stonewall" Jackson*); Benny Baker (*Barney*); Larry Crabbe (*Jake*); Grant Withers (*Lieut. Loomis*); Irving Bacon (*Happy*); Barbara Barondess (*Dode*); Sheila Bromley (*Hazel*); Wilma Francis (*Ruby*); Ethel Sykes (*Bernice*); Murray Alper (*Mattie*); Jack Chapin (*Herb*); Wesley Barry (*Texas*); Nick Lukats (*Tim*); Purnell Pratt (*Father*); Jack Adair (*Sydney*); Josephine McKim, Jennifer Gray, Barbara Koshay, Irene Bennett, Terry Ray [Ellen Drew] and Louise Stanley (*Girls in Sailboat*); Paul Barrett (*Toad*); Roy Crane (*Shorty*); Joe Ploski (*Chowoski*); Frank Arthur Swales, John Morley, Henry Arthur and Frank Losee (*Sailors*); Harry Burns (*Curio Dealer*); Carlos Barbe (*Tenor*); Lowell Drew (*First Guest*); Charles Requa (*Second Guest*); Billy Dooley (*Drunk*); Clarence L. Sherwood (*Waiter*); Robert Cummings (*First Officer*); Edward Earle (*Second Officer*).

It seems that Hollywood's censoring Hays Office had problems with Paramount's various screen adaptations of the 1933 Kenyon Nicholson-Charles Robinson play about girl-happy Navy men on leave, *Sailor, Beware!*, for that studio was forced to change the title, as well as much of the hit play's risqué content, to pacify Production Code requirements of the mid–'30s. In the adaptation devised by Dorothy Parker, Alan Campbell and Harry Ruskin, Buster/Larry portrays an arrogant heartbreaker named Jake, whose celebrated success with the opposite sex contrasts sharply with the film's central male character, Dud "Dynamite" Jones (Lew Ayres). Dynamite's a shy sailor whose romantic luck changes when his fishing scow runs into a boat full of debutantes in the fog. His apologetic concern for their welfare quickly incurs their adoration, impressing his fellow seamen when the women accompany him back to his ship. Especially upset at this unexpected turn of events is Jake, whose romantic luck appears to have temporarily run out, but who bets Dynamite that he cannot score with Billie "Stonewall" Jackson (Mary Carlisle), a Panama City taxi dancer with an aversion to sailors. If he's successful, Dynamite must prove it by producing her "Miss Panama" ribbon. Surprisingly, Dynamite's boy-next-door charm and sincerity win Stonewall's affections, but her girlfriends interfere, and when she finds out about Jake's bet, she breaks off with Dynamite. Brawls and misunderstandings eventually lead to explanations and

Lady Be Careful. Mary Carlisle and BC (Paramount Pictures, 1936).

forgiveness. At the story's conclusion, Dynamite and Stonewall are not only reunited romantically, but also officially engaged.

At 71 minutes, *Lady Be Careful* was best suited for double-feature engagements. A pleasantly innocuous service comedy, it added no luster to Crabbe's career as Paramount continued to cast him in B-pictures.

Rose Bowl (O'Reilly's Luck)

A Paramount Picture: 1936

Credits—Director: Charles Barton; Assistant Director: Eddie Montagne; Executive Producer: William Le Baron; Producer: A. M. Botsford; Screenwriter: Marguerite Roberts; Additional screenwriting contributions: Francis Wallace and Ray Harris; Based on the novel *O'Reilly of Notre Dame* by Francis Wallace; Cinematographer: Henry Sharp; Editor: William Shea; Art Directors: Hans Dreier and Earl Hedrick; Set Decorator: A.E. Freudeman; Music Director: Boris Morros; Song: "Sons of Sierra" by Charley Kisco and Leo Robin; Running Time: 75 minutes.

Cast—Eleanore Whitney (*Cheers Reynolds*); William Frawley (*Soapy Moreland*); Tom Brown (*Paddy O'Reilly*); Benny Baker (*August "Dutch" Schultz*); Larry Crabbe (*Ossie Merrill*); Nydia Westman (*Susie Reynolds*); Nick Lukats (*Donovan*); Priscilla Lawson (*Florence Taylor*); Adrian Morris (*Doc*); James Conlin (*Browning Hills*); Louis Mason (*Thornton Chauffeur*); Terry Ray [Ellen Drew] (*Mary Arnold*); John Sheehan (*Orville Jensen*); Joe Ploski (*Swenski*); Hugh McArthur (*Russell*); Charles Judels (*Mr. Schultz*); Sid Saylor, George Ovey, Milburn Stone, Henry Roquemore and Jerry Fletcher (*Members of Rubber Band*); Bodil Ann Rosing (*Mrs. Schultz*); Billy Lee (*Little Boy*); Ray Wehba, Donald McNeil, Gil Kuhn, Phil J. Duboski, Gene Hibbs, Joe Preininger, Charles Williams, Owen Hansen, Jim Henderson, Boyd Morgan, Nick Pappas, Angelo Peccianti, James Jones, Leavitt Thurlow, Jr., Miles Norton, Lyman H. Russell, Edward Shuey, Glen Galvin, David Newell, David Horsley, Lon Chaney, Jr. and Tod Goodwin (*Football Players*); Bert Moorhouse, Earl Jamison, Hal Price, Arthur Rowlands, Anthony Pawley, Donald Kerr and Buck Mack (*Reporters*); Pat O'Malley, Hooper Atchley and Charles Sherlock (*Photographers*); Herbert Ashley (*Pitt Fan*); Bernard Suss (*Spectator*); Thomas Pogue (*Rooter*); Edward Peil, Jr. (*Undergraduate*); Gertrude Messinger and June Johnson (*Girls*); Joseph Sawyer and Garry Owen (*Announcers*); Ray Hanford (*Football Fan*); Jack Murphy (*Player*); Spec O'Donnell (*Underclassman*); Paul Parry (*Manager*); Bud Flanagan [Dennis O'Keefe] (*Jones*); William Moore (*Holt*); Paul Kruger (*Team Manager*); Harry Depp (*King*); William Jeffrey (*Hay*); Wheaton Chambers (*Wallace*); Antrim Short (*Assistant Director*); Frances Morris (*Assistant Publicity Woman*); Richard Kipling (*Barber*); Charles Wilson (*Burke*); Carmen Dirigo (*Hairdresser*).

At Paramount, Buster/Larry continued to be cast in secondary roles in routine pictures like this collegiate romantic comedy, based on a 1931 novel called *O'Reilly of Notre Dame*.

The movie is set in 1933, when football star Ossie Merrill (Crabbe) graduates from a small-town high school. He and quarterback Paddy O'Reilly (Tom Brown) are rivals for the same girl, Cheers Reynolds (Eleanore Whitney). However, romantic developments are put on hold when Ossie leaves for a California college, and Paddy attends one on the East Coast.

Three years later, Ossie returns to be greeted with a hero's welcome, while Paddy, almost unnoticed, is back in town with his college buddy,

August "Dutch" Schultz (Benny Baker), who's romantically obsessed with actress Florence Taylor (Priscilla Lawson of "Princess Aura" fame). To complicate things, Cheers still loves Ossie, who has not even cared enough to write her during his long absence, while she practically ignores the torchbearing Paddy. Dutch attempts to bring his friend and Cheers together at a football game, but his plan backfires. Eventually, Paddy's college is invited to play in the New Year's Rose Bowl game, wherein the Easterners are triumphant. Finally, Cheers realizes that Paddy is the right man for her, returning Ossie's class ring and freeing him to play the field.

By now, it was stretching things a bit to accept Buster, in *Rose Bowl's* opening scenes, as a high school boy, causing moviegoers initially to wonder if he's not actually the football team's *coach*. In essence, the actor was simply duplicating his previous assignment in *Lady Be Careful*, i.e., playing the callous Casanova who fails to win the film's leading lady.

Arizona Mahoney (Arizona Thunderbolt)

A Paramount Picture: 1936

Credits—Director: James Hogan; Assistant Director: Fritz Collings; Executive Producer: William Le Baron; Producer: A. M. Botsford; Associate Producer: Daniel Keefe; Screenwriters: Robert Yost and Stuart Anthony; Based on the *McCall's* magazine story "Stairs of Sand" by Zane Grey; Cinematographer: George Clemens; Editor: James Smith; Art Directors: Hans Dreier and Robert Odell; Set Decorator: A. E. Freudeman; Music Director: Boris Morros; Running Time: 61 minutes

Cast—Joe Cook (*Arizona Mahoney*); Robert Cummings (*Phil Randall*); Larry Crabbe (*Kirby Talbot*); Marjorie Gateson (*Safrony Jones*); June Martel (*Sue Beatrice Bixby*); Dave Chasen (*Flit Smith*); John Miljan (*Cameron Lloyd*); Fred Kohler, Sr. (*Gil Blair*); James Burtis (*Terry*); Richard Carle (*Sheriff*); Irving Bacon (*Smoky*); Billie Lee (*Kid*); Frank Mayo (*Lefty*); James Mason (*Ramsey*); Jack Perrin (*Stevens*); Charles Williams (*Tim*); Frank McGlynn, Sr. (*Sleepy*); Paul "Tiny" Newland (*Boots*); Johnny Eckert, Al Burk, Frank Cordell, Bill Hurley, Spike Spackman and Cecil Kellogg (*One Picture Stock Players*); Si Jenks (*Stagecoach Driver*); Vic Potel (*Stagecoach Helper*); Ricardo Mandia (*Bum*); Anna Demetrio (*Indian Woman*); Charlene Wyatt (*Indian Child*); Dot Farley (*Woman at Circus*); Jimmy Conlin (*Man in Hay Bill Gag*); James C. Morton (*Bald-Headed Man*); John "Skins" Miller (*Thin Man*); Harry Tyler (*Bidder on Horses*); Chester Gan (*Chinese Man*).

This was an uneasy blend of comedy with standard movie–Western elements, based on the Zane Grey story previously filmed in 1929 under its original title, *Stairs of Sand*, starring Wallace Beery, Jean Arthur and Phillips Holmes.

It begins with a stagecoach robbery, engineered by masked Kirby Talbot (third-billed Crabbe). The heist nets him an express box containing

Arizona Mahoney. **June Martel and BC (Paramount Pictures, 1936).**

$10,000 in gold certificates belonging to passenger Sue Bixby (June Martel), payment for the sale of 500 head of cattle from the ranch she has inherited from her father. A letter in the box informs Kirby that the payment covers cattle stolen from the Bixby ranch by a gang of rustlers headed by Cameron Lloyd and Gil Blair (John Miljan and Fred Kohler, Sr.).

Introducing a bizarre note to the proceedings, the stagecoach victims are aided by the arrival of circus performer Arizona Mahoney (Joe Cook), who appears astride an elephant named "Jenny," along with his shy and bumbling sidekick Phil Randall (Robert Cummings). Phil and Sue are immediately attracted to one another.

Due to his disguise, Kirby, who poses as Sue's ranch foreman, goes unrecognized when she eventually reaches her destination,. That night, he and cohorts Flit Smith and Smoky (Dave Chasen and Irving Bacon) steal back the Bixby cattle from Blair and Lloyd. After Kirby overhears plans for his own killing hatched by Blair and Lloyd, he's involved in a gun battle during which Phil is wounded. Kirby escapes and takes Phil to Sue, who nurses him back to health. A contrite Kirby now admits to his guilt in the stagecoach robbery, and confesses that he was neither her father's foreman nor his friend. He tells her that, after her father's death, the ranch was taken over by strangers who stole the Bixby cattle.

At gunpoint, Kirby demands that Lloyd surrender the deed, and he consents to stay on until she can sell the ranch. When Lloyd's men attack the property, Arizona comes to their aid with his elephant, and is instrumental in destroying the bunkhouse with his cannon. Kirby manages to shoot both Lloyd and Blair, and Sue looks forward to a more peaceful future with Phil.

King of Gamblers *(Czar of the Slot Machines)*

A Paramount Picture: 1937

Credits—Director: Robert Florey; Assistant Director: John Burch; Executive Producer: William Le Baron; Producer: Paul Jones; Screenwriter: Doris Anderson; From a story by Tiffany Thayer, with treatment contributions by Ben Hecht and Charles MacArthur; Cinematographer: Harry Fischbeck; Editor: Harvey Johnston; Art Directors: Hans Dreier and Robert Odell; Set Decorator: A. E. Freudeman; Music Director: Boris Morros; Songs: "Hate to Talk About Myself" by Ralph Rainger, Leo Robin and Richard A. Whiting, and "I'm Feelin' High" by Burton Lane and Ralph Freed; Running Time: 78 minutes.

Cast—Claire Trevor *(Dixie Moore)*; Lloyd Nolan *(Jim Adams)*; Akim Tamiroff *(Steve Kalkas)*; Larry Crabbe *(Eddie)*; Helen Burgess *(Jackie Nolan)*; Porter Hall *(George Kramer)*; Harvey Stephens *(J.G. Temple)*; Barlowe Borland *(Mr. Parker)*; Purnell Pratt *(Strohm)*; Colin Tapley *(Joe)*; Paul Fix *(Charlie)*; Cecil Cunningham *(Big Edna)*; Robert Gleckler *(Ed Murkil)*; Nick Lukats *(Taxi Driver)*; Fay Holden *(Nurse)*; John Patterson *(Freddie)*; Evelyn Brent *(Cora)*; Estelle Ettere *(Laura)*; Priscilla Lawson *(Grace)*; Harry Strang *(Simeley)*; Richard Terry *(Solly)*; Connie Tom *(Tika)*; Harry Worth *(Chris)*; Alphonse Martell *(Headwaiter)*; Aileen Ransom *(Hatcheck Girl)*; George Magrill *(Tough Waiter)*; Wally Maher *(Mechanic)*; Garry Owen *(Fred)*; Mildred Gover *(Maid)*; Frank Reicher *(Temple's Valet)*; Priscilla Moran *(Secretary)*; Gertrude Messinger *(Telephone Operator)*; Frank Puglia *(Barber)*; Ralph M. Remley *(Customer)*; Henry Roquemore and Stanley Blystone *(Men at Table)*; Russell Hicks *(Man at Temple's Table)*; Natalie Moorhead, Lelah Tyler, Rita La Roy and Helen Davis *(Women at Table)*; Ethel Clayton, Gloria Williams.

Perhaps coincidentally, this hard-hitting crime drama bore more than a passing resemblance to another 1937 melodrama, the Bette Davis vehicle, *Marked Woman*. And yet, while that Warner Bros. picture dealt with nightclub clip-joint hostesses tied in with mobsters, *King of Gamblers* centers on Steve Kalkas (Akim Tamiroff), a gangster who rules the slot-machine combines and exacts revenge when innocent children are killed in a barbershop bombing.

Central to the action is the Palm Parade night club, run by maitre 'd Eddie (Crabbe), and where the star attraction is songstress Dixie Moore (Claire Trevor). As in *Marked Woman*, there's a young, pretty, innocent,

King of Gamblers. BC, Claire Trevor and Lloyd Nolan (Paramount Pictures, 1937).

Jackie (Helen Burgess), who's victimized by mobsters and ends up dead. And there's reporter Jim Adams (Lloyd Nolan), who wants to marry Dixie, despite her involvement with Kalkas. Ultimately, Kalkas is killed in the elevator shaft intended for Jim, leaving him to anticipate a better future with Dixie.

Reportedly, the film's original opening scene, in which Louise Brooks played a woman named "Joyce Beaton," who jilts Jim, was cut from the movie's release print.

Helen Burgess, a promising young actress seen to advantage the previous year in Cecil B. DeMille's *The Plainsman*, died of pneumonia at 18, just days before the preview screening of *King of Gamblers*.

And once again, "Larry Crabbe" played a tough guy employed by mobsters, but with little to do, despite his fourth-billed position in the movie's cast.

Murder Goes to College

A Paramount Picture: 1937

Credits—Director: Charles Riesner; Assistant Director: Johnny Burch; Executive Producer: William Le Baron; Producer: William Lackey; Screenwriters: Brian

Marlow, Robert Wyler and Eddie Welch; Based on the novel by Kurt Steel; Cinematographer: Henry Sharp; Editor: Edward Dmytryk; Art Directors: Hans Dreier and Earl Hedrick; Set Decorator: A. E. Freudeman; Music Director: Boris Morros; Running Time: 71 minutes.

　　Cast—Roscoe Karns (*Sim Perkins*); Marsha Hunt (*Nora Barry*); Lynne Overman (*Henry "Hank" Hyer*); Larry Crabbe (*Strike Belno*); Astrid Allwyn (*Greta Barry*); Harvey Stephens (*Paul Broderick*); Purnell Pratt (*President Arthur L. McShean*); Barlowe Borland (*Dean Wilfred Everett Olney*); Earl Foxe (*Tom Barry*); Anthony Nace (*Howard Sayforth*); Terry Ray [Ellen Drew] (*Lil*); Nick Lukats (*Drunk*); Jack Chapin (*Taxi Driver*); Charles Wilson (*Inspector Simpson*); John Indrisano (*Joe Torelli*); James Blaine and Robert Perry (*Detectives*); Ray Turner (*Decker*); James B. Carson (*Waiter*); Tom O'Grady and Paul "Tiny" Newland (*Bouncers*); Edward Emerson (*Young Drunk*); Dale Armstrong (*Announcer*); Dorothy Tennant (*Dowager*); Jack Baxley (*Concessionaire*); Ernie Alexander (*Taxi Driver*); Carl McBride (*Bartender*); Firlie Banks (*Greta's Maid*); Walter Soderling (*Janitor*); Sonny Bupp (*Boy*); Jack Cheatham (*Garage Superintendent*); Charles Sherlock, Ron Wilson, Stanley Blystone, Lelah Tyler.

　　This adaptation of a 1936 Kurt Steel mystery novel of the same title centers on the character of ex-showgirl Greta Barry (Astrid Allwyn), the

Murder Goes to College. Astrid Allwyn, BC and James B. Carson (Paramount Pictures, 1937).

faithless wife of college math professor Tom Barry (Earle Foxe), who runs a numbers racket in cahoots with the notorious Strike Belno (Crabbe). Behind Tom's back, Greta's having an affair with Strike, as well as being the object of admiration of unemployed private eye Henry "Hank" Hyer (Lynne Overman). After Hank follows her to Strike's Ringside Café, she obliges him with a dance before cutting out for a rendezvous with Strike. Hank and his boozy reporter-pal Sim Perkins (Roscoe Karns) follow them to the college, where they hear a gunshot and witness Strike making a hasty departure.

Tom is dead, and Strike appears to be the killer. Hank interrogates the other faculty members, including Paul Broderick (Harvey Stephens), another of Greta's lovers. Hank, who believes Strike innocent, agrees to work for both the gangster and the college to prove that the killer is not from the campus, thus saving the institution from a scandal. Searching for evidence, Hank and Sim find the murder weapon in a college trash can and, in a gathering of all the suspects, Hank exposes the guilty ones. It seems that Greta, who hated Tom, framed Strike and stole his gun, enabling Broderick to shoot her husband, with an eye to taking over the numbers racket. Unpaid for all his crime-solving efforts, Hank is consoled by the attentions of the deceased's pretty sister Nora Barry (Marsha Hunt).

For a change, Buster found himself in a better-than-average programmer. *Variety*'s critic was reminded of *The Thin Man* as he praised director Charles Riesner for the mystery's "brisk pace," also noting that "Larry Crabbe makes an excellent menace as the racketeer involved in the slaying." Film historians might now credit the film's pace to its editor, future director Edward Dmytryk (*Crossfire, Murder My Sweet*).

In an era in which mystery and detective series were popular, Paramount had high hopes for *Murder Goes to College*, featuring the wry comedy team of Roscoe Karns and Lynne Overman. But a follow-up entitled *Partners in Crime* (also 1937) did poorly, marking an end to this "series."

Forlorn River (River of Destiny)

A Paramount Picture: 1937

Credits—Director: Charles Barton; Assistant Director: Eddie Montagne; Producer: William Lackey; Screenwriters: Stuart Anthony and Robert Yost; Based on the novel by Zane Grey; Cinematographer: Harry Hallenberger; Editor: John Link; Art Directors: Hans Dreier and William Flannery; Set Decorator: A. E. Freudeman; Music Director: Boris Morros; Running Time: 56 minutes.

Cast—Larry Crabbe (*Nevada*); June Martel (*Ina Blaine*); Harvey Stephens (*Les Setter*); John Patterson (*Ben Ide*); Sid Saylor (*Weary Pierce*); William Duncan (*Blaine*); Raphael Bennett (*Bill Hall*); Ruth Warren (*Millie Moran*); Lew Kelly (*Sheriff Jim*

Henry Warner); Chester Conklin (*Sheriff Grundy*); Barlowe Borland (*Cashier*); Larry Lawrence (*Ed*); Lee Powell (*Duke*); Oscar G. Hendrian (*Sam*); Robert Homans (*Jeff Winters*); Purnell Pratt (*David Ward*); Tom Ung (*Barber*); Merrill McCormick (*Chet Parker*); Vester Pegg (*Hank Gordon*); Spike Spackman, Jack Moore, Cecil Kellogg, Frank Cordell and Bob Clark (*Cowboys*); Jay Wilsey (*Pete Hunter*); Gordon Jones (*Lem Watkins*); Bill Hurley.

For a change, Paramount unexpectedly cast Crabbe as the nominal hero of this inauspicious little Zane Grey Western. It was, like most of the studio's Grey-based program pictures, a remake of a silent picture, in this case the 1926 *Forlorn River*, which starred Jack Holt. As in 1935's *Nevada*, Crabbe is once again cast as a hero by that name. But, although actor Sid Saylor is again playing his pal, Saylor's character name differs from the earlier Western, and there appears to be no further continuity linking the two Grey yarns.

Cowboy Nevada and his sidekick Weary Pierce intercept bank bandit Les Setter (Harvey Stephens) with stolen money, at first with the idea of keeping the loot, but then turning it over to the sheriff. Intent on revenge, Setter kills government horse-buyer David Ward (Purnell Pratt), impersonating the dead man to sell the horses for personal gain. In good faith that he's dealing with a government man, rancher Blaine (William Duncan) does business with Setter.

Nevada and Weary visit their old friend Ben Ide (John Patterson) and his fiancée Ina Blaine (June Martel), whose father takes them on to help with his horse roundup. Because Nevada knows the true identity of Setter/Ward, the latter tries unsuccessfully to have him killed. Still determined to get even with Nevada for that bank-robbery business, Setter now gets his men to steal a hundred horses during the roundup and see that Nevada gets the blame. Nevada and Weary are subsequently arrested, but get free again after a gun is smuggled in to them by Weary's girlfriend Millie Moran (Ruth Warren), the Blaines' cook. Escaping from jail in time to stop Setter from stealing all the horses, Weary and Nevada are exonerated, and the latter's rewarded by the sheriff, who makes him his deputy.

Variety's critic lauded Buster's performance, but called *Forlorn River* "a weak B-production, geared for such spots where this type of film is needed."

Sophie Lang Goes West

A Paramount Picture: 1937

Credits—Director: Charles Riesner; Assistant Director: Roland Asher; Executive Producer: William Le Baron; Producer: Stuart Walker; Screenwriters: Doris Anderson, Brian Marlow and Robert Wyler; Based on characters created by Frederick Irving

Anderson; Cinematographer: Ted Tetzlaff; Editor: Chandler House; Art Directors: Hans Dreier and Robert Odell; Set Decorator: A. E. Freudeman; Costumes: Edith Head and Travis Banton; Music Director: Boris Morros; Running Time: 65 minutes.

Cast—Gertrude Michael (*Sophie Lang*); Lee Bowman (*Eddie Rollyn*); Sandra Storme (*Helga Roma*); Larry Crabbe (*Steve Clayson*); Barlowe Borland (*Archie Banks*); Robert Cummings (*Curly Griffin*); Jed Prouty (*J.H. Blaine*); C. Henry Gordon (*Sultan of Padaya*); Rafael Corio (*Laj*); Guy Usher (*Inspector Parr*); Fred Miller, Herbert Ransom, John Marston and Howard Mitchell (*Policemen*); Nick Lukats (*Taxi Driver*); Archie Twitchell (*Clark*); Daisy Bufford (*Maid*); "Pop" Byron (*Conductor*); Francis Sayles (*Baggage Man*); Oscar Smith (*Waiter*); Henry Leonard and Bhogwan Singh (*Servants*); Galan Galt (*Cop*); Al Hill (*Marty*); James Quinn (*Cameraman*); Albert Logan (*Pullman Porter*); Kid Herman and James Adamson (*Porters*); Harry Tenbrook (*Painter*); Nick Copeland (*Simmons*); Lynn Bailey (*Actress*); Frank Shannon (*Detective*); Ralph McCullough (*Hotel Clerk*); James Craig (*Waiter*); Philip Harrison, Betty Healy, John "Skins" Miller, Elsa Connor, Gloria Williams.

This third—and weakest—of the Sophie Lang crime-comedy series was also its last. Although Paramount contract star Carole Lombard had refused to take the title role in 1934's introductory picture, *The Notorious*

Sophie Lang Goes West. BC and Gertrude Michael (Paramount Pictures, 1937).

Sophie Lang, Gertrude Michael played that cinematic jewel thief with enough glamour and style to warrant a successful sequel.

In this 1937 follow-up, Sophie (Michael) is retired from crime, but highly suspect by the cops whenever a theft takes place. Thus, Sophie heads West when the police force her to flee her hotel, and in so doing becomes entangled with two attractive men: Eddie Rollyn (Lee Bowman), another reformed crook, and Steve Clayson (Crabbe), the boyfriend of film star Helga Roma (Sandra Storme)—all on a train bound for Hollywood.

Also aboard: the Sultan of Padaya (C. Henry Gordon), who's in possession of the "Star of the World," a large gem whose theft he tries to engineer, since his impoverished country needs the insurance money. Add a suspicious insurance agent named Archie Banks (Barlowe Borland), and *Sophie*'s screenwriting team of Doris Anderson, Brian Marlow and Robert Wyler develop a sprawling and convoluted yarn that meanders all over movieland before a fadeout that romantically unites reformees Sophie and Eddie over a bottle of champagne.

As he often did when playing a heavy, Buster sports a moustache with a suave flair. As he would later comment, these villainous roles were always more enjoyable than impersonating the hero.

Thrill of a Lifetime

A Paramount Picture: 1938

Credits—Director: George Archainbaud; Assistant Director: Joseph Lefert; Executive Producer: William Le Baron; Producer: Fanchon; Screenwriters: Seena Owen, Grant Garrett, Paul Gerard Smith and Maxwell Shane; Cinematographer: William C. Mellor; Editor: Doane Harrison; Art Directors: Hans Dreier and Franz Bachelin; Set Decorator: A. E. Freudeman; Costumes: Edith Head; Music Director: Boris Morros; Musical Arrangers: Victor Young and Arthur Franklin; Songs: "Thrill of a Lifetime" by Frederick Hollander, Sam Coslow and Carmen Lombardo; "Sweetheart Time" and "Paris in Swing" by Frederick Hollander and Sam Coslow; "If We Could Run the Country for a Day" and "It's Been a Whole Year" by the Yacht Club Boys; Dance Director: LeRoy Prinz; Fanchonette dances: Carlos Romero; Running Time: 75 minutes.

Cast—The Yacht Club Boys: Jimmy Kern (*Jimmy*), Charlie Adler (*Charlie*), George Kelley (*Kelly*) and Billy Mann (*Red*); Judy Canova (*Judy*); Ben Blue (*Skipper*); Eleanore Whitney (*Betty Jane*); Johnny Downs (*Stanley*); Betty Grable (*Gwen*); Leif Erickson (*Howard "Howdy" Nelson*); Larry Crabbe (*Don*); The Fanchonettes (*Themselves*); Dorothy Lamour (*Herself*); Zeke Canova and Anne Canova (*Themselves*); Tommy Wonder (*Billy*); Franklin Pangborn (*Sam Wattle*); June Shafer (*Receptionist*); Howard Mitchell (*Businessman*); Si Jenks (*Messenger Boy*); Marie Burton, Paula De Cardo, Norah Gale, Harriette Haddon, Lola Jensen, Gwen Kenyon, Joyce Mathews, Helaine Moler, Priscilla Moran, Suzanne Ridgway, Alma Ross, Dorothy White, Virginia

Thrill of a Lifetime. Betty Grable, BC and Constance Moore (Paramount Pictures, 1938).

Pound [Adrian Booth], Blanca Vischer, Yvonne Duval, Barbara Salisbury, Cynthia Hobart, Billy Daniels, Bill Roberts, Frank Abel, Lee Bennett, Carlyle Blackwell, Jr., Art Bronson, Bob Heasley, Russell Lee, Bud McTaggart, Gene Morgan, Bob Parrish, Mark Logan.

In his fifth year at the studio, Paramount finally allowed "Larry Crabbe" a change of pace by casting him in this musical comedy, where he could once again don swim trunks and display—if briefly—his swimming-and-diving form. Billed eighth in the cast, he had little to do except look good in and out of the water. *Variety* had high praise for the film's comedy stars Judy Canova and Ben Blue, while noting that "Crabbe does some very graceful diving from a high board." For a more strenuous acting assignment, he'd soon be back at Universal in a double-header loanout for the action-packed serials *Red Barry* and a sci-fi sequel, *Flash Gordon's Trip to Mars*.

Thrill of a Lifetime centers on Camp Romance, an island retreat where young singles congregate, looking for love. It's run by Howard "Howdy" Nelson (Leif Erickson), a budding writer who's trying to interest a theatrical agency in his play *There Ain't No Such Thing as Love*. By mistake, he invites the Yacht Club Boys to his camp, somehow confusing that comic singing quartet with big-time theatrical agents, the Wattle brothers. At the agency, Howdy meets a song-and-dance team consisting of sisters Judy and Betty Jane (Judy Canova and Eleanore Whitney) and Stanley (Johnny Downs), who are having problems with agent Sam Wattle (Franklin Pangborn), who wants to book the act, but without goofy Judy. This leads to a plan to take Judy to Camp Romance, where perhaps she'll find a mate and settle for domesticity over show business. And, while Howdy gets his lifeguard Don (Crabbe) to lavish attention on her, Judy takes a shine to bumbling Skipper (Ben Blue), who captains the camp's boat service. At the same time, Judy helps Howdy's adoring secretary Gwen (Betty Grable) make her boss notice her in a romantic scene.

Further complications ensue before Howdy's play is staged, attracting the interest of Wattle, who arranges a New York engagement. And, of course, the predictable romantic pairs find one another before the movie's 75 minutes have concluded.

Daughter of Shanghai (Daughter of the Orient)

A Paramount Picture: 1938

Credits—Director: Robert Florey; Assistant Director: Stanley Goldsmith; Executive Producer: William Le Baron; Producer: Edward T. Lowe; Screenwriters: Gladys Unger, Garnett Weston and William Hurlbut; Cinematographer: Charles Schoenbaum; Editor: Ellsworth Hoagland; Art Directors: Hans Dreier and Robert Odell; Set Decorator: A. E. Freudeman; Music Director: Boris Morros; Running Time: 67 minutes.

Cast—Anna May Wong (*Lan Ying Lin*); Charles Bickford (*Otto Hartman*); Larry Crabbe (*Andrew Sleete*); Cecil Cunningham (*Mrs. Mary Hunt*); J. Carrol Naish (*Frank Borden*); Anthony Quinn (*Harry Morgan*); John Patterson (*James Lang*); Evelyn Brent (*Olga Derey*); Philip Ahn (*Kim Lee*); Fred Kohler (*Captain Gulner*); Guy Bates Post (*Lloyd Burkett*); Virginia Dabney (*Rita*); Ching Wah Lee (*Quan Lin*); Frank Sully (*Jake*

Kelly); Ernest Whitman (*Sam Blike*); Maurice Liu (*Ah Fong*); Mrs. Wong Wing (*Amah*); Paul Fix (*Miles*); Gwen Kenyon (*Phone Girl*); Charles Wilson (*Schwartz*); John Hart (*Sailor*); Layne Tom, Jr. (*Chinese Candy Vendor*); Michael Wu (*Yung Woo*); Mae Busch (*Lil*); Bill Powell (*Carib Waiter*); Carmen Bailey, Paulita Arvizu, Carmen La Roux and Tina Menard (*Dancers*); Gino Corrado (*Interpreter*); Alex Woloshin and Agostino Borgato (*Gypsies*); Bruce Wong (*Chinese*); Andre P. Marsaudon (*South American*); Billy Jones, Jimmie Dundee and Chick Collins (*Seamen Who Fight*); Harry Strang (*Sailor*); Lee Shumway (*Ship's Officer*); Pierre Watkin (*Mr. Yorkland*); Rebecca Wassem, Marie Burton, Paula De Cardo, Alma Ross, Blanca Vischer, Norah Gale, Harriette Haddon, Joyce Mathews, Helaine Moler.

This San Francisco–based crime drama really had nothing to do with Shanghai. In fact, the movie was filmed as *Across the River*, a title so lackluster that Paramount flacks, with an eye to then-current events, came up with something reflective of the Sino-Japanese war.

Of course, the "daughter" in question is the yarn's heroine, Lan Ying Lin (Anna May Wong), whose importer-father is killed for refusing to help

Daughter of Shanghai. Maurice Liu, BC and J. Carrol Naish (Paramount Pictures, 1938).

smuggle illegal aliens into the California port city. Assigned to the case is Detective Kim Lee (Philip Ahn), whose initial meeting with the family and their friend Mary Hunt (Cecil Cunningham) fails to impress Lan Ying, who sets out to crack the smuggling ring on her own. Her immediate quarry is Otto Hartman (Charles Bickford), a shady fellow whom her father believed to be behind that operation. Tracking him to the Central American port where Hartman operates a nightclub, she infiltrates his world by hiring on as a dancer—only to discover that he *isn't* behind the smuggling ring, after all.

A similar quest brings Kim Lee to Hartman's club, where he recognizes Lan Ying among the dancers. Subsequently, the two collaborate to hide aboard the smuggling ship *Jenny Hawk*, where Lan Ying masquerades as a man. Both are discovered and caught by the smugglers, but manage to escape. Eventually, the once-trusted Mrs. Hunt turns out to be queen of the smuggling racket.

Buster Crabbe, although billed third after Wong and Bickford, has little to do as one of Cunningham's henchmen in this routine time-passer.

Flash Gordon's Trip to Mars

A Universal serial: 1938

(Later re-edited into the feature films *Rocket Ship* aka *Mars Attacks the World, Space Soldiers' Trip to Mars* and *The Deadly Ray from Mars.*)

Chapter Titles: 1—"New Worlds to Conquer"; 2—"The Living Dead"; 3—"Queen of Magic"; 4—"Ancient Enemies"; 5—"The Boomerang"; 6—"Tree Men of Mars"; 7—"The Prisoner of Mongo"; 8—"The Black Sapphire of Kalu"; 9—"Symbol of Death"; 10—"Incense of Forgetfulness"; 11—"Human Bait"; 12—"Ming the Merciless"; 13—"The Miracle of Magic"; 14—"A Beast at Bay"; 15—"An Eye for an Eye."

Credits—Directors: Ford Beebe and Robert Hill; Producer: Barney A. Sarecky; Screenwriters: Ray Trampe, Noman S. Hall, Wyndham Gittens and Herbert Dalmus; Based on the *Flash Gordon* comic strip by Alex Raymond; Cinematographer: Jerome Ash; Editors: Saul A. Goodkind, Alvin Todd, Louis Sackin and Joe Gluck; Special Effects: Kenneth Strickfaden and Eddie Keys; Shown in 15 chapters running approximately 20 minutes each.

Cast—Larry "Buster" Crabbe (*Flash Gordon*); Jean Rogers (*Dale Arden*); Charles Middleton (*Emperor Ming*); Frank Shannon (*Dr. Zarkov*); Beatrice Roberts (*Queen Azura*); Donald Kerr ("*Happy*" *Hapgood*); C. Montague Shaw (*The Clay King*); Richard Alexander (*Prince Barin*); Wheeler Oakman (*Tarnak*); Kane Richmond (*Stratosled Captain*); Kenneth Duncan (*Airdrome Captain*); Warner Richmond (*Zandar*); Jack Mulhall (*Flight Commander*); Lane Chandler (*Soldier*); Anthony Warde (*Mighty Toran*); Ben Lewis (*Pilot*); Stanley Price, Earl Douglas, Charles "Bud" Wolfe, Edwin Stanley, Lou Merrill, James C. Eagels, Hooper Atchley, James G. Blaine, Wheaton Chambers, Ray Turner, Edwin Parker, Jerry Frank, Herb Holcombe, Reed Howes, Jerry Gardner, Tom Steele.

Flash Gordon's Trip to Mars. **Frank Shannon, Donald Kerr, Jean Rogers and BC (Universal Pictures, 1938).**

Flash Gordon's Trip to Mars begins where its 1936 predecessor ended, with Flash, Dale and Dr. Zarkov (Buster, Jean Rogers and Frank Shannon) back from the planet Mongo—but not for long. Soon, they're drawn back into outer space by a powerful light beam that has set off a succession of natural disasters on Earth. Mistakenly calculating that the light beam derives from Mongo, the trio sets off in Zarkov's rocket ship, discovering en route that newspaper reporter "Happy" Hapgood (the serial's comic relief, Donald Kerr) has stowed away on board.

  Nearing Mongo, Zarkov finds that the destructive light beam is actually being directed from Mars, motivating their change of course to that planet. After a Martian ray causes their ship to crash in a remote valley, they learn that their old nemesis Ming the Merciless (Charles Middleton) still lives, and on Mars, where he has established a nefarious alliance with Azura (Beatrice Roberts), the Martian Queen of Magic.

  Now targeted by the soldiers of Ming and Azura, the Earthlings take refuge in a cave, where they're soon overpowered by the subterranean Clay People. Their King (C. Montague Shaw) informs them that his people live under a curse by Azura, who owes her magic powers to a white sapphire that she closely guards. It seems that the only salvation for the Clay People would be the destruction of that precious stone, along with a black sapphire in the possession of the planet's woods-dwelling Tree People.

While Dale and Happy are held captive by the Clay People, Flash and Zarkov are sent forth to secure the two magic stones. Eventually, after many dangerous encounters with the Tree People, they claim the black sapphire.

With the discovery that their old colleague Prince Barin (Richard Alexander) is also on Mars, Flash and Zarkov team up with him. Meanwhile, Ming turns against Azura, arranging her demise in an attack on the Clay People. Before she dies, the atoning queen turns over the white sapphire to Flash. Both magic stones are then destroyed in an electrical chamber, after which the Clay People are restored to their natural bodies.

The megalomaniacal Ming now declares himself ruler of Mars, while Flash informs a gathering of Martian noblemen of Ming's treachery. Ming isolates himself in his laboratory, increasing his nitron ray attacks on Earth. But Barin destroys the ray with a well-aimed stratosled bomb, while Ming himself is killed by a disintegrating-ray machine operated by his once-faithful aide Tarnak (Wheeler Oakman). Their mission accomplished, Flash, Dale, Zarkov and Happy return to Earth, leaving Barin in charge of the Tree People.

Unlike the original 1936 serial, *Flash Gordon's Trip to Mars* eschews romantic exchanges between Flash and Dale to concentrate on action and adventure elements. And, mysteriously, the very blonde and long-haired Jean Rogers of the earlier serial here appears in a dark, styled cut that little resembles the original Dale Arden.

Confident of their Flash Gordon franchise, Universal reined in the budget on this sequel, allotting only $175,000, half of the expenditure lavished on their 1936 original. More episodic in structure than its predecessor, this sequel nevertheless benefits from faster, if choppy, editing. With most of the 1936 cast back for an encore, the major newcomer here is Beatrice Roberts' Queen Azura, a bit of a disappointment in her acting, as well as a lack of either exotic makeup or costuming.

The film's special effects are undeniably rudimentary by latter-day standards. And, although 1938 serial audiences were less demanding in their expectations, as *Variety* reported on reviewing *Mars Attacks the World*, a 70-minute feature edited from this full-length serial: "Plenty of titters from the audience at this theatre over some of the stilted acting and other heroics."

In his comprehensive book *Science Fiction Serials*, Roy Kinnard observes that *Mars Attacks the World* "is worth noting, since it contains upgraded special effects footage not used in the serial, including a couple of impressive rear-projection shots depicting Zarkov's rocketship flying over a city as it blasts off from Earth."

Tip-Off Girls

A Paramount Picture: 1938

Credits—Director: Louis King; Assistant Director: George "Dink" Templeton; Executive Producer: William Le Baron; Associate Producer: Edward T. Lowe; Screenwriters: Maxwell Shane, Robert Yost and Stuart Anthony; Based on the *American Magazine* article "Hunting the Highway Pirates" by William E. Frazer; Cinematographer: Theodor Sparkuhl; Editor: Ellsworth Hoagland; Art Directors: Hans Dreier and Robert Odell; Set Decorator: A. E. Freudeman; Music Director: Boris Morros: Running Time: 62 minutes.

Cast—Mary Carlisle (*Marjorie Rogers*); Lloyd Nolan (*Bob Anders*); Roscoe Karns (*Tom Benson*); Larry Crabbe (*Red Deegan*); J. Carrol Naish (*Joseph Valkus*); Evelyn Brent (*Rena Terry*); Anthony Quinn (*Marty*); Benny Baker (*Scotty*); Harvey Stephens (*Jason Baardue*); Irving Bacon (*Sam*); Gertrude Short ("*Boots" Milburn*); Archie Twitchell (*Hensler*); Barlowe Borland (*Blacky*); Pierre Watkin (*George Murkil*); John Hart, Harry Templeton, Vic Demoruelle, Jr., Jack Pennick, Ethan Laidlaw and Stanley King (*Truck Drivers*); Stanley Price (*Louis*); Phillip Warren (*Steve*); Wade Boteler (*Pete*); John Patterson (*Jim*); Frank Austin (*Gus*); Richard Allen (*Police Lieutenant*); Stanley Andrews (*Police Sergeant*); Oscar G. Hendrian (*Hijacker*); Barbara Jackson (*Nurse*); Wally Dean (*First Businessman*); Field Norton (*Second Businessman*); Frank Mayo (*Third Businessman*); Pat West and Al Herman (*Proprietors*); Wally Maher (*Garage Attendant*); Harry Fleischmann and Willard Kent (*Cops*); Joyce Mathews (*Tessie*); Ruth Rogers, Laurie Lane, Margaret Randall and Cheryl Walker (*Waitresses*); Lola Jensen, Paula De Cardo, Marion Weldon, Gloria Williams.

Originally shot under the working title of *Highway Racketeers*, this well-produced B-picture was renamed the more intriguing *Tip-Off Girls* prior to its spring 1938 release. Actually, the plural is inaccurate, for reference is made to only one such woman, a gangster's moll named Rena Terry (Evelyn Brent). Rena's the girl friend of Red Deegan (Buster), overseer of the truck-robbing operations of master hijacker Joseph Valkus (J. Carrol Naish). Rena's ploy is to pose as a helpless hitchhiker (sometimes with an injury) who, once offered a lift from a trucker, tips off the vehicle's whereabouts to the gang, who then steal the truck, often reaping large profits, depending on the contents.

When some of the truck drivers are killed in the hijackings, the FBI dispatches agents Bob Anders and Tom Benson (Lloyd Nolan, Roscoe Karns) as undercover investigators. Posing as truckers, they intercept a tip from Rena and hijack a Deegan truck loaded with whiskey. Deegan catches them attempting to sell the liquor and, impressed with their thieving skills, he hires them. Bob not only becomes one of Deegan's most trusted employees, but also finds romance with Valkus's secretary, Marjorie Rogers (Mary Carlisle), who's quite ignorant of her boss's criminal career. When Bob shares an evening's assignment with the distrustful Rena, they're stopped by a policeman friend of Bob's, and whom Bob pretends to knock out, while passing the cop information implicating Valkus. But Deegan's hireling Marty (Anthony Quinn) and Rena overhear Tom phoning a hijacking tip to the authorities, and bring him to Valkus, who's already suspicious of Bob. Unaware of the FBI connection, Valkus assumes the two men are in the employ of rival hijackers, and he forces Tom and Marjorie to drive a truckload of hijackers to meet that "rival" gang—and into a police blockade. Meanwhile, Valkus tries to force Bob to reveal the identity of his real boss, but is shot by cops summoned by Marjorie's receptionist-pal "Boots" Milburn (Gertrude Short). Bob then leads a police chase after the trucks, resulting in a highway accident and the arrest of Rena, Deegan and their colleagues. Bob and Marjorie finally find a quiet moment to get hitched.

Variety's critic had high praise for *Tip-Off Girls*: "Though melodrama of a familiar brand, it is so well done that it has a freshness of appeal." Both Carlisle and Crabbe were cited for "above average" performances.

Hunted Men (Crime Gives Orders)

A Paramount Picture: 1938

Credits—Director: Louis King; Assistant Director: Joseph Lefert; Executive Producer: William Le Baron; Producer: Harold Hurley; Associate Producer: Stuart Walker; Screenwriters: Horace McCoy and William R. Lipman; Based on the play *Queen's Local* by Albert Duffy and Marian Grant; Cinematographer: Victor Milner; Editor: Anne Bauchens; Art Directors: Hans Dreier and Franz Bachelin; Set Decorator: A. E. Freudeman; Music Director: Boris Morros; Running Time: 65 minutes.

Cast—Mary Carlisle (*Jane Harris*); Lloyd Nolan (*Joe Albany*); Lynne Overman (*Peter Harris*); J. Carrol Naish (*Morton Rice*); Anthony Quinn (*Mac*); Dorothy Peterson (*Mary Harris*); Delmar Watson (*Robert Harris*); Johnny Downs (*Frank Martin*); Larry Crabbe (*James Flowers*); Regis Toomey (*Donavan*); Louise Miller (*Virgie*); Fern Emmett (*Miss Quinn*); George Davis (*Waiter*); Hooper Atchley (*Headwaiter*); Laurie Lane (*First Girl*); Mary Parker (*Second Girl*); Dick Rush (*Policeman*); Howard Mitchell (*Doorman*); Zeffie Tilbury (*Flower Woman*); Phillip Warren (*Gangster*); Robert E. Homans (*Traffic Cop*); Stanley Price (*Taxi Man*); Janet Waldo.

By now "Larry Crabbe" was getting used to being loaned to Universal for the strenuous lead in a serial, only to return to supporting roles in Paramount B-pictures. In *Hunted Men*, his assignment is even smaller than customary, and he's killed off early in the story. Nevertheless, the actor made the most of his footage, sufficient for *Variety* to cite him, along with J. Carrol Naish, for contributing "strong bits."

Hunted Men. Lloyd Nolan, BC, Phillip Warren, Anthony Quinn and J. Carrol Naish (Paramount Pictures, 1938).

In this hard-hitting little melodrama, filmed under the title *Crime Gives Orders*, Lloyd Nolan stars as racket boss Joe Albany, who bumps off night-club partner James Flowers (Crabbe) when he finds him stealing money from their joint business venture. On the lam, Joe hides out with the suburban family of hardware salesman Peter Harris (Lynne Overman), who accepts him as "Charles Edwards," a fellow conventioneer. The Harris home becomes Joe's hideout for several weeks when his lawyer, Morton Rice (Naish), advises him to remain there. Eventually, Harris and his wife Mary (Dorothy Peterson) are informed of Joe's true identity, but not their children, Jane (Mary Carlisle) and Robert (Delmar Watson), who have grown fond of "Charles." In fact, Jane admits she's fallen in love with Joe. It's a potential relationship that the racketeer reluctantly discourages, lest he cause her future unhappiness.

Young Robert, who idolizes Joe, unwittingly causes his discovery when a photo he's taken of the fugitive falls into the hands of police, who close in on the Harris home. When Joe's ordered out of the house with his hands up, he refuses to do so, deliberately reaching into his pocket and causing the cops to shoot him down.

The movie's critics admired its blend of toughness and sentiment, singling out Victor Milner's cinematography and Anne Bauchens' editing. But there was some criticism of the picture's harsh finale.

Red Barry

A Universal serial: 1938

Chapter Titles: 1—"Millions for Defense"; 2—"The Curtain Falls"; 3—"The Decoy"; 4—"High Stakes"; 5—"Desperate Chances"; 6—"The Human Target"; 7—"Midnight Tragedy"; 8—"The Devil's Disguise"; 9—"Between Two Fires"; 10—"The False Trail"; 11—"Heavy Odds"; 12—"The Enemy Within"; 13—"Mission of Mercy."

Credits—Directors: Ford Beebe and Alan James; Associate Producer: Barney A. Sarecky; Screenwriters: Norman S. Hall and Ray Trampe; Based on the comic strip by Will Gould; Cinematographer: Jerome Ash; Editors: Saul A. Goodkind, Louis Sackin and Alvin Todd; Art Director: Ralph De Lacy; Music: Charles Previn; Shown in 13 chapters running approximately 20 minutes each.

Cast—Larry "Buster" Crabbe (*Red Barry*); Edna Sedgwick (*Natacha*); Frances Robinson (*Mississippi*); Cyril Delevanti (*Wing Fu*); Frank Lackteen (*Quong Lee*); Wade Boteler (*Inspector Scott*); Hugh Huntley (*Valentine Vane*); Philip Ahn (*Hong Kong Cholly*); William Ruhl (*Mannix*); William Gould (*Commissioner*); Wheeler Oakman (*Weaver*); Stanley Price (*Petrov*); Earl Douglas (*Igor*); Charles Stevens (*Captain May*); Eric Wilton (*Tubbs*); Rita Gould (*Mama Sonja*).

Universal had experienced great success bringing such popular Sunday-supplement comic strips as *Flash Gordon, Ace Drummond, Jungle Jim* and *Tim Tyler's Luck* to the screen, and the studio now turned to the less fanciful crime melodrama *Red Barry,* based on Will Gould's mystery-adventure strip about underworld intrigue in San Francisco's Chinatown. With Buster happy to shed his Flash Gordon tights and return to his natural brown hair as the detective of the serial's title, *Red Barry* appeared aimed chiefly at juvenile audiences. In his 1977 book *Cliffhanger,* serials maven Alan G. Barbour dismisses this one as "an inferior mish-mash of intrigue in a Chinatown setting."

The plot is triggered by the theft of $2 million in negotiable bonds from a Russian envoy en route to San Francisco by ship. In Chinatown, master importer Wing Fu (Cyril Delevanti, misspelled "Syril" throughout the serial's credits) awaits delivery of the bonds, needed to finance combat planes for the ongoing war in China. Meanwhile, murders in Chinatown draw an assignment for police detective Red Barry (Buster), known as "possibly the cleverest man on the force."

Working from the Gould strip, screenwriters Norman S. Hall and Ray Trampe manage to devise a nearly endless succession of action-heavy hazards, traps and challenges for detective Red as those coveted bonds change

Red Barry. BC in the serial's title role (Universal Pictures, 1938).

hands many times before justice triumphs. Among those importantly involved in their pursuit: Russian dancer Natacha (Edna Sedgwick) and her sidekicks Igor (Earl Douglas) and Petrov (Stanley Price); Red's friend, the snoopy newspaperwoman Mississippi (Frances Robinson); Wing Fu's enterprising son, Hong Kong Cholly (Philip Ahn); master villain Quong Lee (Frank Lackteen); the anachronistically dandy, British-toned detective

Valentine Vane (Hugh Huntley); and a rather suspicious-acting theatre manager named Mannix (William Ruhl).

Buster acquits himself well in this change-of-pace role, from the physical demands necessarily placed upon any serial star to the minimal acting demands of such unlikely cliff hanging adventures. However, not a few of the suspenseful chapter endings, when reprised at the beginning of succeeding episodes, turn out to be almost inconsequential, barely giving Red Barry a moment's pause in his pursuit of the crooks—and those elusive bonds.

Illegal Traffic

A Paramount Picture: 1938

Credits—Director: Louis King; Assistant Directors: George Hippard and Harry Scott; Executive Producer: William Le Baron; Associate Producer: William C. Thomas; Screenwriters: Robert Yost, Lewis Foster and Stuart Anthony; Cinematographer: Henry Sharp; Editor: Harvey Johnston; Art Directors: Hans Dreier and John Goodman; Set Decorator: A. E. Freudeman; Music Director: Boris Morros; Running Time: 67 minutes.

Cast—J. Carrol Naish (*Lewis Zomar*); Mary Carlisle (*Carol Butler*); Robert Preston (*Charles "Bent" Martin*); Judith Barrett (*Marie Arden*); Pierre Watkin (*Jigger*); Larry Crabbe (*Steve*); George McKay (*Frank "Old Man" Butler*); Richard Denning (*Silk Patterson*); Phillip Warren (*Dittmar*); Sheila Darcy (*Mathilde*); Dolores Casey (*Mamie*); Richard Stanley [Dennis Morgan] (*Cagey Miller*); John Hart (*Davis*); Regis Toomey (*Windy*); William B. Davidson (*Dalton*); Joseph Crehan (*Chief Daley*); Monte Blue (*Captain Moran*); Archie Twitchell (*Duke*); Morgan Conway (*State's Attorney Ryan*); Howard Mitchell (*Sea Captain*); Jean Fenwick (*Stenographer*); John Locke (*Headwaiter*); Andre P. Marsaudon, Albert Pollet and Pat West (*Waiters*); Stanley Price (*Police Broadcaster*); Dick Rush (*State Patrolman*); Emory Parnell (*Lieutenant*); Robert Ryan (*Irishman*); Helaine Moler and Moselle Kimbler (*Nurses*); Marie Burton, Paula De Cardo, Harriette Haddon, Ruth Rogers, Gloria Williams, Mike Donovan.

Lewis Zomar (J. Carrol Naish) heads a transport company that helps criminals escape the law. A police investigation goes undercover with agent Charles "Bent" Martin (Robert Preston) by planting him in Zomar's employ. Bent worms his way into Zomar's good graces, during which he becomes romantically involved with Carol Butler (Mary Carlisle), whose father Frank (George McKay) runs an air strip and coffee shop connected to Zomar's illegal business.

Zomar takes an interest in the innocent Carol and makes her his personal secretary, causing his girlfriend Marie (Judith Barrett) to become jealous. When Marie goes out with Bent, it angers Carol, who doesn't realize that they're doing a job for Zomar. In order to trap Zomar, Bent and his agency boss formulate a plan involving an assisted prison break. In a bar with Marie, Bent feigns drunkenness, passing out and allowing Marie to find his F.B.I. agent card, of which she informs Zomar. The crime boss packs Marie off to Canada, empties his safe and bumps off his interfering partner Jigger (Pierre Watkin).

Forcing Bent to go to the coffee shop, Zomar shoots him, ordering Frank and Carol to take him away. But Bent manages to follow Zomar's getaway car in a plane he's piloting, forcing the car to a stop and gunning down the escaping Zomar before crash-landing safely. With Carol by his side, Bent recovers in a hospital bed.

Merely "doing time" at Paramount, in between serial-starring loanouts to Universal, "Larry Crabbe" hovers around on the periphery of *Illegal Traffic* as one of crime boss Naish's chief lieutenants. *Variety* observed that he "seems miscast," which may have signified that Buster was simply phoning it in.

Unmarried (Night Club Hostess)

A Paramount Picture: 1939

Credits—Director: Kurt Neumann; Assistant Director: Russell Mathews; Executive Producer: William Le Baron; Screenwriters: Lillie Hayward and Brian Marlow; Story: Grover Jones and William Slavens McNutt; Cinematographer: Harry Fischbeck; Editor: Stuart Gilmore; Art Directors: Hans Dreier and Robert Odell; Set Decorator: A. E. Freudeman; Music Director: Boris Morros; Running Time: 65 minutes.

Cast—Helen Twelvetrees (*Pat Rogers*); Buck Jones (*Slag Bailey*); Donald O'Connor (*Ted Streaver at 12*); John Hartley (*Ted Streaver as an Adult*); Robert Armstrong (*Pins Streaver*); Sidney Blackmer (*Cash Enright*); Larry Crabbe (*Buzz Kenton*); Edward Pawley (*Swade*); William Haade (*Waiter*); Phillip Warren (*Joe*); Dorothy Howe (*Betty Reed*); Lucien Littlefield (*School Principal*); Louise Carter (*Mrs. Charles*); Kathryn Bates (*Mrs. Smith*); Sarah Edwards (*Mrs. Jones*); Gordon Hart (*Bartender*); Stanley Blystone (*First Man*); George Melford (*Second Man*); Emory Parnell and Pat O'Malley (*Policemen*); Robert Homans (*Watchman*); Roland Drew (*Sportsman*); "Pop" Byron (*Turnkey*); Janet Waldo (*Secretary*); Larry McGrath (*Referee*); Franklin Parker (*Announcer*); Sam Ash (*Small-Town Announcer*); Jack Roper (*Spider*); Frank Hagney (*Second Referee*); Davison Clark (*Officer*); Spencer Charters (*Judge*); James Flavin (*Oil Driller*); Clarence Wilson (*Grocery Clerk*); Hamilton McFadden (*Assistant Coach*); John Conte (*Announcer*); Paula De Cardo, Norah Gale, Gwen Kenyon and Judy King (*Girls*).

As the careers of Westerns star Buck Jones and Helen Twelvetrees waned in the late thirties, Paramount teamed them in a remake of the studio's 1932 drama *Lady and Gent* that had earlier starred George Bancroft and Wynne Gibson. Cast as a prizefighter, Crabbe briefly displays his still-well-maintained swimmer's form in a pugilistic battle with Jones—and later, a beat-up, "cauliflower" face, courtesy of the studio's makeup department.

Unmarried. BC and Buck Jones (Paramount Pictures, 1939).

The "unmarried" ones of the title are longtime New York sweethearts Slag Bailey (Jones), a third-rate fighter, and nightclub hostess Pat Rogers (Twelvetrees), who take on the job of raising young Ted Streaver (Donald O'Connor), the orphaned son of Slag's late manager Pins Streaver (Robert Armstrong), who was killed in a robbery attempt. What begins as an upstate visit to check out Pins' deserted house, following his death, becomes a years-long dedication to helping young Ted get a good education. Later, in college, the youth becomes a popular football star, falling under the influence of shady fight promoter Cash Enright (Sidney Blackmer), who hopes to lure Ted away from school for the fight game. Slag tries to intervene on Ted's behalf, precipitating an altercation in which the veteran fighter is knocked out by his foster son. A contrite Ted now realizes how much he owes Slag and Pat for their dedication to his upbringing, and determines to complete his education. The long-unwed couple finally decide to make it legal.

Billed seventh as "Larry Crabbe," Buster first appears in the ring with Jones, followed by a brief scene, dancing in Twelvetrees' nightclub with singer Dorothy Howe. He reappears late in the movie as a beat-up has-been, serving as a lesson to the grown-up Ted (John Hartley). Once again, Paramount wasted their contractee's potential.

Million Dollar Legs

A Paramount Picture: 1939

Credits—Directors: Nick Grinde and (uncredited) Edward Dmytryk; Assistant Directors: Joseph Lefert and Alvin Ganzer; Executive Producer: William Le Baron; Associate Producer: William C. Thomas; Screenwriters: Lewis R. Foster, Richard English, Erwin Gelsey and Louis S. Kaye; Cinematographer: Harry Fischbeck; Editors: Arthur Schmidt and Stuart Gilmore; Art Directors: Hans Dreier and William Flannery; Set Decorator: A. E. Freudeman; Running Time: 65 minutes.

Cast—Betty Grable (*Carol Parker*); John Hartley (*Greg Melton*); Donald O'Connor (*Sticky Boone*); Jackie Coogan (*Russ Simpson*); Dorothea Kent (*Susie Quinn*); Joyce Mathews (*Bunny Maxwell*); Peter Lind Hayes (*Freddie Fry*); Larry Crabbe (*Coach Baxter*); Richard Denning (*Hunk Jordan*); Phillip Warren (*Buck Hogan*); Edward Arnold, Jr. (*Blimp Garrett*); Thurston Hall (*Gregory Melton, Sr.*); Roy Gordon (*Dean Wixby*); Matty Kemp (*Ed Riggs*); William Tracy (*Egghead Jackson*); Russ Clark (*Referee*); Wallace Rairden (*Crandall*); John Hart (*Haldeman*); Anthony Marsh (*MacDonald*); Tom Seidel (*Greene*); Lambert Rogers (*Murray*); Rob Ireland (*Hall*); Roger Laswell (*Alden*); Bill Boggess (*Wells*); Ken Nolan (*Thurston*); Bill Wilkerson (*Rich*); James Kelso (*Carpenter*); Si Jenks (*Bus Driver*); William Conselman, Jr. (*Husky Student*); Byron Foulger (*Mr. Day*); Jack Smart (*Splash Gordon*); Pat West (*George*); Billy Gilbert (*Dick Schultz*); Dorothy Moore (*Stella Cinders*); George Magrill (*Bystander*); Nick Copeland (*Seller*); George Anderson (*President Greene*); Charles Regan, Allen Fox, Russell Wade, Tom Dugan, Florence Farley, Eve Carlton.

Paramount's 1932 W. C. Fields comedy, also called *Million Dollar Legs*, bears no resemblance to this 1939 picture, despite the studio's puzzling recycling of its title. In fact, aside from one long shot of *Legs* star Betty Grable's celebrated underpinnings, the title is quite meaningless. Even worse, in production, the movie was called *Campus Dormitory*.

This *Million Dollar Legs* is an unpretentious sports comedy centering on Middleton College, where campus leader and basketball star Greg Melton (John Hartley) rebels against the preferential treatment afforded by his philanthropic father's wealth. Greg's girlfriend, Carol Parker (Grable), urges him to set an example by joining the crew team organized by Freddie Fry (Peter Lind Hayes), and the newly formed team begins training under Coach Baxter (Crabbe). Misunderstandings ensue when Greg learns that Freddie conspired with Carol to attract him to the crew, causing him mistakenly to think they only wanted him for his wealth.

Meanwhile, Gregory Melton, Sr. (Thurston Hall) gives the college a new basketball building as a ploy to lure the student athletes back to the

Million Dollar Legs. Roy Gordon, BC and Matty Kemp (Paramount Pictures, 1939).

court and away from their leaking boats and broken-down boathouse. Acting under Melton's influence, Dean Wixby (Roy Gordon) finds a reason to prevent Freddie from serving as coxswain in the upcoming race, replacing him with the incompetent Egghead Jackson (William Tracy). But Freddie manages to sabotage Egghead's health and lead his teammates to victory by shouting commands through a loudspeaker from Carol's moving car. The crew team scores a victory, causing Melton to withdraw his opposition to that sport.

Former film editor Edward Dmytryk, who had only directed one previous feature, the 1935 independent Western *The Hawk*, took over the direction of *Million Dollar Legs* on short notice. It was later revealed that Paramount executive Harold Hurley decided to replace the picture's nominal director, Nick Grinde, halfway through production, with the announcement that Grinde was suffering "a serious throat infection." More likely: a serious *career* infection!

Million Dollar Legs not only marked an inauspicious end to Buster's

Paramount contract, but it also enabled the actor to consider resuming the more familiar sobriquet of Larry "Buster" Crabbe.

Buck Rogers

A Universal serial: 1939

(Later re-edited into the feature films *Destination Saturn* and *Planet Outlaws*—aka *Buck Rogers Conquers the Universe*)

Chapter Titles: 1—"Tomorrow's World"; 2—"Tragedy on Saturn"; 3—"The Enemy's Stronghold"; 4—"The Sky Patrol"; 5—"The Phantom Plane"; 6—"The Unknown Command"; 7—"The Primitive Urge"; 8—"Revolt of the Zuggs"; 9—"Bodies Without Minds"; 10—"Broken Barriers"; 11—"A Prince in Bondage"; 12—"War of the Planets."

Credits—Directors: Ford Beebe and Saul A. Goodkind; Producer: Barney A. Sarecky; Screenwriters: Norman E. Hall and Ray Trampe; Based on the *Buck Rogers* comic strip, written by Philip Nowlan and drawn by Dick Calkins; Cinematographer: Jerome Ash; Editors: Alvin Todd, Louis Sackin and Joseph Gluck; Art Directors: Jack Otterson and Ralph De Lacy; Music Director: Charles Previn; Shown in 12 chapters running approximately 20 minutes each.

Cast—Larry "Buster" Crabbe (*Buck Rogers*); Constance Moore (*Wilma Deering*); Jackie Moran (*Buddy Wade*); Jack Mulhall (*Capt. Rankin*); Anthony Warde (*Killer Kane*); Philson [Philip] Ahn (*Prince Tallen*); C. Montague Shaw (*Dr. Huer*); Guy Usher (*Aldar*); William Gould (*Marshall Kragg*); Henry Brandon (*Capt. Lasca*); Wheeler Oakman (*Patten*); Kenneth Duncan (*Lt. Lacy*); Carleton Young (*Scott*); Reed Howes (*Roberts*); Karl Hackett, Stanley Price, David Sharpe.

In view of their success with two *Flash Gordon* serials, Universal hit upon the idea of yet another sci-fi chapterplay, this one based on the popular *Buck Rogers* comic strip. First published in 1929, the *Buck Rogers* strip was written by Philip Nowlan and drawn by Dick Calkins, derived from Nowlan's novel *Armageddon 2419 A.D.* The serial's visual appearance outclassed the same studio's pair of *Flash* adventures, with production designers Jack Otterson and Ralph De Lacy making a concerted effort not to have their sets and spaceships looking like *Flash Gordon* leftovers. As frequently happened, stock footage from Fox's 1930 futuristic musical *Just Imagine* was employed to represent a city of tomorrow, with additional recycling of Franz Waxman's flavorful score from *Bride of Frankenstein*.

To further differentiate from the *Flash* serials, Buster is here allowed to retain his natural brown hair, other comparisons remaining unavoidable. Not that that factor deterred our Latino neighbors: As Roy Kinnard reveals in *Science Fiction Serials*, "Mexican posters are in existence proving that south of the border *Buck Rogers* was re-titled and marketed as a *Flash Gordon* serial"! Kinnard also describes how the 12-part *Buck Rogers* was originally intended as a 13-part serial: "An extra episode, consisting mainly of

Buck Rogers. Henry Brandon, Philson Ahn, David Sharpe, BC and Constance Moore (Universal Pictures, 1939).

re-cap footage from previous chapters, was prepared, and was originally intended to be Chapter 7—a 22-minute chapter of which bootleg 16mm prints have circulated."

Television has twice to date utilized the *Buck Rogers* name: first in a live 1950–51 series called *Buck Rogers in the 25th Century* that starred Robert Pastene, and again under that title in a 1979–81 series, with Gil Gerard as Buck. In a couple of well-publicized episodes, Buster was enterprisingly engaged to guest star as "Brigadier Gordon" (Flash?).

The serial's plot begins with Buck Rogers and his young assistant Buddy Wade (Jackie Moran) crashing their giant dirigible into an Arctic mountain, precipitating the leakage of an experimental "nirvano gas," which leaves them in a state of suspended animation for 500 years. When they're eventually found and revived by scientists, they learn that the world has been taken over by the obsessive Killer Kane (Anthony Warde) and his super-gangsters.

Taken to the scientists' Hidden City (within a mountain), they encounter the brilliant inventor Dr. Huer (C. Montague Shaw) and his attractive assistant Wilma Deering (Constance Moore), whom they offer to help resist Kane. To enlist further aid, Buck, Buddy and Wilma head for Saturn in their spaceship. They're pursued by Kane's men, who bomb their vehicle, but the trio nevertheless manages to land safely on Saturn via their de-gravity belts.

Captain Lasca (Henry Brandon), Kane's henchman, captures them, but all are, in turn, imprisoned by the Saturnians, who take them before the Council of the Wise for sentencing. But Buck and his companions manage to escape, returning to Earth in one of Lasca's spaceships.

When Buck and Buddy learn that Saturn's Prince Tallen (Philson Ahn) has arrived to sign a peace treaty with Killer Kane, they infiltrate the enemy's stronghold to forestall any such union. With their de-gravity belts, they spirit Prince Tallen away through a window, only to be overpowered by Kane's guards, employing paralyzer rays.

Buddy rescues Buck and Tallen with his disintegrator gun, heading back to the Hidden City in one of Kane's spaceships. But before they can get there, they're attacked by another spaceship piloted by the unaware Wilma. The trio lands in a mountainous area, where they're attacked by Kane's men. Now aware of what's happening, Wilma scares the enemy spaceship away and rescues her friends, who bring Tallen to the Hidden City, securing Saturn's aid to combat Kane.

Traveling to Saturn to firm up the alliance, Buck, Wilma and Tallen are attacked by Lasca and his men and brought before the Saturnian Council of the Wise, where Tallen, given a mind-altering device, orders his friends' incarceration. Using Tallen to shield them, Buck and Wilma escape through an underground tunnel, returning to the Council to correct the situation, now that Tallen has regained his reason.

In this vein of cliffhanging exploits, the perilous space adventures of Buck, Wilma and Buddy continue until, eventually, Lasca and his men are captured. The help of Saturnian forces result in a heavy air battle and the defeat of Killer Kane. With a return to peace on Earth, Buck and Wilma are free to concentrate on a more personal relationship.

Colorado Sunset

A Republic Picture: 1939

Credits—Director: George Sherman; Assistant Director: William O'Connor; Producer: Harry Grey; Associate Producer: William Berke; Screenwriters: Betty Burbridge and Stanley Roberts; Story: Luci Ward and Jack Natteford; Cinematographer: William Nobles; Editor: Lester Orlebeck; Music Director: Raoul Kraushaar; Songs: "Colorado Sunset," "On the Merry Way Back Home," "I Want to Be a Cowboy's

Sweetheart," "Poor Little Dogie," "Beautiful Isle of Somewhere," "Autry's Our Man" and "Seven Years with the Wrong Woman" by Con Conrad and L. Wolfe Gilbert; Running Time: 64 minutes.

Cast—Gene Autry (*Gene*); Smiley Burnette (*Frog*); June Storey (*Carol Haines*); Barbara Pepper (*Ginger*); Larry "Buster" Crabbe (*Dave Haines*); Robert Barrat (*Dr. Rodney "Doc" Blair*); Patsy Montana (*Herself*); Purnell Pratt (*Mr. Hall*); William Farnum (*Sheriff*); Kermit Maynard (*Drake*); Jack Ingram (*Clanton*); Elmo Lincoln (*Burns*); Frankie Marvin (*Frankie*); The CBS-KMBC Texas Rangers.

Apart from his ongoing sideline as a serials hero, the Crabbe screen image was now so well-identified with B-movie villainy that Republic Pictures engaged the newly freelancing actor to play a sinister role in a Gene Autry vehicle.

This time, billed once again as Larry "Buster" Crabbe, he's a shady deputy sheriff named Dave Haines, who's in cahoots with town vet Dr. Rodney "Doc" Blair (Robert Barrat) in fomenting a dairy war between farmers and cattle ranchers. Gene and his singing cowboys, The Texas Trou-

Colorado Sunset. June Storey, BC, Gene Autry and Barbara Pepper (Republic Pictures, 1939).

badours, become involved when they try to settle down on a newly purchased ranch whose "cattle" turn out to be dairy cows.

Placing blame on the local Hall Trucking Company, Blair promotes setting up a protective organization. But Gene opposes that proposal, and Blair retaliates by using the radio station operated by Haines' sister Carol (June Storey) to wage a raid on Gene's ranch. After Gene apprehends Blair's hireling Clanton (Jack Ingram) and turns him in to the town sheriff (William Farnum), Blair kills the lawman and sets his own man free.

Gene now suspects that Blair and Haines are behind the cattle raids, and he readily accepts an opportunity to run against Haines for the now-vacant position of sheriff. Winning the election, Gene persuades the ranch owners do business with the unfairly maligned Hall Trucking Company, and he sets up an ambush in which the hijackers are apprehended and the dairy war is ended.

Variety dubbed *Colorado Sunset* "on a par with previous Autry Westerns."

Call a Messenger

A Universal Picture: 1939

Credits—Director: Arthur Lubin; Assistant Director: Henry Spitz; Associate Producer: Ken Goldsmith; Screenwriter: Arthur T. Horman; Story: Sally Sandlin and Michel Kraike; Cinematographer: Elwood Bredell; Editor: Charles Maynard; Art Directors: Jack Otterson and Ralph De Lacy; Set Decorator: R. A. Gausman; Gowns: Vera West; Music Director: Hans J. Salter; Running Time: 65 minutes.

Cast—Billy Halop (*Jimmy Hogan*); Huntz Hall (*Pig*); Robert Armstrong (*Kirk Graham*); Mary Carlisle (*Marge Hogan*); Anne Nagel (*Frances O'Neill*); Victor Jory (*Ed Hogan*); Larry Crabbe (*Chuck Walsh*); El Brendel (*Baldy*); Jimmy Butler (*Bob Pritchard*); George Offerman, Jr. (*Big Lip*); Hally Chester (*Murph*); William Benedict (*Trouble*); David Gorcey (*Yap*); Harris Berger (*Sailor*); Jimmy O'Gatty (*Al*); Joe Gray (*Nails*); Cliff Clark (*Sergeant Harrison*); John Hamilton (*Lieutenant Nelson*); J. Anthony Hughes (*Gardner*); Kay Sutton (*Virginia*); James Morton and Frank O'Connor (*Cops*); Sherwood Bailey (*Sweeney*); Joey Ray and Lyle Moraine (*Clerks*); Ruth Rickaby (*Miss Clarington*); Frank Mitchell (*Barber*); James Farley (*Desk Sergeant*); Payne Johnson (*Kid*); Jack Gardner (*Paymaster*); Kernan Cripps (*Police Officer*); Russ Powell (*Watchman*); Wilson Benge (*Butler*); Louise Franklin (*Maid*).

Using familiar screen performers formerly associated with both Warner Bros.' defunct Dead End Kids pictures, as well as Universal's own Little Tough Guys series, screenwriter Arthur T. Horman came up with this supporting-bill crime drama. And, for a studio that had now starred Buster as the superhero of no less than three adventure serials, it's surprising that he was cast in the same sort of supporting villain role that had dogged his years at Paramount. It would be his *only* non-serial movie at Universal.

Central to the story is young street gang leader Jimmy Hogan (Billy Halop), who bungles a Postal Telegraph Service robbery and gets arrested. Former street kid Kirk Graham (Robert Armstrong), who's now the district manager, wants to help Jimmy, and offers him a choice between a messenger job and reform school. Jimmy opts for the job, convincing his fellow gang members to follow his example.

While Jimmy's going straight, he's upset that his sister Marge (Mary Carlisle) is involved with gangster Chuck Walsh (Buster), who has promised to get their brother Ed (Victor Jory) released from jail. Jimmy introduces Marge to fellow messenger Bob Pritchard (Jimmy Butler), who helps her forget about Walsh.

Call a Messenger. BC as Chuck Walsh (Universal Pictures, 1939).

And, although Walsh makes good on securing Ed's freedom, he then secures Ed's allegiance to the Walsh gang, engaging his help with a succession of postal robberies. However, when Walsh makes plans to rob Jimmy's office, Ed stages a protest, and is shot by Walsh. But Jimmy pursues the gang leader and, with the aid of his fellow messengers, brings the culprits to justice.

As the dastardly Walsh, "Larry Crabbe" once again sports his by-now-signature bad-guy moustache. After this picture, he would give his screen villainy a temporary rest.

Sailor's Lady

A 20th Century–Fox Picture: 1940

Credits—Director: Allan Dwan; Assistant Director: Aaron Rosenberg; Executive Producer: Sol M. Wurtzel; Screenwriters: Frederick Hazlitt Brennan; Lou Breslow, Niven Busch and Owen Francis; Story: Frank Wead; Cinematographer: Ernest

Sailor's Lady. Jon Hall, BC and Nancy Kelly (20th Century–Fox Pictures, 1940).

Palmer; Editor: Fred Allen; Art Directors: Richard Day and Lewis Creber; Set Decorator: Thomas Little; Costumes: Herschel; Music Director: Samuel Kaylin; Song: "A Sailor's Luck" by Val Burton, Will Jason and Ben Ryan; Technical Advisor: Lieut. Comdr. A. J. Bolton, U.S.N.; Running Time: 66 minutes.

Cast—Nancy Kelly (*Sally Gilroy*); Jon Hall (*Danny Malone*); Joan Davis (*Myrtle*); Dana Andrews (*Scrappy Wilson*); Mary Nash (*Miss Purvis*); Larry Crabbe (*Rodney*); Katharine [Kay] Aldridge (*Georgine*); Harry Shannon (*Father McGann*); Wally Vernon (*Goofer*); Bruce Hampton (*Skipper*); Charles D. Brown (*Captain Roscoe*); Selmer Jackson (*Executive Officer*); Edgar Dearing (*Mulcahy*); Edmund MacDonald (*Barnacle*); William B. Davidson (*Judge Hinsdale*); Kane Richmond (*Division Officer*); William Conselman, Jr., Charles Tannen, Murray Alper, John Kellogg, Bud Carpenter, Tommy Seidel, Lyle Moraine, Gene Garrick and Don Forbes (*Sailors*); Gladys Blake (*Beauty Shop Operator*); Matt McHugh and Harvey Parry (*Taxi Drivers*); Ralph Dunn and Ward Bond (*Shore Patrol*); Gladden James (*Juvenile Officer*); Bert Moorhouse (*Paymaster*); Lester Dorr (*Assistant Paymaster*); Donald Barry (*Second Paymaster*); Alan Davis (*Officer of the Day*); Kitty McHugh (*Proprietress*); Marie Blake and Frances Morris (*Beauty Operators*); Ruth Warren (*Mother*); Eddie Acuff (*Escort*); Pat Flaherty (*Chief Petty Officer*); Edward Earle (*Lieutenant Commander*); Robert Shaw (*Ensign*); Emmett Vogan (*Ship's Doctor*); Billy Wayne (*Sail Maker*); Irving Bacon (*Storekeeper*); Peggy Ryan (*High School Girl*); Walter Miller (*Policeman*); Dick Rich (*Beany*); Gaylord Pendleton (*Sailor #111*); James Flavin (*Motorcycle Cop*); Ruth Clifford (*Maid*);

Harry Strang (*Marine Orderly*); George Wolcott (*Telephone Man*); Pierre Watkin (*Rear Admiral of Arizona*); Cyril Ring (*Lieutenant Commander of Arizona*); J. Anthony Hughes (*Lieutenant Senior Grade of Arizona*).

Before returning to Universal for his third and last crack at playing Flash Gordon, Buster made his only appearance in a 20th Century–Fox picture, in which he was billed not only under the film's stars, Nancy Kelly and Jon Hall, but also under co-stars Joan Davis and Dana Andrews. Filmed under the unwieldy working title of *Sweetheart of Turret One*, this is an unpretentious military-comedy programmer that billed Buster as "Larry Crabbe."

With the U.S.S. *Dakota* due to dock shortly, the sweethearts of the fleet keep the local beauty parlors busy, especially nervous Sally Gilroy (Nancy Kelly), who anticipates marriage to her sailor beau, Danny Malone (Jon Hall). Meanwhile, aboard ship, Danny's buddy Scrappy Wilson (Dana Andrews) learns that, because of back alimony, his pay has been withheld. The anti-marriage sailor now plots with his pal Goofer (Wally Vernon) to save Danny from a similar fate by planting Navy property in Danny's duffel bag, thus getting him arrested for theft. Scrappy tries to discourage Sally by informing her that Danny will be in the brig for a month.

Taking advantage of the situation, sailor Rodney (Buster) attempts to divert Sally's affections to himself, but Danny engineers a trip ashore, taking Sally to their "dream house." Sally surprises Danny with a baby boy she has decided to adopt, because her friends, the parents, were killed in an auto accident. Danny's not keen on the idea, but she insists.

Their snippy neighbor Miss Purvis (Mary Nash) then shows up to inform Sally that the juvenile court has placed her in charge of little "Skipper" (Bruce Hampton). Complicating matters, the shore patrol arrives to arrest Danny for skipping out with another sailor's pass. Sally is motivated to visit Danny's commanding officer, Captain Roscoe (Charles D. Brown), whom she informs that she and Danny are already married, and that he only came ashore to visit his "sick child."

When Danny arrives home to find Rodney befriending little Skipper, it takes the arrival of Father McGann (Harry Shannon) to calm him down with the suggestion that hosting a party for Miss Purvis might win her over. It's a plan that's ruined when Barnacle (Edmund MacDonald) starts a fight with Danny. Sally then breaks off with him, and the enterprising Rodney proposes to her, using the persuasion that she needs a husband to keep Skipper. But Danny returns and they reconcile—until he learns of Rodney's proposal. This results in a pitched battle between the two men, who are carted away by the shore patrol.

Additional plot complications (yes, dear reader, there are more!) knock

Buster out of the competition for Nancy Kelly who, of course, ends up with co-star Jon Hall.

Flash Gordon Conquers the Universe

A Universal serial: 1940

(Later edited into the feature films *Perils From the Planet Mongo* and *Purple Death from Outer Space*)

Chapter Titles: 1—"The Purple Death"; 2—"Freezing Torture"; 3—"Walking Bombs"; 4— "The Destroying Ray"; 5—"The Palace of Terror"; 6—"Flaming Death"; 7—"The Land of the Dead"; 8—"The Fiery Abyss"; 9—"The Pool of Peril"; 10—"The Death Mist"; 11—"Stark Treachery"; 12—"Doom of the Dictator."

Credits—Directors: Ford Beebe and Ray Taylor; Assistant Directors: Edward Tyler and Charles Gould; Associate Producer: Henry MacRae; Screenwriters: George H. Plympton, Basil Dickey and Barry Shipman; Based on the *Flash Gordon* comic strip by Alex Raymond; Cinematographers: Jerome H. Ash and William Sickner; Editors: Saul A. Goodkind, Alvin Todd, Louis Sackin and Joe Gluck; Art Director: Harold MacArthur; Special Effects: Kenneth Strickfaden; Shown in 12 chapters running approximately 20 minutes each.

Cast—Larry "Buster" Crabbe (*Flash Gordon*); Carol Hughes (*Dale Arden*); Charles Middleton (*Emperor Ming*); Anne Gwynne (*Sonja*); Frank Shannon (*Dr. Zarkov*); Lee Powell (*Roka*); Roland Drew (*Barin*); Shirley Deane (*Aura*); Donald Curtis (*Capt. Ronal*); Don Rowan (*Capt. Torch*); Sigurd Nilssen (*Count Korro*); Michael Mark (*Karn*); William Royle (*Capt. Sudin*); Victor Zimmerman (*Thong*); Edgar Edwards (*Turan*); Tom Chatterton (*Mr. Arden*); Harry C. Bradley (*Keedish*); Mimi Taylor (*Verna*); Byron Foulger (*Drulk*); Ben Taggart (*Gen. Lupi*); Earl Dwire (*Zandar*); Luli Deste (*Queen Fria*); Jack Roper (*Giant*); Charles Sherlock, Paul Reed, Harold Daniels, Edward Payson, Reed Howes, Clarice Sherry, Jack Gardner, Joey Ray, Paul Douglas, Ernie Adams, Edward Mortimer, Robert Blair, Bill Hunter, Charles Waldron, Jr., Pat Gleason, Frank Hagney, Ray Mala, Chief Yowlachie, John Hamilton, Herbert Rawlinson, Jeanne Kelly [Jean Brooks], Allan Cavan, John Elliott, Roy Barcroft, Carmen D'Antonio.

Following the release of its *Buck Rogers* serial, Universal initially planned a sequel—until its mediocre box-office reception changed corporate thinking towards producing, instead, a third *Flash Gordon* serial.

In its art direction and cinematography alone, this one stood head and shoulders above 1938's *Flash Gordon's Trip to Mars*. Like its predecessors, *Flash Gordon Conquers the Universe* cut costs by utilizing sets already constructed for previous Universal features (*Tower of London* and *Green Hell*), as well as recycling rocket ship footage from the original 1936 *Flash Gordon*. It also employed mountain-climbing sequences from 1929's *White Hell of Pitz Palu*, a German production released in the U.S. by Universal. This third serial's musical score will ring familiar to those conversant with themes

Flash Gordon Conquers the Universe. **Carol Hughes and BC (Universal Pictures, 1940).**

from *Bride of Frankenstein* and *Son of Frankenstein*, in addition to Liszt's "Les Preludes."

Because Jean Rogers was by now under contract to 20th Century–Fox and therefore no longer available, actress Carol Hughes here replaced her as Dale Arden, while Roland Drew took over for Richard Alexander as Prince Barin. Although it made a profit, *Flash Gordon Conquers the Universe* was the least successful of the three *Gordon* serials. Universal considered producing a fourth in the series, but never did so.

Despite the fact that 1938's *Flash Gordon's Trip to Mars* depicted the *death* of Ming by a disintegrating-ray machine, here we have the merciless one inexplicably restored to life and power as supreme dictator of the planet Mongo. With complete disregard for the events covered in the second Flash Gordon serial, screenwriters George H. Plympton, Basil Dickey and Barry Shipman begin by having Ming dispatch a rocket ship to Earth carrying a deadly plague known as the Purple Death. Suspecting that their old nemesis is behind this disaster, Flash and Dale Arden (Buster Crabbe and Carol

Hughes) set out with Dr. Zarkov (Frank Shannon) in the latter's spaceship for Mongo.

Joining forces with Prince Barin (Roland Drew) of the forest kingdom of Arboria, and Queen Fria (Luli Deste), ruler of icy Frigia, they invade Ming's palatial sanctuary, where they succeed in wrecking part of the megalomaniac's powerful machinery.

Learning that the mineral polarite, an antidote for the Purple Death, lies in Frigia, the Earthlings journey there, where they're menaced by one of Ming's rocket ships, commanded by the determined Captain Torch (Don Rowan).

There ensues a succession of perilous adventures, captures and escapes before culminating in the destruction of Ming (again!) as an explosives-bearing rocket ship crashes into the emperor's tower. Finally, Flash, Dale and Dr. Zarkov are free to return home, their Earth-saving mission accomplished.

Jungle Man (Drums of Africa)

A Producers Releasing Corp. Picture: 1941

Credits—Director: Harry Fraser; Assistant Director: Robert Ray; Executive Producer: George R. Batcheller; Producer: T. H. Richmond; Screenwriter: Rita Douglas; Cinematographer: Mervyn Freeman; Editor: Holbrook Todd; Art Director: John Huff; Running Time: 63 minutes.

Cast—Buster Crabbe (*Dr. Robert "Junga" Hammond*); Charles Middleton (*Father Jim Graham*); Sheila Darcy (*Betty Graham*); Vince Barnett (*Buck*); Weldon Heyburn (*Bruce Kellogg*); Robert Carson (*Andy*); Paul Scott (*William Graham*); Hal Price (*Floyd Shackelford*).

Fresh from shooting his last Flash Gordon serial for Universal—and with his hair still mostly blond—Buster now took a big step downward when he agreed to star in this low-grade jungle drama for the "Poverty Row" company Producers Releasing Corp. Nearly half of the 63-minute feature consists of stock footage of jungle animals and location scenery, edited to give this studio-bound cheapie some sense of authenticity. Unfortunately, some of the extra material is as poorly shot as *Jungle Man*'s dramatic scenes. But, then, Rita Douglas' script doesn't give director Harry Fraser a whole lot to work with.

Seeking a legendary "City of the Dead," photographer Bruce Kellogg (Weldon Heyburn) and his friend Andy (Robert Carson) prepare for an African expedition. They're joined by Bruce's bored fiancée Betty Graham (Sheila Darcy), who persuades her father William (Fred Scott) that they should accompany the others. Graham sees it as an opportunity to look up his brother Jim (Charles Middleton), a missionary in Africa for the past 30 years.

The scene shifts to the Dark Continent, where Father Jim visits with the American Dr. Robert Hammond (Buster Crabbe), familiarly known as "Junga," who has spent five years there devising a cure for the dreaded

Jungle Man. BC as Dr. Robert "Junga" Hammond (PRC Pictures, 1941).

malaria fever. Hammond anticipates the arrival from the U.S. of a batch of the experimental serum he has developed, in the hope of warding off an anticipated epidemic. As drums herald the arrival of the Kellogg–Graham expedition, Hammond is annoyed at this intrusion, but joins in the celebrations as Dr. Jim is reunited with the other members of his family.

While Bruce and Andy search for their Lost City, fickle Betty (never mind Bruce) finds herself attracted to Hammond, who saves her from being mauled by a predatory lion. Hammond is responsive to Betty's attentions—until he receives the news that the ship carrying his precious serum has been sunk off the coast.

Meanwhile, Bruce and Andy have survived jungle perils to reach their destination, and are photographing the ruins. Back at camp, Hammond is called to a neighboring village, where a new case of the fever has turned up. Betty insists on accompanying him. At the same time, marauding members of an enemy tribe threaten the settlement. Betty is again saved from the lions by Hammond.

Bruce and Andy return to camp, where the former is stricken with fever, moving Hammond to attempt a dive to the shipwreck for the sunken box of serum. By now, Betty, too, has come down with the illness. But Hammond returns with the serum to administer it successfully, bringing about Betty's recovery. They embrace. THE END.

Filmed under the title *King of the Tropics*, this silly grade-Z melodrama holds barely enough interest to keep its audience from snoozing, not helped much by the cast members. Hardly worth a mention is the reunion of Buster with his Flash Gordon series nemesis, Charles Middleton, who here plays a sympathetic part. From here on, Buster would spend the better part of the forties toiling away in the quickies churned out by PRC.

Billy the Kid Wanted

A Producers Releasing Corp. Picture: 1941

Credits—Director: Sherman Scott [Sam Newfield]; Assistant Director Melville De Lay; Producer: Sigmund Neufeld, Screenwriter: Fred Myton; Cinematographer: Jack Greenhalgh; Editor: Holbrook N. Todd; Art Director: Vin Taylor; Music: Johnny Lange and Lew Porter; Running Time: 64 minutes.

Cast—Buster Crabbe (*Billy the Kid*); Al "Fuzzy" St. John (*Fuzzy*); Dave O'Brien (*Jeff*); Glenn Strange (*Matt Brawley*); Charles King (*Jack Saunders*); Slim Whitaker (*Sheriff*); Howard Masters (*Stan Harper*); Choti Sherwood (*Jane Harper*); Joel Newfield (*Child Joey Harper*); Budd Buster (*Storekeeper*); Frank Ellis (*Bart*); Kenne Duncan, Curley Dresden, Wally West, Pascale Perry, Reed Howes, Art Dillard, Steve Clark, Chick Hannon, Arch Hall, George Morrell, Ray Henderson.

With *Billy the Kid Wanted*, filmed under the tentative title *Billy the Kid's Oklahoma Justice*, Buster Crabbe took over for Western star Bob Steele, who had portrayed the title character in the first six entries in this low-budget PRC series. Incidentally, there was no relation between this "Billy the Kid" and that notorious 19th-century American outlaw (1859–81) of the same name. Indeed, controversy would eventually move series producer Sigmund Neufeld to change the character's moniker to "Billy Carson." Character actor Al "Fuzzy" St. John, who had played sidekick "Fuzzy" opposite Bob Steele, continued in the role throughout Crabbe's tenure in the series.

Buster's first appearance as Billy is appropriately dramatic: He bursts onscreen with a sheriff's posse in hot pursuit when he's mistaken for a bank robber. Eluding his pursuers, Billy joins pals Fuzzy and Jeff (Dave O'Brien) at their campsite. Later, Billy and Jeff rally to Fuzzy's aid when he crosses unscrupulous Matt Brawley (Glenn Strange), the powerful president of a land company who uses his company store and water rights to keep the locals in debt to him. They confer with victimized rancher Stan Harper (Howard Masters), whom Billy determines to help by robbing Brawley's store of supplies, which he delivers to the homesteaders.

Brawley enlists outlaw leader Jack Saunders (Charles King) to get rid of Billy, while offering marksman Billy money to kill Saunders. At the same time, he alerts the crooked sheriff to arrest Billy for the expected "murder." But before a gunfight can take place, Jeff pretends to denounce Billy, joining Saunders' gang.

Crosses and double-crosses keep the plot moving until the bad guys are ultimately overcome, with Saunders killed and Stan appointed sheriff. Order is restored, and the movie closes with Billy, Jeff and Fuzzy bidding goodbye to the Harper family as they ride off to further adventures.

The character of "Jeff" would remain as a sidekick to Billy, but he would be played by an array of different actors as the series continued.

Variety's prescient critic "Wear." observed, "It looks like it might be the start of a series from this producer, with Buster Crabbe. Crabbe fits nicely into the title role, although not looking particularly like a cow puncher."

Billy the Kid's Round-Up

A Producers Releasing Corp. Picture 1941

Credits—Director: Sherman Scott [Sam Newfield]; Assistant Director: Melville De Lay; Producer: Sigmund Neufeld; Screenwriter: Fred Myton; Cinematographer: Jack Greenhalgh; Editor: Holbrook N. Todd; Art Director: Vin Taylor; Music: Johnny Lange and Lew Porter; Running Time: 58 minutes.

Cast—Buster Crabbe (*Billy the Kid*); Al "Fuzzy" St. John (*Fuzzy Q. Jones*); Carleton Young (*Jeff*); Joan Barclay (*Betty*); Glenn Strange (*Vic Landreau*); Charles King

(*Ed Slade*); Slim Whitaker (*Sheriff Jim Hanley*); John Webster (*Dan Webster*); Dennis Moore, Kenne Duncan, John Elliott, Curley Dresden, Dick Cramer, Wally West, Tex Palmer, Tex Cooper, Horace B. Carpenter, Jim Mason, Ray Henderson, Tex Phelps, Tom Smith, Augie Gomez, Oscar Gahan, George Morrell, Art Dillard, Denver Dixon.

While in production, this movie was called *Billy the Kid's Oklahoma Justice*, the same "working title" as its predecessor, *Billy the Kid Wanted*. But, once again, the "Oklahoma" reference was overruled, and this time discarded for good. With actor Carleton Young here replacing Dave O'Brien as Billy's pal Jeff, the series' producers were apparently unmindful or uncaring of how confusing these casting switches might prove to audiences. Glenn Strange, who had last been seen as villainous Matt Brawley in *Billy the Kid Wanted*, and now portrayed unscrupulous saloon owner Vic Landreau, would again play a bad guy in the series' next feature, *Billy the Kid Trapped*, in which yet *another* actor would impersonate Jeff!

With outlaws beginning to downgrade the county, Billy (Buster), Fuzzy (Al "Fuzzy" St. John) and Jeff are drawn into the plot when a mysterious killer shoots Sheriff Jim Hanley (Slim Whitaker) near their campsite, then attempts to kill Billy. They capture the gunman, who is forced to admit that he was hired by Vic Landreau. Billy confronts Vic, who denies any complicity. After learning that Sheriff Jim was murdered, Billy is warned to leave town by Deputy Sheriff Ed Slade (Charles King).

Vic now turns to persecuting Dan Webster and his daughter Betty (John Webster and Joan Barclay), who run the local newspaper. His thugs vandalize the printing presses and kidnap Betty, who is rescued by Billy and Fuzzy. In retaliation, they kidnap Ed, forcing him to write a confession about his alliance with Vic—which Betty plans to publish. Despite further vandalizing of their printing presses, Betty and her father are aided by Billy, Fuzzy and Jeff, and manage to turn out a limited edition of the paper headlining Ed's confession.

In a fight with Vic, Billy beats the saloon owner and escorts him to jail. The film concludes with Fuzzy's election to town sheriff, while Billy and Jeff head off to further adventures.

Variety's critic "Mori." found the picture "conventional," while observing, "Crabbe photographs well and gives a good account of himself in the top assignment as a quick-shooting, hard-riding sagebrush stalwart."

Billy the Kid Trapped

A Producers Releasing Corp. Picture: 1942

Credits—Director: Sherman Scott [Sam Newfield]; Assistant Director: Melville De Lay; Producer: Sigmund Neufeld; Screenwriter: Joseph O'Donnell; Cinematographer: Jack Greenhalgh; Editor: Holbrook N. Todd; Music: Johnny Lange and Lew Porter; Running Time: 59 minutes.

Cast—Buster Crabbe (*Billy the Kid*); Al "Fuzzy" St. John (*Fuzzy Jones*); Bud McTaggart (*Jeff Walker*); Anne Jeffreys (*Sally*); Glenn Strange (*Stanton*); Walter McGrail (*Judge McConnell*); Ted Adams (*Sheriff Masters*); Jack Ingram (*Red Barton*); Milton Kibbee (*Judge Clarke*); Eddie Phillips (*Dave*); Budd Buster (*Montana*); Jack Kenney, Jimmie Aubrey, Wally West, Bert Dillard, Kenne Duncan, George Chesebro, Carl Mathews, Richard Cramer, Curley Dresden, Horace Carpenter, Jim Mason, Hank Bell, Oscar Gahan, Herman Hack.

It's amusing to note the lack of continuity from movie to movie in this ongoing series. At the close of the previous entry, *Billy the Kid's Round-Up*, Fuzzy became a town's new sheriff, while his buddies Billy and Jeff (now played by Bud McTaggart) went their own way. At the start of *Billy the Kid Trapped*, the three pals are about to be hanged for a killing of which they're innocent (what happened to Fuzzy's sheriff's job?).

It seems that there's a look-alike gang of outlaws in the region, responsible for impersonating the trio and framing them for their *own* criminal

Billy the Kid Trapped. Al "Fuzzy" St. John, BC, Bud McTaggart and Ted Adams (PRC Pictures, 1942).

activities. Escaping from their imminent lynching, Billy, Fuzzy and Jeff rescue Sheriff Masters (Ted Adams) from a shootout involving the look-alike gang, and convince him of their innocence.

From this point on, screenwriter Joseph O'Donnell and director Sherman Scott (a pseudonym for the series' ubiquitous Sam Newfield) stack the plot complications to bring in character actor Glenn Strange as "Stanton," ruthless leader of the impersonator-gang whom Billy eventually brings to justice.

Anne Jeffreys, who portrays "Sally," the film's token female, would go on to a bigger career (in RKO features and TV) than perhaps any other Billy the Kid leading lady.

Variety's critic "Eddy." called this one "An average Western, helped by exciting gunplay and a creditable story," and he added, "Acting is all good for a horse opera, with Buster Crabbe carrying off top honors with the fattest part."

Billy the Kid's Smoking Guns

A Producers Releasing Corp. Picture: 1942

Credits—Director: Sherman Scott [Sam Newfield]; Assistant Director: Melville De Lay; Producer: Sigmund Neufeld; Screenwriter: George Milton; Cinematographer: Jack Greenhalgh; Editor: Holbrook N. Todd; Music: Johnny Lange and Lew Porter; Running Time: 63 minutes.

Cast—Buster Crabbe (*Billy the Kid*); Al "Fuzzy" St. John (*Fuzzy*); Dave O'Brien (*Jeff*); John Merton (*Morgan*); Milton Kibbee (*Dr. Elmo Hagen*); Ted Adams (*Sheriff Carson*); Karl Hackett (*Hart*); Frank Ellis (*Carter*); Slim Whitaker (*Roberts*); Budd Buster (*Rancher*); Joel Newfield (*Dickie Howard*); Joan Barclay (*Mrs. Howard*); Richard Fraser, Lester Mathews, Robert O. Davis, Bert Dillard.

Billy, Fuzzy and Jeff (once again played by Dave O'Brien, of *Billy the Kid Wanted*) are mistaken for outlaws and pursued to the county line by a posse. Gunshots draw them to the aid of Dickie Howard (Joel Newfield), a little boy, and his wounded father, whose wagon was attacked by murderous thieves. Sheriff Carson (Ted Adams) arrives on the scene, arrests the trio for the ambush and takes them to the office of the villainous Dr. Elmo Hagen (Milton Kibbee), who kills Howard while Billy, Fuzzy and Jeff escape from their captor. Escorting Billy home, they rescue Mrs. Howard (Joan Barclay) from an attack by Hagen's men. She tells the trio of being victimized by the Ranchers Cooperative Association, which plots to cheat ranchers of their property.

Morgan (John Merton), head of the corrupt Association, is about to foreclose on the landowners in cahoots with Dr. Hagen, the local mastermind, who directs his henchmen to kill Billy, Jeff and Fuzzy because of their interference with his plans. To foil Morgan, the trio open up their own general store, employing a pair of supply wagons, one of which is a decoy. But a spy among the ranchers reports their activities to Dr. Hagen and Morgan, and the real supply wagon is attacked.

Suspicious of the death rate among Dr. Hagen's patients, Billy visits the physician's office, holding him at gunpoint while he uncovers a cache of firearms and incriminating death certificates for the deceased ranchers. Ultimately, Billy rallies the nearly decimated ranchers against Morgan and his gang in a gun battle that results in Jeff being wounded. Fuzzy unknowingly takes him to Dr. Hagen, and only a last-minute rescue by Billy prevents his friend's murder. Finally, Morgan and Dr. Hagen are jailed, the ranchers' homes are saved, and Billy, Fuzzy and Jeff move on.

Jungle Siren

A Producers Releasing Corp. Picture: 1942

Credits—Director: Sam Newfield; Assistant Director: Melville De Lay; Producer: Sigmund Neufeld; Screenwriters: George W. Sayre and Sam Robins; Story: George W. Sayre and Milton Raison; Cinematographer: Jack Greenhalgh; Editor: Holbrook N. Todd; Art Director: Fred Preble; Song "Song of the Jungle" by John Lang and Lew Porter; Running Time: 68 minutes.

Cast—Ann Corio (*Kuhlaya*); Buster Crabbe (*Capt. Gary Hart*); Evelyn Wahl (*Frau Anna Lukas*); Paul Bryar (*Sgt. Mike Jenkins*); Milton Kibbee (*Dr. Hanigan*); Arno Frey (*Herr George Lukas*); Jess Brooks (*Chief Selangi*); Manart Kippen (*Major Renault*); James Adamson (*Johnny*); Greco (*Greco the Chimpanzee*).

After four successive B-Westerns, Buster undoubtedly welcomed the opportunity to trade in his saddle gear for tropical duds. Despite the similarity in titles, there's no connection between this picture and the actor's 1941 PRC drama *Jungle Man* outside of their shared African (studio set) locales. For a change, Crabbe relinquished top billing to his distaff co-star, former burlesque queen Ann Corio, the nominal "siren" of the title. A decorative movie star of short duration, she also headlined several other minor-league pictures (e.g., *Call of the Jungle, Swamp Woman*) and even chanced the stage in *White Cargo* and *Cat on a Hot Tin Roof,* before retiring to private life.

Amid World War II, Yanks Capt. Gary Hart and Sgt. Mike Jenkins (Buster Crabbe and Paul Bryar) join forces with the Free French Engineering Corps to survey a piece of land near Carraby, an African jungle community. They're warned to beware of Chief Selangi (Jess Brooks), a local tribal leader who has been collaborating with the Nazis.

Jungle Siren. **Paul Bryar, Ann Corio and BC (PRC Pictures, 1942).**

When their native bearers are frightened off by a masked tribesman, Gary and Mike encounter Kuhlaya (Ann Corio), a white woman raised in the jungle by Dr. Hanigan (Milton Kibbee) after Selangi murdered her missionary parents. Kuhlaya takes the two men to Carraby, where they find rooms at a hotel operated by the German spy George Lukas and his wife Anna (Arno Frey and Evelyn Wahl).

While Lukas works with Selangi to dispose of Kuhlaya, Gary and Mike, Anna makes a play for Gary, warning him of the danger at hand. Kuhlaya turns wild with jealousy when she sees the pair together, but nevertheless rescues Gary from a murderous attack by Selangi's tribesmen. When Lukas offers to help Mike and Gary reclaim their abandoned equipment, the suspicious Kuhlaya arrives in time to prevent their being ambushed.

While Mike and Gary continue their survey work, the latter is increasingly attracted to the smitten Kuhlaya. Selangi now steps up his terrorist tactics, kidnapping Gary, Mike and Harrigan, as well as two engineering workers, whom he poisons. Anna attempts to free the hostages, but is shot by her treacherous husband.

Kuhlaya challenges the powers of Selangi by shooting one of his followers with an arrow and daring the chief to restore him to life. Selangi's failure to do so causes his tribesmen to lose faith in him, freeing Gary, who shoots Selangi before he can kill Kuhlaya. With French planes heading their way to secure the community, Gary and Kuhlaya look forward to legalizing their relationship.

Law and Order

A Producers Releasing Corp. Picture: 1942

Credits—Director: Sherman Scott [Sam Newfield]; Assistant Director: Melville De Lay; Producer: Sigmund Neufeld; Screenwriter: Sam Robins; Cinematographer: Jack Greenhalgh; Editor: Holbrook N. Todd; Running Time: 57 minutes.

Cast—Buster Crabbe (*Billy the Kid/Ted Morrison*); Al "Fuzzy" St. John (*Fuzz "Fuzzy" Jones*); Tex [Dave] O'Brien (*Jeff*); Sarah Padden (*Aunt Mary*); Wanda McKay (*Linda*); Charles King (*Mil Crawford*); Hal Price (*Simms*); John Merton (*Turtle*); Kenne Duncan (*Durgan*); Ted Adams (*Sheriff*); Budd Buster, Kermit Maynard.

In an opening similar to previous entries in this Billy the Kid series, Billy, Fuzzy and Jeff (now portrayed by Dave O'Brien) are arrested by the cavalry for crimes of which they're innocent. But this time there's a twist: Cavalry commander Ted Morrison is Billy's identical twin (a dual role for Buster), moving Billy to steal his uniform to facilitate their escape. In so doing, the three are fired upon by unknown gunmen. When Billy finds a wedding invitation in Ted's coat pocket—to the union of Ted's blind but wealthy Aunt Mary (Sarah Padden) and her long-time beau George Fremont—he reasons that there's a link between the old lady and the would-be killers' attempt on Ted's life. Apparently, the gunmen mistook Billy for Ted, and it turns out that "George Fremont" is actually an impersonator in league with justice of the peace Mil Crawford (Charles King), who has his sights set on Mary's fortune.

Meanwhile, the real Fremont is ambushed as he nears town by stagecoach with Ted, and despite the efforts of Billy, Jeff and Fuzzy to save them, both men are murdered by Crawford's men. In an effort to solve the mystery of Ted's killing, Billy visits Mary in the guise of her nephew, while Crawford, suspicious of the impersonation, plots Billy's demise. Billy, as "Ted," and the three pals enlist the aid of Fremont's niece Linda (Wanda McKay) to help identify the false Fremont as an imposter and prove the culpability of Crawford.

Fuzzy and Jeff manage to disarm the gang members, while Billy prevents Crawford's escape. With Linda left to care for Aunt Mary, Billy, Fuzzy and Jeff head off to further escapades.

Variety dubbed *Law and Order* "worthy Western material, suitable for average demands."

Wildcat

A Pine-Thomas Production, released by Paramount Pictures: 1942

Credits—Director: Frank McDonald; Assistant Director: Edward Mull; Producers: William H. Pine and William C. Thomas; Screenwriters: Maxwell Shane and Richard Murphy; Based on the story "Roaring Gold" by North Bigbee; Cinematographer: Fred Jackman, Jr.; Editor: William Ziegler; Art Director: F. Paul Sylos; Set Decorator: Ben Berk; Music Director: Freddie Rich; Running Time: 73 minutes.

Cast—Richard Arlen (*Johnny Maverick*); Arline Judge (*Nan Dearing*); William Frawley (*Oliver Westbrook*); Larry "Buster" Crabbe (*Mike Rawlins*); Arthur Hunnicutt (*Watchfob Jones*); Elisha Cook, Jr. (*Harold "Chicopee" Nevins*); Ralph Sanford (*Grits O'Malley*); Alec Craig (*Joseph D. Campbell*); John Dilson (*Gus Sloane*); Will Wright (*Paw Smithers*); Jessica Newcombe (*Maw Smithers*); Billy Benedict (*Bud Smithers*).

Wildcat. Richard Arlen, Arline Judge, Arthur Hunnicutt and BC (Paramount Pictures, 1942).

Amidst his ongoing series of PRC program Westerns, Buster accepted a very subsidiary role in the Richard Arlen vehicle *Wildcat*, jointly produced by the team known as "the dollar Bills," William H. Pine and William C. Thomas, for Paramount release.

Arlen plays an itinerant oil worker named Johnny Maverick, who teams up with "Chicopee" Nevins (Elisha Cook, Jr.), a footloose youth, to find oil. When they learn that two competing companies are offering $25,000 to the first person to drill a new oil well, Johnny and Chicopee also happen to discover signs of oil on a farmer's stream, and manage to negotiate a purchase of that land—with money that they don't have.

After Chicopee is killed in an oil rig "accident," Johnny discovers that his old nemesis, Mike Rawlins (Buster Crabbe), is out to sabotage his current plans. Complicating things further is the arrival of a pair of con artists, Nan Dearing (Arline Judge) and Oliver Westbrook (William Frawley), who attempt to capitalize on Johnny's enterprise by having Nan pretend to be Chicopee's sister to realize the late partner's share in their oil business.

While Rawlins tries to discourage Johnny's hopes of bringing in a gusher, Nan finds herself falling for Johnny. Rawlins tries to buy him out, but Johnny throws nitroglycerine down the well and induces a gusher. But when it ignites, Johnny confronts Rawlins, who's rendered unconscious by an explosion. Johnny tries to cap the oil blaze, but he's pinned under a fallen pipe. Having heard about the fire, Nan arrives on the scene in time to maneuver the crane that frees Johnny from the pipe. The rig is then successfully capped, smothering the fire and leaving Nan and Johnny to face a lucrative future with their oil rigs—and each other.

For Richard Arlen, this was only one of many action dramas made under contract to Paramount in the early forties; but for Buster Crabbe, his talents were better used at PRC. *Variety*'s critic "Walt." opined that "Arlen does well as the two-fisted and aggressive tool-dresser, getting fine support from Miss Judge, Frawley, Crabbe, Cook and Ralph Sanford."

Sheriff of Sage Valley

A Producers Releasing Corp. Picture: 1942

Credits—Director: Sherman Scott [Sam Newfield]; Assistant Director: Melville De Lay; Executive Producer: Leon Fromkess; Producer: Sigmund Neufeld; Screenwriters: George W. Sayre and Milton Raison; Cinematographer: Jack Greenhalgh; Editor: Holbrook N. Todd; Song: "The Man Who Broke My Heart" by Johnny Lange and Lew Porter; Running Time: 57 minutes.

Cast—Buster Crabbe (*Billy the Kid/Kansas Ed*); Al "Fuzzy" St. John (*Fuzzy Jones*); Tex [Dave] O'Brien (*Jeff*); Maxine Leslie (*Janet*); Charles King (*Sloane*); John

Merton (*Nick*); Kermit Maynard (*Slim*); Hal Price (*Harrison*); Curley Dresden, Jack Kirk, Lynton Brent, Budd Buster, Art Dillard, Ray Henderson, Al Taylor, Frank Ellis, Jack Evans, Bert Dillard, Carl Matthews, Dan White, Merrill McCormick.

In an era wherein special effects experts were enabling movie stars to appear opposite themselves in dual roles (e.g., *The Prisoner of Zenda*, *A Stolen Life* and *The Dark Mirror*), Buster now was able to confront his own alter-image, courtesy of an offbeat George W. Sayre–Milton Raison script and the combined efforts of cameraman Jack Greenhalgh and film editor Holbrook N. Todd.

In a storyline that begins with a stagecoach robbery that intercepts the local ranchers' payroll and kills the Sage Valley sheriff, Buster takes on the double acting assignment of combining his ongoing Billy the Kid role with that of an outlaw known as Kansas Ed. Their obvious resemblance is ultimately explained when the deservedly shot and dying Ed reveals that Billy is his brother. In between, *Sheriff of Sage Valley* is an action-oriented yarn with brawls, gunshots and confused identities.

As in many of this long-running series of B-Westerns, former genre star Kermit Maynard plays a supporting role. Perhaps producer Sigmund Neufeld considered the Maynard name a good-luck charm.

Variety's "Char." called this one "an indie-made Western that ranks with the best in the field, although palpably having cost less than most."

The Mysterious Rider (Billy the Kid in the Mysterious Rider/Panhandle Trail)

A Producers Releasing Corp. Picture: 1942

Credits—Director: Sherman Scott [Sam Newfield]; Assistant Director: Melville De Lay; Producer; Sigmund Neufeld; Screenwriter: Steve Braxton; Cinematographer: Jack Greenhalgh; Editor: Holbrook N. Todd; Running Time: 54 minutes.

Cast—Buster Crabbe (*Billy the Kid/Bill Andrews*); Al "Fuzzy" St. John (*Fuzzy Q. Jones*); Caroline Burke (*Martha Kincaid*); John Merton (*Dalton*); Edwin Brien (*Johnny Kincaid*); Jack Ingram (*Trigger Lawson*); Slim Whitaker (*Rufe*); Ted Adams (*Marshal*); Frank Ellis, Karl Hackett, Art Dillard, Augie Gomez, Jimmy Aubrey.

Once again, Billy's accused of lawless behavior, sending him and sidekick Fuzzy to evade the law, this time in the ghost town of Laramie, whose few remaining inhabitants try to locate a vein of gold found by a murdered rancher named Kincaid. Billy finds the dead man's gold map hidden inside his broken violin, but meets frustration in his efforts to identify the killer as former sheriff Dalton Sykes (John Merton). The latter, meanwhile, gains the confidence of the murder victim's daughter Martha (Caroline Burke), who tells him about the map. Eventually, Billy captures Sykes and turns the coveted map over to Kincaid's offspring, Martha and Johnny (Edwin Brien).

After six films, and a succession of different actors portraying Billy's sidekick "Jeff," it was decided to abandon that character altogether. Henceforth, Buster's sole onscreen pal would be "Fuzzy," in the person of crusty Al St. John.

The Kid Rides Again

A Producers Releasing Corp. Picture: 1943

Credits—Director: Sherman Scott [Sam Newfield]; Assistant Director: Melville De Lay; Producer: Sigmund Neufeld; Screenwriter: Fred Myton; Cinematographer: Jack Greenhalgh; Editor: Holbrook N. Todd; Music: Leo Erdody; Running Time: 60 minutes.

Cast—Buster Crabbe (*Billy the Kid*); Al "Fuzzy" St. John (*Fuzzy Jones*); Iris Meredith (*Joan Ainsley*); Glenn Strange (*Tom Slade*); Charles King (*Vic*); I. Stanford Jolley (*Mort Slade*); Ed Peil, Sr. (*Ainsley*); Ted Adams (*Sheriff*); Slim Whitaker (*Texas Sheriff*); Karl Hackett, Kenne Duncan, Curley Dresden, Snub Pollard, John Merton.

The story begins with Billy's escape from jail, serving time for a robbery he didn't commit. A tip from his pal Fuzzy sends Billy to the outlaw community of Sundown, the home of brothers Mort and Tom Slade (I. Stanford Jolley and Glenn Strange). Billy is certain that the Slade gang is responsible for framing him, and he's intent on seeking retribution and clearing his name.

Billy also suspects the Slades of victimizing local ranchers by attacking their properties and taking over the mortgages of ranchers unable to keep up their payments. Billy and Fuzzy overhear Mort's plan to destroy town banker Ainsley (Ed Peil, Sr.), warning him and his daughter Joan (Iris Meredith) of their imminent danger, although Billy's outlaw reputation damages his credibility.

A succession of action-driven events spurs the plot onward before Billy is forced to kill Mort Slade in self-defense, restoring law and order to Sundown.

Variety's critic found *The Kid Rides Again* a formulaic entry for action addicts, citing Al "Fuzzy" St. John "the only standout in the cast," while concluding that "Buster Crabbe makes a handsome but colorless title character."

Queen of Broadway

A Producers Releasing Corp. Picture: 1943

Credits—Director: Sam Newfield; Assistant Director: Melville De Lay; Screenwriters: Rusty McCullogh and George Wallace Sayre; Producer: Bert Sternbach; Cinematographer: Jack Greenhalgh; Editor: Holbrook N. Todd; Art Director: Fred Preble; Set Decorator: Harry Reif; Music Score: Leo Erdody; Music Director: David Chudnow; Running Time: 63 minutes.

Cast—Rochelle Hudson (*Sherry Baker*); Buster Crabbe (*Ricky Sloane*); Paul Bryar (*Rosy*); Emmett Lynn (*Chris*); Donald Mayo (*Jimmy Carson*); Isabel La Mal (*Mrs. Barnett*); Blanche Rose (*Mrs. Ogilvie*); Henry Hall (*Judge John Morse*); John Dilson (*Bickel*); Milton Kibbee (*Joe*); Vince Barnett (*Schultz*); Jack Mulhall (*Bookie*); Snowflake (*Mose*).

Although credited to Rusty McCullough and George Wallace Sayre, the screenplay for *Queen of Broadway* owes a lot to the once-familiar writings of Damon Runyon, especially the 1934 Shirley Temple vehicle *Little Miss Marker*, whose plot echoes this one in its tale of a lovable child changing the lives of Broadway bookies and gamblers. And, for Buster Crabbe, it must have been a relief to exchange his customary saddle duds for suits, neckties and the inevitable fedoras worn in the movies of the '40s.

The title role of Sherry Baker (Rochelle Hudson) is a math whiz who handicaps tables for sporting events, a knack that makes her Broadway

Queen of Broadway. **Rochelle Hudson and BC (PRC Pictures, 1943).**

office a popular hangout for bookies, although she herself neither bets nor gambles. Complicating her busy life is the appearance of a six-year-old named Jimmy Carson (Donald Mayo), sent to her office by his dying mother to place a bet. When they discover the mother dead, Sherry and her side-kicks Chris (Emmett Lynn) and Rosy (Paul Bryar) take the boy under their wing to prevent his being sent to an orphanage. This turn of events also impacts on the somewhat contentious relationship of Sherry and her long-time boyfriend Ricky Sloane (Buster Crabbe), who owns a football team.

In Runyon fashion, the boy quickly endears himself to one and all, soft-ening their toughened personalities, and challenging their mental resources when the authorities wrest little Jimmy from their protective "custody" to place him in a hated orphanage.

To solve the dilemma of a so-called proper home for the child, Ricky weds Sherry. But misunderstandings ensue, and it takes yet another plot cri-sis before the newly united trio actually assume the status of a happy family.

Veering as it does between comedy and melodrama, *Queen of Broad-way* offers reasonable entertainment with slightly better production values than the customary low-budget PRC movie of 1943.

Fugitive of the Plains *(Raiders of Red Rock)*

A Producers Releasing Corp. Picture: 1943

Credits—Director: Sam Newfield; Assistant Director: Melville De Lay; Producer: Sigmund Neufeld; Screenwriter: George W. Sayre; Cinematographer: Jack Greenhalgh; Editor: Holbook N. Todd; Music: Leo Erdody; Running Time: 56 minutes.

Cast—Buster Crabbe (*Billy the Kid*); Al "Fuzzy" St. John (*Fuzzy Q. Jones*); Max-ine Leslie (*Kate*); Jack Ingram (*Dillon*); Kermit Maynard (*Spence*); Karl Hackett (*Sher-iff Packard*); Hal Price (*Sheriff Conley*); George Chesebro (*Baxter*); Frank Ellis (*Dirk*); John Merton (*Deputy*).

Produced in December of 1942, this feature was copyrighted in 1943, the year it was reportedly released—although not shown in Los Angeles until 1946!

Bandits have been terrorizing towns along the Mexican-American bor-der, and Billy is getting the blame. To clear his name, he sets out with his buddy Fuzzy for Red Rock County, where they find the body of the sher-iff's deputy, pinned with a note attributing responsibility to "Billy the Kid." Following the real killer's trail, Billy discovers that the party he's after is a woman bandit leader named Kate (Maxine Leslie).

Seeking evidence, Billy impresses Kate sufficiently to be accepted into her gang of henchmen, despite the protestations of Dillon (Jack Ingram), her most treacherous hireling. Kate directs Billy to hold up a stagecoach, while Dillon tips off the town sheriff, so that Billy will be captured. But Fuzzy foils the plot, and he and Billy take two of Kate's men prisoner, informing her that they were captured during the attempted stage robbery.

Kate now sets her sights on robbing the local bank, but two more of her hired guns disappear, and she becomes suspicious of Billy, who has already warned the sheriff of Kate's robbery plot. As the gang is chased out of town, Kate is wounded in the shootout, but prevents Dillon's killing Billy before she dies. Finally, Billy is able to clear his name.

Western Cyclone (Billy the Kid in Western Cyclone/Frontier Fighters)

A Producers Releasing Corp. Picture: 1943

Credits—Director: Sam Newfield; Assistant Director: Melville De Lay; Producer: Sigmund Neufeld; Screenwriter: Patricia Harper; Cinematographer: Robert Cline; Editor: Holbrook N. Todd; Music: Leo Erdody; Running Time: 62 minutes.

Western Cyclone. Hal Price, BC, Al "Fuzzy" St. John, Marjorie Manners and Karl Hackett (PRC Pictures, 1943).

Cast—Buster Crabbe (*Billy the Kid*); Al "Fuzzy" St. John (*Fuzzy Q. Jones*); Marjorie Manners (*Mary Arnold*); Karl Hackett (*Governor Jim Arnold*); Milton Kibbee (*Senator Peabody*); Glenn Strange (*Dirk Randall*); Charles King (*Ace Harmon*); Hal Price (*Sheriff*); Kermit Maynard (*Hank*); Frank Ellis, Frank McCarrroll, Artie Ortego, Herman Hack, Al Haskell.

Although Buster's Billy the Kid bears no connection to the notorious real-life outlaw of that name, he's nevertheless suspected of similar behavior in this series entry when he poses as a masked bandit to hold up a stagecoach. His motive: to impress upon stage passenger Senator Peabody (Milton Kibbee) the difficulties faced by the state's Governor Arnold (Karl Hackett), due to an increase of criminal activity in the region.

After Billy's later framed for murder and sentenced to be executed, he and pal Fuzzy escape from jail and rescue Arnold's daughter Mary (Marjorie Manners), who has been kidnapped. Finally, Billy manages to bring to justice culprits Randall (Glenn Strange) and Harmon (Charles King), clearing his name and ending the area's crime wave.

Variety's critic "Char." singled out *Western Cyclone* as "one of the best of the 'Billy the Kid' series ... not only because it has plenty of action and lively dialog, but also as a result of the laugh value. Crabbe, as usual, gives a fine performance, including in the fist battles he indulges."

The Renegades (The Renegade/Code of the Plains)

A Producers Releasing Corp. Picture: 1943

Credits—Director: Sam Newfield; Assistant Director: Melville De Lay; Producer: Sigmund Neufeld; Screenwriter: Joe O'Donnell; Story: George Milton; Cinematographer: Robert Cline; Editor: Holbrook N. Todd; Music Director: David Chudnow; Running Time: 58 minutes.

Cast—Buster Crabbe (*Billy the Kid*); Al "Fuzzy" St. John (*Fuzzy Q. Jones*); Lois Ranson (*Julie Martin*); Karl Hackett (*John Martin*); Ray Bennett (*Mayor Hill*); Frank Hagney (*Saunders*); Jack Rockwell (*Sheriff*); Tom London (*Pete*); George Chesebro (*Bart*); Jimmy Aubrey, Carl Sepulveda, Dan White, Wally West, Milburn Morante.

The town of Pine Bluffs is secretly victimized by its own Mayor Hill (Ray Bennett), who masterminds a robbery of the local bank, leaving its depositors in chaos. Billy the Kid and Fuzzy rally to the aid of bank president John Martin (Karl Hackett), whose life is endangered by a lynch mob organized by the mayor's henchman Pete (Tom London).

A succession of underhanded dealings involve Martin's daughter Julie (Lois Ranson) before an ambush and gun battle lead to the capture of Pete and his gang, and the eventual exposure and arrest of Mayor Hill.

The Renegades. Al "Fuzzy" St. John, Karl Hackett and BC (PRC Pictures, 1943).

Cattle Stampede

A Producers Releasing Corp. Picture: 1943

Credits—Director: Sam Newfield; Assistant Director: Melville De Lay; Producer; Sigmund Neufeld; Screenwriter; Joe O'Donnell; Cinematographer: Robert Cline; Editor: Holbrook N. Todd; Running Time: 58 minutes.

Cast—Buster Crabbe (*Billy the Kid*); Al "Fuzzy" St. John (*Fuzzy Jones*); Frances Gladwin (*Mary Dawson*); Charles King (*Brandon*); Ed Cassidy (*Sam Dawson*); Hansel Werner (*Ed Dawson*); Ray Bennett (*Stone*); Frank Ellis (*Elkins*); Steve Clark (*Turner*); Roy Brent (*Slater*); John Elliott (*Doctor*); Budd Buster (*Jensen*); Tex Cooper, Ted Adams, Frank McCarroll, Ray Jones, Rose Plumer, George Morrell, Glenn Strange, Hal Price, Curley Dresden, Cactus Mack, Art Dillard, Carl Mathews, Roy Bucko.

While in production, this movie was known as *Thundering Cattle*, a title that might have led audiences to expect more from its cattle sequences than was evident in the finished product.

The plot kicks off on a busy note and immediately thickens: Billy's the target of an outlaw gang that intends to kidnap him for the expected reward, considering the kid's reputation. But Billy and sidekick Fuzzy are tipped off by Ed Dawson (Hansel Werner), a stranger who seeks a favor from them. Having escaped from the gang, he begs their support in helping his father and sister, Sam and Mary Dawson (Ed Cassidy and Frances Gladwin), deal with Coulter, a land baron intent on raiding their cattle drives. Consequently, Billy becomes their new cattle boss, though his identity is kept secret.

With Coulter out to take over the Dawson ranch by whatever means, and eventually control the whole territory, Billy and Fuzzy organize the other local ranchers into a trail patrol. Further attacks on the herds are lessened, but they still continue. Coulter now attempts to make a deal with Billy, and when Billy pretends to rob a stagecoach (giving the money to Fuzzy to secure in a bank), Mary recognizes Billy and thinks he's betrayed them.

She unwisely confides in Coulter, who takes her hostage, ordering Sam to sign over the Dawson ranch or forfeit Mary's life. Tipped off as to her whereabouts, Billy and Fuzzy head for Coulter's ranch, where a gunfight ensues. Finally, the outlaws are brought to justice, Mary is freed, and their next cattle drive takes place without incident. Billy and Fuzzy head back to their independent way of living.

Blazing Frontier

A Producers Releasing Corp. Picture: 1943

Credits—Director: Sam Newfield; Assistant Director: Melville De Lay; Producer; Sigmund Neufeld; Screenwriter: Patricia Harper; Cinematographer: Robert Cline; Editor: Holbrook N. Todd; Running Time: 59 minutes.

Cast—Buster Crabbe (*Billy the Kid*); Al "Fuzzy" St. John (*Fuzzy Q. Jones*); Marjorie Manners (*Helen*); Milton Kibbee (*Lem Barstow*); I. Stanford Jolley (*Luther Sharp*); Frank Hagney (*Tragg*); Kermit Maynard (*Pete*); George Chesebro (*Slade*); Frank Ellis (*Biff*); Hank Bell, Jimmy Aubrey, Charles King, Curley Dresden, Cactus Mack, Frank McCarroll.

Reaching for a fresh variation on the formulaic plots of this series, Patricia Harper devised a story and screenplay dealing with a railroad company and its interest in the rights to ranchers' property. As usual, human greed is the plot-twisting factor in *Blazing Frontier* (a meaningless title), with Billy hired by the ranchers' lawyer to investigate the railroad's possible involvement in a land swindle. Benefiting the most, it turns out, is a railroad agent named Luther Sharp (I. Stanford Jolley), who's in league with Tragg (Frank Hagney), chief of the railroad detectives. Their ploy: a secretly added clause in the ranchers' contracts allowing for a raise in the asking price for their land. The result is a growing number of homeless settlers who form a justifiably angry mob.

Tragg, however, counters with a gang of bullies that drives the settlers out of town, while he issues warrants for their arrest. Billy's outlaw reputation moves Tragg to offer him a job driving away the settlers, but he declines the assignment, bringing in Fuzzy, who is introduced as a ruthless killer. Eventually, Billy and Fuzzy see to it that Sharp and Tragg are brought to justice.

Devil Riders

A Producers Releasing Corp. Picture: 1943

Credits—Director: Sam Newfield; Assistant Director: Melville De Lay; Producer: Sigmund Neufeld; Screenwriter; Joe O'Donnell; Cinematographer:: Robert Cline; Editor: Bob Crandall; Song: "It Don't Mean Anything Now" by Lew Porter and Franklyn J. Tableporter; Running Time: 56 minutes.

Cast—Buster Crabbe (*Billy Carson*); Al "Fuzzy" St. John (*Fuzzy Q. Jones*); Patti McCarthy (*Sally Farrell*); Charles King (*Del Stone*); John Merton (*Jim Higgins*); Kermit Maynard (*Red*); Frank LaRue (*Tom Farrell*); Jack Ingram (*Turner*); George Chesebro (*Curley*); Ed Cassidy (*Doc*); Frank Ellis, Al Ferguson, Bert Dillard, Bud Osborne, Artie Ortego, Herman Hack, Roy Bucko, Buck Bucko.

With this late-1943 release, PRC's ongoing "Billy the Kid" series suddenly underwent a name change, becoming the "Billy Carson" series. Understandably, labeling a cowboy hero with the name of a notorious Western outlaw (no matter how unrelated) bothered parents and educators to the extent that nothing would do but a moniker switch for the character. And so PRC complied, supplying Buster Crabbe's on-screen "Billy" with the surname of "Carson," and removing all references to his previous "outlaw" reputation.

Here we have Billy and Fuzzy as partners in a Pony Express line who are suddenly confronted with the competition of a stagecoach business run by the enterprising Tom Farrell (Frank LaRue), who has also been commissioned to build new roads through an outlaw area called the Badlands. It's a territory ruled by cattle rustler Del Stone (Charles King) and lawyer Jim Higgins (John Merton), who set out to foil Farrell's plans.

Stone sends masked riders to attack the first stagecoach, but Billy manages to rout them single-handedly, thus saving passenger Sally Farrell (Patti McCarthy), Tom's daughter, from possible harm.

Director Sam Newfield manages to pack a near-record amount of fast-moving action scenes into the mere 56 minutes of this B-Western before a windup which has the bad guys defeated and Billy and Fuzzy going into business with Farrell.

Variety called *Devil Riders* "an okay amalgam of action and comedy," citing Al St. John's comic talents, and concluding, "Photography is better than in the usual buckskin meller."

Nabonga (Nabonga Gorilla/The Girl and the Gorilla/Gorilla/The Jungle Woman)

A Producers Releasing Corp. Picture: 1944

Credits—Director: Sam Newfield; Assistant Director: Melville De Lay; Producer: Sigmund Neufeld; Screenwriter: Fred Myton; Cinematographer: Robert Cline; Editor: Holbrook N. Todd; Special Effects: Gene Stone; Art Director: Paul Palmentola; Music Score: Willy Stahl; Music Director: David Chudnow; Running Time: 73 minutes.

Cast—Buster Crabbe (*Ray Gorman*); Fifi D'Orsay (*Marie*); Barton MacLane (*Carl Hurst*); Julie London (*Doreen Stockwell*); Bryant Washburn (*Hunter*); Herbert Rawlinson (*T.F. Stockwell*); Prince Modupe (*Tobo*); Jackie Newfield (*Doreen as a Child*); Nbonga (*Sampson, the Gorilla*).

In 1944, this silly jungle melodrama may have provided mild escape from the sacrifices and deprivations of wartime. Viewed today, it's mainly good for a few unintended laughs, with its ridiculous dialogue, low-budget

Nabonga. Julie London, BC and "Nbonga" (PRC Pictures, 1944).

studio-jungle settings and interpolated stock footage of African wildlife. Added to which, sound engineer Corson Jowett aids verisimilitude with the ever-present background sounds of birds, monkeys and predatory beasts of the jungle. As to why the movie is entitled *Nabonga*, who knows? Portraying the giant gorilla identified as "Sampson" is a well-hidden performer identified in the credits simply as "Nbonga," but spelled differently from the film's on-screen title.

The story opens with a small chartered plane battling a powerful storm as it flies over the African jungle, before it's forced to crash-land. Its sole passengers are T. F. Stockwell (Herbert Rawlinson), fleeing with a fortune in stolen jewels and securities, and his small daughter Doreen (Jackie Newfield). Although both they and their pilot survive the crash, Stockwell subsequently shoots the pilot when he's discovered with his loot. Doreen, meanwhile, has wandered into the jungle and befriended a wounded gorilla.

Many years later, adventurer Ray Gorman (Buster Crabbe) arrives at a nearby jungle village to track down the missing embezzler, attracting the attention of hunter Karl Hurst (Barton MacLane) and his girlfriend Marie (Fifi D'Orsay), who soon get wind of Gorman's treasure hunt. The latter is also intrigued by local tales of a white witch, who turns out to be the now-grown Doreen (young Julie London in her movie debut).

Accompanied by the native bearer Tobo (Prince Modupe), Gorman explores deep into the jungle, secretly followed by Hurst and Marie. Gorman meets Doreen, a pretty young adult in a flowered sarong, but her protective gorilla-friend Sampson kills Tobo, a fact that simply gives Gorman momentary pause.

Gorman locates Doreen's jewels in a cave, but has trouble making her understand that they don't really belong to her, despite her late father's promises. Hurst and Marie manage to steal the loot but, in a succession of unbelievable events, Marie is killed by Sampson, who then takes care of Hurst, before succumbing himself. Gorman is left to console Doreen, whom he promises to take back to civilization.

During *Nabonga*'s production, Buster must have been reminded of his early starring vehicle, *King of the Jungle*, an outdoor melodrama boasting much more respectable production values than this modest programmer.

Thundering Gun Slingers

A Producers Releasing Corp. Picture: 1944

Credits—Director: Sam Newfield; Assistant Director: Melville De Lay; Producer: Sigmund Neufeld; Screenwriter: Fred Myton; Cinematographer: Robert Cline; Editor: Holbrook N. Todd; Running Time: 58 minutes.

Cast—Buster Crabbe (*Billy Carson*); Al "Fuzzy" St. John (*Doc Fuzzy Jones*); Frances Gladwin (*Beth Halliday*); Karl Hackett (*Jeff Halliday*); Charles King (*Steve Kirby*); Jack Ingram (*Vic*); Kermit Maynard (*Ed Slade*); Budd Buster (*Sheriff*); George Chesebro (*Dave Carson*); Hank Bell, Ray Henderson, Cactus Mack, Augie Gomez, Roy Bucko, Jack Kinney, Wally West.

The story begins with the lynching of cattle thief Dave Carson (George Chesebro), the latest episode in a wave of vigilante activity secretly fomented by saloon owner Steve Kirby (Charles King), whose goal is to get local ranchers to undersell their land. News of his uncle's hanging brings Billy Carson (Buster Crabbe) to town to investigate, and although Kirby's men attempt to ambush Billy, those plans are thwarted by the intervention of Doc Fuzzy Jones (Al "Fuzzy" St. John). Instrumental to the plot are cattle owner Jeff Halliday (Karl Hackett) and his daughter Beth (Frances Gladwin), whom Billy mistakenly believes is responsible for his uncle's death.

Murder, treachery and double dealing spur the plot of this standard entry in the series, culminating in a rousing brawl, with justice, of course, triumphant.

Variety's "Merr." had no good words for *Thundering Gun Slingers*, dismissing it as "a below-par equiner, which, judging from inferior quality of production, was given smaller budget and less shooting time than even the average Western." In summation, he called it "a shoddy job."

Frontier Outlaws

A Producers Releasing Corp. Picture: 1944

Credits—Director: Sam Newfield; Assistant Director: Melville De Lay; Producer: Sigmund Neufeld; Screenwriter: Joseph O'Donnell; Cinematographer: Robert Cline; Editor: Holbrook N. Todd; Running Time: 58 minutes.

Cast—Buster Crabbe (*Billy Carson*); Al "Fuzzy" St. John (*Fuzzy Jones*); Frances Gladwin (*Pat Clark*); Marin Sais (*Ma Clark*); Charles King (*Barlow*); Jack Ingram (*Taylor*); Kermit Maynard (*Wallace*); Edward Cassidy (*Sheriff*); Emmett Lynn (*Judge James Ryan*); Budd Buster (*Clerk*); Bert Dillard, Dan White, Tex Williams, Ray Henderson, Carl Mathews, Artie Ortego, Silver Tip Baker, Tex Cooper, Silver Hart, Jess Cavan, Wally West, Herman Hack, George Morrell, Horace B. Carpenter, Jimmy Aubrey.

By now, Buster's onscreen billing in this series had expanded to read "Buster Crabbe, King of the Wild West and His Horse Falcon." Perhaps it was producer Sigmund Neufeld's idea to rival the fame of cowboy star Roy Rogers' celebrated mount "Trigger." Whatever the case, "Falcon" never achieved the legendary status among screen equines.

Frontier Outlaws presents Billy Carson as a gold miner up against the master plotting of crooked banker Barlow (Charles King) and his partner

Frontier Outlaws. BC and Al "Fuzzy" St. John (PRC Pictures, 1944).

Taylor (Jack Ingram), who hope to achieve complete control of the area known as Wolf Valley. To facilitate their plans, they hire gunman Rusty Bradford, whose efforts to intimidate the defiant Billy lead to a shoot-out resulting in Bradford's death.

Screenwriter Joseph O'Donnell's subsequent plotting packs so many melodramatic twists into this series entry that it's amazing to realize it's all unfolding in less than an hour of screen time. And, for a change, Billy has a love interest in the person of rancher's daughter Pat Clark, portrayed by Frances Gladwin. The actress had already played the female lead (a different character altogether, by the name of "Beth Halliday") in this series' previous release, *Thundering Gun Slingers*, a factor that never seemed to bother producer Neufeld. Aside from the roles of Billy and Fuzzy, PRC's Billy the Kid/Billy Carson Westerns maintained a regular stock company of character actors who were routinely assigned to various roles throughout the series.

Variety's critic "Char." waxed uncharacteristically enthusiastic over *Frontier Outlaws*: "In other respects a very good Western, this one's value is enhanced markedly by its comedy, notably a courtroom scene that's of big-time caliber for laughs."

Valley of Vengeance (Vengeance)

A Producers Releasing Corp. Picture: 1944

Credits—Director: Sam Newfeld; Assistant Director: Melville De Lay; Producer: Sigmund Neufeld; Screenwriter: Joseph O'Donnell; Cinematographer: Jack Greenhalgh, Editor: Holbrook N. Todd; Special Effects: Ray Mercer; Running Time: 57 minutes.

Cast—Buster Crabbe (*Billy Carson*); Al "Fuzzy" St. John (*Fuzzy Jones*); Evelyn Finley (*Helen Miller*); Donald Mayo (*Young Billy*); David Polonsky (*Young Fuzzy*); Glenn Strange (*Marshal Baker*); Charles King (*Burke*); John Merton (*Kurt*); Lynton Brent (*David Carr, aka Andrew Carberry*); Jack Ingram (*King Brett*); Bud Osborne (*Dad Carson*); Nora Bush (*Ma Carson*); Steve Clark (*Happy*); Budd Buster, Hank Bell, John Elliott, Ben Corbett, Artie Ortego, Bob Cason, Tex Cooper, Wally West, George Morrell, Herman Hack, Buck Bucko, Pascale Perry, Morgan Flowers, Ray Henderson, Merrill McCormick, Tom Smith, Ray Jones.

For *Valley of Vengeance,* Joseph O'Donnell devised an original story and screenplay with an unusual angle (for the Billy Carson series), containing a flashback sequence in which Billy and Fuzzy are shown as childhood pals 20 years earlier. It seems that, as children, they were traveling West with their respective families when they were victimized by an attorney named Andrew Carberry (Lynton Brent), who fleeced the settlers of their land deeds before directing his gang to attack their wagons, killing the parents and leaving the two boys to be adopted by different families. Thus separated as children, Billy and Fuzzy are reunited by chance many years later. (Billy as a boy is portrayed by Donald Mayo, the orphaned child at the center of Buster's 1943 film *Queen of Broadway.*)

The main storyline of *Valley of Vengeance* centers on the efforts of Billy and Fuzzy to track down those responsible for their families' deaths so many years earlier. In so doing, they discover that the murderous Carberry is now known as Dave Carr, whose accidental killing leaves them to contend with an even more nefarious foe in town boss King Brett (Jack Ingram), whose secretary Helen (Evelyn Finley) aids them in their quest for justice.

Variety was less critical than usual of this entry in the Billy Carson series, labeling it "a fairly entertaining hoss opera." Calling the settings "better than average," they noted that "Buster Crabbe and Al 'Fuzzy' St. John, with the aid of a good supporting cast ... give neat performances."

The Contender

A Producers Releasing Corp. Picture: 1944

Credits—Director: Sam Newfield; Assistant Director: Melville De Lay; Producer: Bert Sternbach; Screenwriters: George Sayre, Jay Doten and Raymond Schrock; Cinematographer: Robert Cline; Editor: Holbrook N. Todd; Special Effects: Ray Mercer; Art Director: Paul Palmentola; Set Decorator: Elias H. Reif; Music: Albert Glasser and David Chudnow; Technical Advisor: Art Lasky; Running Time: 63 minutes.

Cast—Buster Crabbe (*Gary Farrell*); Arline Judge (*Linda Martin*); Julie Gibson (*Rita Langdon*); Donald Mayo (*Mickey Farrell*); Roland Drew (*Kip Morgan*); Milton Kibbee (*Pop Turner*); Glenn Strange (*Biff*); Sam Flint (*Commandant*); Duke York (*Bomber Brown*); George Turner (*Sparky*).

Shot under the working title *Ringside*, this modest boxing drama afforded Buster another opportunity to heal his saddle sores and exercise his acting muscles in a character rife with moods and temperament. He plays widower Gary Farrell, a truck driver whose efforts to give his son

The Contender. Roland Drew, Arline Judge, Donald Mayo, BC and Glenn Strange (PRC Pictures, 1944).

Mickey (Donald Mayo, who teamed with Buster in 1943's *Queen of Broadway*) a decent life involve an upscale military-school education that Gary can ill afford. To finance the boy's tuition, his father enters a boxing competition with the moral support of Pop Turner (Milton Kibbee), a former fight manager currently employed by Gary's trucking company.

At the same time, Gary becomes friends with sports reporter Linda Martin (Arline Judge), winning $500 in the boxing match. His success in the ring attracts the interest of manager Kip Morgan (Roland Drew), who contracts Gary for future fights. It also draws the attention of Rita Langdon (Julie Gibson), an opportunistic beauty who makes a play for the boxer.

Gary trains seriously and wins several matches, with only Bomber Brown (Duke York) remaining between him and the world champ. But Brown declines to fight Gary until Linda instigates a disagreement between the two that culminates in a ring challenge. Meanwhile, Gary indulges in undisciplined nights of alcoholic excess with Rita, who is also enjoying his expensive gifts.

Nevertheless, Gary defeats Brown in the ring. It's a victory that leads him to overconfident arrogance—and suspension by the boxing commission for his unprofessional behavior. After a bored Rita ends their relationship and Morgan dissolves their partnership, Linda tries to help Gary turn his life around by publicly criticizing him in her column. An unpleasant confrontation between the boxer and his little boy leads Gary to disappear for a while.

The friendless Gary now determines to fight his way back to the top. Employing a new name, he engages in a series of unsuccessful matches until he's finally tracked down by Linda, Kip and his old friend Biff (Glenn Strange), who find the remorseful Gary now welcoming their love and support.

Variety called Buster Crabbe "okay as the vacillating pug," but thought Sam Newfield's direction "generally hazy, with clips from actual fights awkwardly inserted into the continuity."

Fuzzy Settles Down

A Producers Releasing Corp. Picture: 1944

Credits—Director: Sam Newfield; Assistant Director; Melville De Lay; Producer: Sigmund Neufeld; Screenwriter: Louise Rousseau; Cinematographer: Jack Greenhalgh; Editor: Holbrook N. Todd; Special Effects: Ray Mercer; Set Decorator: George Milo; Running Time: 55 minutes.

Cast—Buster Crabbe (*Billy Carson*); Al "Fuzzy" St. John (*Fuzzy Jones*); Patti McCarty (*Edith Martin*); Charles King (*Lafe Barlow*); John Merton (*Pete*); Frank McCarroll (*Rusty*); Hal Price (*Sheriff*); John Elliott (*John Martin*); Ed Cassidy (*Weaver*); Robert Hill (*Jones*); Ted Mapes, Tex Palmer.

This time, the story's emphasis is on Fuzzy, which is not surprising, in light of the title. The "settling down" comes about when cowboys Billy and Fuzzy are rewarded for apprehending a team of bank robbers, and the latter acquires a town's newspaper by outbidding an outlaw contingent intent on silencing the crusading publication that had threatened their illegal activities. Indeed, that criminal faction was responsible for silencing the paper's previous editor, whose surviving daughter, Edith Martin (Patti McCarthy), becomes Fuzzy's partner in running the paper.

Billy and Fuzzy determine to see the paper continue the late newspaperman's law-and-order policies, and are warned by rancher Lafe Barlow (Charles King), the secret power behind the outlaws, that the publication's editorials might prove life-threatening.

Fuzzy's attacked by the outlaws, but Billy rescues him, only to have the novice newspaperman vanish again, this time with $10,000 belonging to the ranchers and meant for construction of a telegraph line. When the reappearing Fuzzy claims to have been kidnapped, with the money stolen, Barlow accuses him of robbery, and Fuzzy is arrested.

Billy rides out to Barlow's ranch to investigate, finds the stolen money, and convinces Barlow's gunman Pete (John Merton) to testify against his boss. A gunfight at the saloon results in the wounded Pete's shooting Barlow, leaving Fuzzy to run the newspaper with Edith. But Fuzzy really isn't cut out for "settling." At the story's fadeout, he's back on his horse and galloping off to catch up with the departing Billy.

Rustlers' Hideout

A Producers Releasing Corp. Picture: 1944

Credits—Director: Sam Newfield; Assistant Director: Melville De Lay; Producer: Sigmund Neufeld; Screenwriter: Joseph O'Donnell; Cinematographer: Jack Greenhalgh; Editor: Holbrook N. Todd; Special Effects: Ray Mercer; Running Time: 60 minutes.

Cast—Buster Crabbe (*Billy Carson*); Al "Fuzzy" St. John (*Fuzzy Jones*); Patti McCarty (*Barbara Crockett*); Charles King (*Buck Shaw*); John Merton (*Harry Stanton*); Terry Frost (*Jack Crockett*); Hal Price (*Dave Crockett*); Lane Chandler (*Hammond*); Al Ferguson (*Steve*); Frank McCarroll (*Squint*); Ed Cassidy (*Sheriff*); Bud Osborne, Wally West, Steve Clark, John Cason.

In a curious error of inconsistency, onscreen credits list the character played by Buster Crabbe as "Billy *Gibson*," although he's called "Billy Carson" in the movie's dialogue, as well as in its review in the trade paper *Variety*.

Cattle rustling is the focus of this entry in the series, as head wrangler Billy and sidekick Fuzzy lead a drive from Montana to Wyoming, a route frequented by rustlers. This yarn is set in the Wyoming community of Teton City, where the rustling is engineered by saloon keeper Buck Shaw (Charles King) and town banker Harry Stanton (John Merton), with the aid of Shaw's turncoat card dealer Hammond (Lane Chandler).

Plot twists find Billy falsely blamed for Hammond's murder, a master plan implemented by Shaw and Stanton to poison Billy's herd by contaminating a strategic waterhole—a move ultimately thwarted by the intervention of a Teton City businessman curiously named Dave Crockett (Hal Price).

In the words of *Variety*: "Stereotyped plot won't do much for this average mustanger. Buster Crabbe rides again to crab the act of the cattle pilferers."

Wild Horse Phantom

A Producers Releasing Corp. Picture: 1944

Credits—Director: Sam Newfield; Assistant Director: Harold E. Knox; Producer: Sigmund Neufeld; Screenwriter: George Milton; Cinematographer: Jack Greenhalgh; Editor: Holbrook N. Todd; Special Effects: Ray Mercer and Ray Smallwood; Art Director: Paul Palmentola; Running Time: 55 minutes.

Cast—Buster Crabbe (*Billy Carson*); Al "Fuzzy" St. John (*Fuzzy Jones*); Elaine Morey (*Marian Garnet*); Kermit Maynard (*Link Daggett*); Budd Buster (*Ed Garnet*); Hal Price (*Cliff Walters*); Robert Meredith (*Tom Hammond*); Frank Ellis (*Callen*); Frank McCarroll (*Mofett*); Bob Cason (*Lucas*); John Elliott, George Morrell, Jimmy Aubrey, Herman Hack.

When $50,000 is stolen from the Piedmont Bank, Marshal Billy Carson engineers the escape of jailed robber Link Daggett (Kermit Maynard) and his cohorts in the hopes that the escapees will lead them to the money. But things get complicated when model prisoner Tom Hammond (Robert Meredith) is forced to join the fugitives, and it's revealed that the stolen funds belonged to the local ranchers, jeopardizing their ability to pay their mortgages and retain their lands.

Billy tracks the Daggett gang to the Wild Horse Mine, where a proliferation of tunnels confuses Daggett's ability to retrieve the loot. Eventually, of course, the villains are either killed or captured, and the money located in time to meet the deadline for paying off those ranchers' mortgages.

Oath of Vengeance

A Producers Releasing Corp. Picture: 1944

Credits—Director: Sam Newfield; Assistant Director: Harold E. Knox; Producer: Sigmund Neufeld; Screenwriter: Fred Myton; Cinematographers: Robert Cline and

Ernest Smith; Editor: Holbrook N. Todd; Special Effects: Ray Mercer and Ray Small-wood; Art Directors: Paul Palmentola and Harry Reif; Running Time: 57 minutes.

Cast—Buster Crabbe (*Billy Carson*); Al "Fuzzy" St. John (*Fuzzy Jones*); Mady Laurence (*Dale Kirby*); Jack Ingram (*Steve Kinney*); Charles King (*Mort*); Marin Sais (*Ma*); Karl Hackett (*Dan Harper*); Kermit Maynard (*Red*); Hal Price, Frank Ellis, Wally West, Ray Henderson, Frank McCarroll, Buck Bucko, Herman Hack, Jack Evans, Jack Kinney, Hank Bell, Augie Gomez.

In an effort to give up the cowboy life, Fuzzy decides to run a general store in partnership with his buddy Billy Carson. In so doing, they find themselves caught up in a long-simmering feud between the local farmers and ranchers over the theft of cattle. The ranch owners have thus been forced to patronize moneylender Steve Kinney (Jack Ingram), the party secretly responsible for the rustling, along with his crony Mort (Charles King). Chief among the cattle owners is tough-minded Dale Kirby (Mady Laurence), who's instrumental in falsely blaming the farmers for the theft. Her adamant refusal to let Billy settle the feud prolongs animosities and nearly leads to all-out warfare before justice prevails.

Screenwriter Fred Myton solves the likely sedentary future of store-keeper Fuzzy by making him the romantic target of the town's matronly postmistress (Marin Sais), thus motivating his return to the itinerant life.

The Drifter

A Producers Releasing Corp. Picture: 1944

Credits—Director: Sam Newfield; Assistant Director: Melville De Lay; Producer: Sigmund Neufeld; Screenwriters: Patricia Harper and Oliver Drake; Cinematographer: Robert Cline; Editor: Holbrook N. Todd; Running Time: 61 minutes.

Cast—Buster Crabbe (*Billy Carson/Drifter Davis*); Al "Fuzzy" St. John (*Fuzzy Jones*); Carol Parker (*Sally Dawson*); Kermit Maynard (*Jack*); Jack Ingram (*Dirk Trent*); Roy Brent (*Sam*); George Chesebro (*Blackie*); Ray Bennett (*Simms*); Jimmy Aubrey (*Sheriff Perkins*); Slim Whitaker (*Marshal Hodges*); Wally West, Russell Hopton, Ann Brody, Ynez Seabury.

Once again, Buster did double-duty as both law-abiding Billy Carson and the less scrupulous Drifter Davis, a professional bank robber who masks his lawless side by performing as a sharpshooter in a traveling medicine show.

When Davis is caught robbing the Clinton National Bank, he's jailed by Sheriff Perkins (Jimmy Aubrey), who's surprised to encounter Billy the next day, mistaking him for an "escaped" Davis. The confusion is cleared up when the two men come face to face, giving Billy the notion to pose as Davis in order to clear his name and bring outlaw gang members to justice.

From here on, it's a continuing dramedy of errors and mistaken identities as Fuzzy sees a poster advertising Drifter Davis, thinks it's Billy using a "stage name," and goes to see him in person, only to be rebuffed by Billy, who doesn't want his cover blown.

Eventually, the thieving Davis is gunned down by his own cohort, gang leader Dirk Trent (Jack Ingram). Sharp-shooting Billy agrees to remain with the medicine show to help out its owner, Sally Dawson (Carol Parker).

By contemporary standards, the uncredited "special effects" that enable Buster Crabbe to share a film frame with himself looks rather crude, although the film's Billy Carson-Drifter Davis scenes must have confounded 1944 audiences.

Variety opined that "PRC, in trying to build up Buster Crabbe as a Western star, will have to furnish him with better material than this." And they further noted, "The mistaken identity angle has everyone confused—the audience included. Crabbe does the best he can with the stereotyped yarn."

The Drifter. BC and Al "Fuzzy" St. John (PRC Pictures, 1944).

His Brother's Ghost

A Producers Releasing Corp. Picture: 1945

Credits—Director: Sam Newfield; Assistant Director: Harold E. Knox; Producer: Sigmund Neufeld; Screenwriter: George Milton; Cinematographers: Jack Greenhalgh and Allyn C. Jones; Editor: Holbrook N. Todd; Special Effects: Ray Mercer and Ray Smallwood; Art Director: Paul Palmentola; Running Time: 60 minutes.

Cast—Buster Crabbe (*Billy Carson*); Al ""Fuzzy" St. John (*Andy Jones/Jonathan "Fuzzy" Q. Jones*); Charles King (*Thorne*); Karl Hackett (*Doc Packard*); Archie Hall (*Deputy Sheriff Bentley*); Roy Brent (*Yaeger*); Bud Osborne (*Magill*); Bob Cason (*Jarrett*); Frank McCarroll (*Madison*); George Morrell (*Foster*); Frank Ellis, Jimmy Aubrey, Carl Mathews, Ray Henderson, Rube Dalroy, Herman Hack, Charles Soldani, Art Dillard.

Not to be outdone, Al "Fuzzy" St. John here takes on a dual role of his own, doubling as both Jones brothers: Fuzzy (it seems that his formal name is "Jonathan"!) and his twin brother Andy, a well-to-do rancher. As can be expected, confusion and mistaken identities keep the plot spinning as an outlaw gang preys on sharecroppers, aided by Billy—and, eventually Fuzzy, after Andy dies from wounds incurred in a shootout with outlaw raiders.

In the movie's title role, Fuzzy impersonates the deceased Andy to terrify the gang members at their hideout. Amid much gun-slinging, Fuzzy (impersonating Andy) is almost forced into signing over his twin's property to the villainous rancher Thorne (Charles King) before Billy arrives in the nick of time, shooting Thorne. The sharecroppers round up the remainder of the gang, and Fuzzy, now elevated to Wolf Valley's judge and sheriff, restores law and order in the region.

Shadows of Death

A Producers Releasing Corp. Picture: 1945

Credits—Director: Sam Newfield; Assistant Director: Melville De Lay; Producer: Sigmund Neufeld; Screenwriter: Fred Myton; Cinematographers: Jack Greenhalgh and Ernest Smith; Editor: Holbrook N. Todd; Special Effects: Ray Mercer and Ray Smallwood; Art Director: Paul Palmentola; Running Time: 61 minutes.

Cast—Buster Crabbe (*Billy Carson*); Al "Fuzzy" St. John (*Fuzzy Q. Jones*); Dona Dax (*Babs Darcy*); Charles King (*Steve Landreau*); Karl Hackett (*Dave Hanley*); Edward Hall (*Clay Kincaid*); Frank Ellis (*Frisco*); Bob Cason (*Butch*); Emmett Lynn (*Bather*), Ed Peil, Sr., Frank McCarroll.

The fact that many of the same supporting players (i.e., Charles King, Karl Hackett, Kermit Maynard) constantly played different characters in this series apparently offered no problem to producer Sigmund Neufeld.

Nor, obviously, did the arbitrary plot turns that allowed co-star Al "Fuzzy" St. John various, changing professions, despite being cast always as a character by the name of "Fuzzy Jones." Here, Fuzzy is presented as no less than the sleepy town of Red Rock's combined marshal, dentist and justice of the peace!

Shadows of Death hinges on a railroad's plan to extend a line through a new area, threatening changes that inspire contention over land rights and ownership. At the same time, Marshal Fuzzy is angered by the town's new saloon owner (Charles King), who's intent on turning his establishment into a lucrative gambling house. And Fuzzy's pal Billy Carson, in Red Rock to locate a killer, almost finds himself in a romantic triangle when he's introduced to attractive rancher Babs Darcy (Dona Dax), to the annoyance of her long-time suitor Clay Kincaid (Edward Hall).

Action and intrigue fill out the hour-long proceedings before Billy eventually witnesses the marriage of Babs and Clay, officiated by Fuzzy.

Gangster's Den

A Producers Releasing Corp. Picture: 1945

Credits—Director: Sam Newfield; Assistant Director: Jack Vance; Producer: Sigmund Neufeld; Screenwriter: George Plympton; Cinematographers: Jack Greenhalgh and Ernest Smith; Editor: Holbrook N. Todd; Special Effects: Ray Mercer; Running Time: 60 minutes.

Cast—Buster Crabbe (*Billy Carson*); Al "Fuzzy" St. John (*Fuzzy Jones*); Sydney Logan (*Ruth Lane*); Charles King (*Butch*); Emmett Lynn (*Webb*); Kermit Maynard (*Curt*); Edward Cassidy (*Sheriff*); I. Stanford Jolley (*Horace Black*); George Chesebro (*Dent*); Karl Hackett (*Taylor*); Michael Owen (*Jimmy Lane*); Bob Cason (*Burk*); Wally West, Steve Clark, Frank McCarroll, George Kesterson, Horace B. Carpenter, Herman Hack.

Billy and Fuzzy are now owners of a gold mine who rally to the aid of neighboring rancher Ruth Lane (Sydney Logan) when she's menaced by two trespassers. It's suspected that the men were sent by lawyer Horace Black (I. Stanford Jolley), in an effort to drive Ruth and her brother Jimmy (Michael Owen) off their land. Black also makes a failed attempt to buy Billy and Fuzzy's mine, before directing his attention to acquiring the local saloon, beneath which reputedly lies the entrance to a once-prosperous mine. However, saloon owner Taylor (Karl Hackett) refuses to sell.

Black's opportunity arrives when Jimmy gets drunk, gambles away his money and asks him for the loan of $2,000, enabling Black to trick the young man into signing over his ranch (in place of the expected IOU). Black makes another try at getting Taylor to sell, but the latter again turns him down, while confessing to Fuzzy his fears of what Taylor might do next. Eager to leave town, Taylor agrees to sell his saloon to Fuzzy.

The plot thickens when those plans are overheard by Black's eavesdropping henchman Curt (Kermit Maynard), who's then directed to murder Taylor and ambush Fuzzy. Foiling that plan is Ruth, who fires at Curt and his men as they are about to attack, then rides off to alert Billy and Jimmy. After Taylor is murdered by one of Black's men, Black himself dies in a shootout, leaving Fuzzy with a saloon to run. But Fuzzy's had enough of big business, and turns over its operations to his cook Webb (Emmett Lynn).

As one might perceive from the plot description, Fuzzy figures more prominently in the proceedings this time than does Billy Carson.

Stagecoach Outlaws

A Producers Releasing Corp. Picture: 1945

Credits—Director: Sam Newfield; Assistant Director: William O'Connor; Producer: Sigmund Neufeld; Screenwriter: Fred Myton; Cinematographers: Jack Greenhalgh and Ernest Smith; Editor: Holbrook N. Todd; Special Effects: Ray Mercer; Running Time: 58 minutes.

Cast—Buster Crabbe (*Billy Carson*); Al "Fuzzy" St. John (*Fuzzy Jones*); Frances Gladwin (*Linda Bowen*); Ed Cassidy (*Jed Bowen*); I. Stanford Jolley (*Steve Kirby*); Kermit Maynard (*Vic Dawson*); Bob Cason (*Joe Slade*); Robert Kortman (*Matt Brawley*); Steve Clark (*Sheriff*); George Chesebro, Hank Bell, Wally West, Tex Cooper, Victor Cox, Herman Hack, Jimmy Aubrey, Ben Corbett.

The object of contention here is the Red River stagecoach line owned by Jed Bowen (Ed Cassidy), whose daughter Linda (Frances Gladwin) is a coach passenger saved from a kidnapping by cowpoke Billy Carson. Billy's then offered a job protecting the line, but elects to avoid the constrictions of regular employment. Saloonkeeper Steve Kirby (I. Stanford Jolley), the force behind the botched kidnapping, hopes to force Jed to sell for his own nefarious motives.

There's a mistaken-identity subplot involving Billy's old pal Fuzzy Jones, here portrayed as a dimwit charged with minding the local jail, and another in which Billy impersonates a Mexican. And, in a more successful kidnapping effort, Linda is taken hostage by Kirby henchmen Joe and Vic (Bob Cason, Kermit Maynard), but is later rescued by Fuzzy and Billy, who kills Kirby in a shootout. Billy, who seems destined never to get the girl, bids farewell to Jed and Linda, leaving Fuzzy to mind that jail.

Variety's critic "Sten." called *Stagecoach Outlaws* "an average oater," while further noting: "Sets seem to be wearing out. Maybe PRC ought to get some new ones, now that the war is over."

Border Badmen

A Producers Releasing Corp. Picture: 1945

Credits—Director: Sam Newfield; Assistant Director: William O'Connor; Producer: Sigmund Neufeld; Screenwriter: George Milton; Cinematographer: Jack Greenhalgh; Editor: Holbrook N. Todd; Special Effects: Ray Mercer; Music: Frank Sanucci; Running Time: 59 minutes.

Cast—Buster Crabbe (*Billy Carson*); Al "Fuzzy" St. John (*Fuzzy Q. Jones*); Lorraine Miller (*Helen Stockton*); Charles King (*Merritt*); Raphael Bennett (*Deputy Spencer*); Archie Hall (*Gillan*); Budd Buster (*Evans*); Marilyn Gladstone (*Roxie*); Marin Sais (*Mrs. Bentley*); Steve Clark (*Mayor Jed Bates*); Bud Osborne, John Cason, Robert Kortman, Frank Ellis, Ray Jones, Ray Henderson, Wally West.

Fuzzy's belief that he's to inherit money from a late cousin named Silas Stockton sends him and Billy to the town of Silver Creek—and a dizzying succession of dangerous escapades that begin with the cowboy pals' arrest for a murder of which they know nothing. The impending arrival of Stockton's niece Helen (Lorraine Miller) motivates the nefarious plans of five prominent townsmen who plot to gain control of Silver Creek by acquiring the Stockton fortune. To prevent Helen's getting her share of the estate, they formulate a scheme to kidnap her, hiring a woman named Roxie (Marilyn Gladstone) to impersonate her.

The plotting intricacies that ensue are to the credit of screenwriter George Milton, who collaborated inventively with director Sam Newfield to pack a breathtaking amount of action and story twists into less than an hour of continuity.

And yet *Variety* carped: "The most that can be said about *Border Badmen* is that it's just another low-budgeted Buster Crabbe Western, lacking originality."

Fighting Bill Carson

A Producers Releasing Corp. Picture: 1945

Credits—Director: Sam Newfield; Assistant Director: William O'Connor; Producer: Sigmund Neufeld; Screenwriter: Louise Rousseau; Cinematographer: Jack Greenhalgh; Editor: Holbrook N. Todd; Music: Frank Sanucci; Running Time: 54 minutes.

Cast—Buster Crabbe (*Billy Carson*); Al "Fuzzy" St. John (*Fuzzy Jones*); Kay Hughes (*Joanne Darcey*); I. Stanford Jolley (*Clay Allison*); Kermit Maynard (*Cass*); Bob Cason (*Joe*); John L. Buster (*Steve*); Bud Osborne (*Sheriff*); Wally West, Jimmy Aubrey, George Morrell, Ray Jones, Augie Gomez.

The movie's title is hard to explain, considering that protagonist Billy is never referred to as "Bill." Otherwise, this is a routine entry in the series, presenting its nominal hero as a justice-seeker whose pal Fuzzy is a store-keeper delegated to head the new Eureka town bank. Unknown to Fuzzy, his new teller Jeanne Darcey (Kay Hughes) is in cahoots with her prominent uncle, Clay Allison (I. Stanford Jolley), to rob the bank. She also warns him that Billy and Fuzzy are growing suspicious, and Clay orders his henchman Joe (Bob Cason) to "take care of" Billy. A gun battle ensues, and Billy manages to escape, overhearing a conversation linking Jeanne with Clay, and implicating them in the theft.

Finally, Billy overcomes Clay in a fistfight, and Jeanne begs the cowboy's forgiveness for her part in the robbery. But she pays for her sins by intercepting a bullet aimed at Billy by the outlaw Cass (Kermit Maynard), who is then shot down by Billy.

Prairie Rustlers

A Producers Releasing Corp. Picture: 1945

Credits—Director: Sam Newfield; Assistant Directors: William O'Connor and Stanley Neufeld; Screenwriter: Fred Myton; Cinematographers: Jack Greenhalgh and Roy Babbitt; Editor: Holbrook N. Todd; Special Effects: Ray Smallwood; Art Director: Edward C. Jewell; Music Director: Lee Zahler; Song: "It's Over and So Goodbye" by Lew Porter; Running Time: 56 minutes.

Cast—Buster Crabbe (*Billy Carson/Jim*); Al "Fuzzy" St. John (*Fuzzy Jones*); Evelyn Finley (*Helen Foster*); Karl Hackett (*Dan Foster*); I. Stanford Jolley (*Matt*); Bud Osborne (*Bart*); Kermit Maynard (*Vic*); Herman Hack, George Morrell, Tex Cooper, Dorothy Vernon, Tex Williams, Wally West, Ray Jones, John Cason.

In this entry in the Carson series, Buster gets to play not only Billy, but also his look-alike cousin Jim, the murderous leader of a gang of cattle rustlers. With Fuzzy now a café proprietor-cum-deputy sheriff who succeeds to the full position of sheriff when the town's present one is killed by the gang, the scene is set for a tale of lawlessness and a lot of mistaken identity, with more than the usual plot complications involving a cattle rancher named Helen Foster (Evelyn Finley).

Providing an extra challenge for the film's cameramen and editor, Fred Myton's script not only provides a scene in which the two Busters enter into hand-to-hand fisticuffs with one another, but another wherein the cousins exchange clothing.

Variety opined that *Prairie Rustlers* "provides everything that the outdoor film fan wants—plenty of chases, gunplay, mild humor and romance." And, it also noted, "Crabbe knocks himself out in a neat bit of trick photography."

Prairie Rustlers. BC beside himself in a dual role (PRC Pictures, 1945).

Lightning Raiders

A Producers Releasing Corp. Picture: 1946

Credits—Director: Sam Newfield; Assistant Directors: Lou Perloff and Stanley Neufeld; Producer: Sigmund Neufeld; Screenwriter: Elmer Clifton; Cinematographers: Jack Greenhalgh and Roy Babbitt; Editor: Holbrook N. Todd; Special Effects: Ray Mercer and Ray Smallwood; Art Director: Edward C. Jewell; Music: Lee Zahler; Running Time: 59 minutes.

Cast—Buster Crabbe (*Billy Carson*); Al "Fuzzy" St. John (*Fuzzy*); Mady Laurence (*Jane Wright*); Henry Hall (*Wright*); Steve Darrell (*Frank Hayden*); I. Stanford Jolley (*Kane*); Karl Hackett (*Murray*); Roy Brent (*Phillips*); Marin Sais (*Mrs. Murray*); Al Ferguson (*Lorrin*); John Cason.

Billy and Fuzzy try to solve the mystery of stagecoach robberies, the latest of which has targeted the U.S. mail, while overlooking a shipment of gold aboard the same coach. Tracking the thieves, the cowboy pals check out an old mining camp, where they're ambushed by bandits who attempt to burn the mailbag before escaping.

Elmer Clifton's rather simplistic plot now introduces a rancher couple named Murray (Karl Hackett and Marin Sais), owners of a mine whose ore has been downgraded by a phony assayer's report. Murray's on the verge of selling his mine to unscrupulous banker Frank Hayden (Steve Darrell), but Billy prevents his being victimized, pursuing his suspicions that Hayden has been intercepting assayer's reports from the mail, before altering them so that local miners would willingly undersell their property. Finally, Hayden's lawless machinations are uncovered and he is brought to justice.

While acknowledging that Crabbe and St. John had built up quite a following for themselves in this sort of vehicle, *Variety*'s critic called *Lightning Raiders* "a run-of-the-mill Western, but with enough action, gun fights and juvenile comedy to satisfy the customers who go for this type of thing."

Gentlemen with Guns

A Producers Releasing Corp. Picture: 1946

Credits—Director: Sam Newfield; Assistant Director: Stanley Neufeld; Producer: Sigmund Neufeld; Screenwriter: Fred Myton; Cinematographer: Jack Greenhalgh; Editor: Holbrook N. Todd; Special Effects: Ray Mercer and Ray Smallwood; Art Director: Edward C. Jewell; Music: Lee Zahler; Running Time: 53 minutes.

Cast—Buster Crabbe (*Billy Carson*); Al "Fuzzy" St John (*Fuzzy Q. Jones*); Patricia Knox (*Matilda Boggs*); Steve Darrell (*McAllister*); George Chesebro (*Slade*); Karl Hackett (*Justice of the Peace*); Budd Buster (*Sheriff*); Frank Ellis (*Cassady*).

Screenwriter Fred Myton here delivered an offbeat script that centers on Fuzzy, whose bumbling habits begin with burned biscuits and encompass a would-be mail-order bride named Matilda Boggs (Patricia Knox), who's not the woman she initially appears to be. But providing greater problems for Fuzzy is a rancher named McAllister (Steve Darrell), who wants to purchase his water rights and who'll stop at nothing to get what he wants.

Billy Carson gets involved when McAllister's men attempt to intimidate Fuzzy for not cooperating with their boss. The two pals manage to rout McAllister's hoodlums, but Fuzzy is later framed for "killing" the rancher's hireling Slade (George Chesebro), and he's arrested. Unknown to both Fuzzy and the sheriff, Slade only pretended to be dead.

Meanwhile, mail-order bride Matilda arrives, mistaking handsome Billy for her intended, the unprepossessing Fuzzy, who manages to escape from jail and explain his situation to her. She feigns sympathy for Fuzzy, while focused only on his money. Billy helps his buddy hide out from the sheriff's men. Meanwhile, Matilda plots with McAllister, hoping to wed Fuzzy for his property and sell it to McAllister after Fuzzy is hanged for murder. Billy has reason to distrust her, and determines to prevent the wedding, returning Fuzzy to jail. He then produces Slade, bringing him to town in time to prevent Fuzzy's lynching. Fuzzy celebrates his exoneration by beating up McAllister and buying everyone else a drink, while Matilda wisely leaves town on the next stagecoach.

In a very brief review, *Variety* credited Buster with making the most of his material, but noted, "Hasty takes and forced humor give the film a negative standing in the lowest category." Finally, *Gentlemen with Guns* was dismissed as a "hoss opry opus which even the kids will find hard to take."

Ghost of Hidden Valley

A Producers Releasing Corp. Picture: 1946

Credits—Director: Sam Newfield; Assistant Director: Stanley Neufeld; Producer: Sigmund Neufeld; Screenwriter: Ellen Coyle; Cinematographers: Art Reed and Ralph Ash; Editor: Holbrook N. Todd; Special Effects: Ray Mercer and Ray Smallwood; Art Director: Edward C. Jewell; Music: Lee Zahler; Running Time: 57 minutes.

Cast—Buster Crabbe (*Billy Carson*); Al "Fuzzy" St. John (*Fuzzy Q. Jones*); Jean Carlin (*Kaye*); John Meredith (*Henry Trenton*); Charles King (*Ed Dawson*); Jimmy Aubrey (*Tweedle*); Karl Hackett (*Jed*); John Cason (*Sweeney*); Silver Hart (*Stage Guard*); Zon Murray (*Arnold, aka Jim Slade*).

Cattle rustlers rely on the popular legend of a "ghost" haunting the late Dudley Trenton's abandoned Hidden Valley Ranch to mask their stolen herds from possible discovery. Billy and Fuzzy, old friends of Dudley, await the arrival of Henry Trenton (John Meredith), the British son and heir to the property, who is journeying from Oxford. Henry's met by Ed Dawson (Charles King), head of the rustlers, who seeks to protect his illegal activities by ridiculing the Englishman and goading him into a fight, in the hope of chasing him out of town.

Billy and Fuzzy intervene, escorting Henry and his butler Tweedle (Jimmy Aubrey) to the ranch, where they're welcomed by Dawson's niece Kaye (Jean Carlin), who is ignorant of her uncle's illegal activities. Meanwhile, Dawson's boss Arnold (Zon Murray) recommends that Dawson eliminate Henry, a suggestion that repulses Dawson, moving him to end his rustling operation.

Cattle tracks lead Billy and Fuzzy to realize that Hidden Valley Ranch has sheltered stolen herds, and Billy recognizes Arnold as a bad man once run out of Cheyenne by vigilantes. Escorting Kaye home, Henry is introduced to Dawson, whom he recognizes as the man who tried to scare him out of town. Kaye tells her uncle that she's in love with Henry, but is unable to prevent the Englishman from being attacked by the gang, who kidnap Henry and Billy.

Arnold tries to force Henry to sell him the ranch, while Dawson attempts to intervene, but is killed by Arnold. Fuzzy distracts the gang, while Billy helps Henry escape. Arnold then tries to frame Billy for Dawson's murder, but Billy succeeds in proving the real killer to be Arnold, whose real name is Jim Slade. With the rustlers apprehended, Henry and Kaye are free to face a future together at Hidden Valley Ranch.

Variety noted that "story, thesping, even settings, which are ordinarily a cinch for a passable rating in oaters, are all strictly second-rate."

Prairie Badmen

A Producers Releasing Corp. Picture: 1946

Credits—Director: Sam Newfield; Assistant Director: Stanley Neufeld; Producer: Sigmund Neufeld; Screenwriter: Fred Myton; Cinematographer: Robert Cline; Editor: Holbrook N. Todd; Special Effects: Ray Mercer; Music Director: Lee Zahler; Songs: "By the Camp Fire" and "Prairie Pete: The Bad Man" by Lew Porter; Running Time: 56 minutes.

Cast—Buster Crabbe (*Billy Carson*); Al "Fuzzy" St. John (*Fuzzy Jones*); Patricia Knox (*Linda Lattimer*); Charles King (*Cal*); Ed Cassidy (*Doc Lattimer*); Kermit Maynard (*Lon*); John Cason (*Steve*); Steve Clark (*Sheriff*); Frank Ellis (*Bill Thompson*); John L. Buster (*Don Lattimer*).

Centering on a cache of gold bars stolen years earlier from an express office, this entry in the Billy Carson series presents Fuzzy as the salesman for a traveling medicine show who tangles with an outlaw gang. Billy's a passing cowboy who rallies to the aid of show owners Doc Lattimer (Ed Cassidy) and his daughter Linda (Patricia Knox). It seems that Doc once knew a man named Thompson (Frank Ellis), who drew a map pinpointing where the gold is hidden. Since Doc was the last one to see Thompson alive, it's discovered that not only does he have that map, but he also knows the location of the gold—in an abandoned cabin. His son Don (John L. Buster) tries to convince Doc to retrieve the gold so that he can lead a better life; Linda believes that they should hand it over to the sheriff. When Don takes it upon himself to find the gold, he's followed by the outlaw gang and victimized. Billy and Fuzzy rally to his aid, overpowering the outlaws. Finally, Doc turns the long-hidden gold over to the sheriff, receiving an unexpected reward for his efforts.

Variety's critic, referring to the movie as a "routine potboiler," noted: "Fortunately, film doesn't have too much dialog to burden the ungifted cast, and Sam Newfield's well-oiled pacing hides a lot of basic deficiencies."

Terrors on Horseback

A Producers Releasing Corp. Picture: 1946

Credits—Director: Sam Newfield; Assistant Director: Stanley Neufeld; Producer: Sigmund Neufeld; Screenwriter: George Milton; Cinematographer: Jack Greenhalgh; Editor: Holbrook N. Todd; Special Effects: Ray Mercer; Music Director: Lee Zahler; Running Time: 55 minutes.

Cast—Buster Crabbe (*Billy Carson*); Al "Fuzzy" St. John (*Fuzzy Q. Jones*); Patti McCarty (*Roxy*); I. Stanford Jolley (*Grant Barlow*); Kermit Maynard (*Wagner*); Henry Hall (*Doc Jones*); Karl Hackett (*Ed Sperling*); Marin Sais (*Mrs. Bartlett*); Budd Buster (*Sheriff Bartlett*); Steve Darrell (*Jim Austin, aka Buck*); Steve Clark (*Cliff Adams*).

An urgent summons from his pal Fuzzy Jones brings Billy Carson to Canyon City, where he's surprised to find that Fuzzy merely wanted to introduce Billy to his niece Evelyn, scheduled to arrive on the noon coach. When they receive the shocking news that the stagecoach was attacked and robbed of $40,000, with all its passengers killed, Billy investigates. His findings include a .45 caliber pistol and the shell from a .38, while the badly wounded driver recalls that the gang leader was a tall man riding a pinto horse.

Terrors on Horseback. Al "Fuzzy" St. John and BC (PRC Pictures, 1946).

Their pursuit of justice takes Billy and Fuzzy to Pecos City, where they spot a saloon singer named Roxy (Patti McCarty) riding a pinto she rented from the stable of Ed Sperling (Karl Hackett). From this point on, it's a methodical but dangerous procedure of connecting the dots before justice finally triumphs.

Overland Riders

A Producers Releasing Corp. Picture: 1946

Credits—Director: Sam Newfield; Assistant Director: Stanley Neufeld; Producer: Sigmund Neufeld; Screenwriter: Ellen Coyle; Cinematographer: Jack Greenhalgh; Editor: Holbrook N. Todd; Special Effects: Ray Mercer; Music Director: Lee Zahler; Running Time: 52 minutes.

Cast—Buster Crabbe (*Billy Carson*); Al "Fuzzy" St. John; (*Fuzzy Jones*); Patti McCarty (*Jean Barkley*); Slim Whitaker (*Jeff Barkley*); Bud Osborne (*Sheriff*); Jack O'Shea (*Vic Landreau*); Frank Ellis (*Cherokee*); Al Ferguson (*Tug Wilson*); John L. Cason (*Hank Fowler*); George Chesebro (*Jim Rance*); Lane Bradford (*Cowboy*); Wally West.

After five years and some 36 films, Buster finally bade farewell to this long-running PRC Western series, although the earlier-made *Outlaws of the Plains* was actually the last Billy Carson picture to be *released*. Perhaps producer Sigmund Neufeld's writers were finding plot ideas too challenging for Billy and his pal Fuzzy, for there's little new about this one.

At the outset, robbers attack a stagecoach carrying Fuzzy and rancher's daughter Jean Barkley (Patti McCarty), and kill the driver. Billy's arrival on the scene prevents the actual robbery, although Fuzzy's presence on that stage is kept secret from Billy. Eventually, it turns out that Fuzzy was intent on buying land—as were several nefarious others—which might make them rich, as it is situated in a burgeoning railroad's right of way.

Here the chief villain is a supposedly upstanding citizen named Vic Landreau (Jack O'Shea), who's not only leader of the robber gang, but also intent on bringing financial ruin to not a few of his fellow townsmen for his own profit. He's also responsible for the murder of Jean's father Jeff (Slim Whitaker). Only the last-minute intervention of Billy prevents Jean's selling her ranch to Landreau, who's ultimately arrested with his henchmen.

Concerning his farewell to the Billy Carson series, Buster later recalled: "We started my last movie for PRC on Monday, and we had it in the can on Thursday! That's when I decided I'd had enough, and quit. I went in and told them I was through. The next thing I knew, they replaced me with Lash LaRue."

Swamp Fire

A Pine-Thomas Production, released by Paramount Pictures: 1946

Credits—Director: William H. Pine; Assistant Director: Harold Knox; Executive Producers: William H. Pine and William C. Thomas; Associate Producer: L. B. Merman; Screenwriter: Geoffrey Homes; Cinematographer: Fred Jackman, Jr.; Editors: Howard Smith and Henry Adams; Special Effects: Howard A. Anderson and Ray Smallwood; Art Director: F. Paul Sylos; Set Decorator: Louis Diage; Music Score: Rudy Schrager; Running Time: 69 minutes.

Cast—Johnny Weissmuller (*Johnny Duval*); Virginia Grey (*Janet Hilton*); Buster Crabbe (*Mike Kalavich*); Carol Thurston (*Toni Rousseau*); Pedro de Cordoba (*Tim Rousseau*); Marcelle Corday (*Grandmere Rousseau*); William Edmunds (*Emile Ledoux*); Edwin Maxwell (*Capt. Pierre Moise*); Pierre Watkin (*P.T. Hilton*); Charles Gordon (*Hal Payton*); Frank Fenton (*Capt. Pete Dailey*).

Before shooting his last two Tarzan pictures, Johnny Weissmuller took a rare break from 13 successive years as the famed jungle man to star in this

Swamp Fire. BC, Carol Thurston and Johnny Weissmuller (Paramount Pictures, 1946).

independent Pine-Thomas production for Paramount release. Billed third, after distaff star Virginia Grey, Buster may have been surprised to find himself again reporting to PRC studios, where this rural drama was shot, apart from location scenes filmed in the environs of New Orleans.

In the aftermath of his World War II service, Johnny Duval (Weissmuller) returns home to Louisiana's delta country to find that Cajun trapper Mike Kalavich (Crabbe) has been courting Johnny's sweetheart Toni Rousseau (Carol Thurston). But en route up the Mississippi, Johnny is befriended by Janet Hilton (Virginia Grey), a wealthy socialite who pursues him to the point of battling Toni for his affections. Johnny, meanwhile, encounters trouble with the combative Mike, with whom he refuses to fight.

On the eve of Johnny's marriage to Toni, her brother Tim (Pedro de Cordoba) is accidentally killed in a boat accident for which Johnny feels responsible, and he turns to drink. Injured in a traffic accident, Johnny is nursed back to health by Janet, who upbraids Toni and his bar-pilot boss Captain Moise (Edwin Maxwell) for inhibiting Johnny's future potential, refusing to let them visit him.

After his recovery, Janet secures Johnny a job with her father P.T. Hilton (Pierre Watkin), which brings him once again into contention with trapper Mike, who disdains Hilton's posted warnings. After Toni is caught illegally hunting, Johnny is accused of siding with the Hiltons against traditional bayou hunting-fishing rights, and he learns that Janet has deliberately sabotaged his relationship with Toni by intercepting her efforts to contact him.

Mike unsuccessfully tries to foment an uprising among the bayou trappers, setting a swamp fire that sends Toni to the Hiltons' island to warn Johnny. Mike shoots and wounds Toni, and is knocked out by Johnny, who rescues them both from the flames. After Toni recovers, Captain Moise hires Johnny as a tanker pilot.

Sporting a moustache, once again signifying his presence in a villainous role, Buster is most convincing with his Cajun accent. He would later identify Mike Kalavich as one of his favorite movie roles. *Variety* considered him here "a satisfactory villain."

Outlaws of the Plains

A Producers Releasing Corp. Picture: 1946

Credits—Director: Sam Newfield; Assistant Director: Stanley Neufeld; Producer: Sigmund Neufeld; Screenwriter: A. Fredric Evans; Story: Elmer Clifton; Cinematographer: Jack Greenhalgh; Editor: Holbrook N. Todd; Special Effects: Ray Mercer; Music Director: Lee Zahler; Running Time: 56 minutes.

Cast—Buster Crabbe (*Billy Carson*); Al "Fuzzy" St. John (*Fuzzy Q. Jones*); Charles King, Jr. (*Nord Finners*); Karl Hackett (*Reed*); Bud Osborne (*Sheriff*); John Cason (*Chief Standing Pine*); Patti McCarty, Jack O'Shea, Budd Buster, Roy Brent, Slim Whitaker.

Buster's last Billy Carson entry to be shown to the public was this September 1946 PRC release, which was actually completed in January of that year, prior to the already-seen *Overland Riders*. Perhaps producer Sigmund Neufeld considered this tale of widespread con-artistry a more fitting close to Buster's long-running Western series. Whatever the case, *Outlaws of the Plains* veers away from the usual Billy-Fuzzy storyline to focus on the latter's innocent gullibility.

Hearing a spirit voice claiming to be that of the late Chief Standing Pine, Fuzzy is directed to where he can expect to find a sizable vein of gold. Although he finds a few nuggets, Fuzzy's accused of trespassing by landowner Nord Finners (Charles King, Jr.), who offers to sell his claim for $50,000.

A further consultation with Standing Bear elicits the suggestion that Fuzzy also get his friends to invest in the claim—but not Billy Carson, whom the voice claims is "bad medicine." Behind all of this subterfuge is the ghostly voice of an outlaw Billy once ran out of Dodge City.

Billy's skepticism over Fuzzy's spirit-voice directives is verified when a rancher named Reed (Karl Hackett) is killed before he can reveal his knowledge of the deception. Finally, the Finners gang is exposed and the investors' funds recovered. The gold nuggets, it turns out, were merely a plant. And, although the townsfolk are disappointed in their dreams of riches, a railroad representative happens to arrive on the scene, offering $150,000 for the land.

Last of the Redmen (Last of the Redskins)

A Columbia Picture: 1947

Credits—Director: George Sherman; Assistant Directors: Leonard Shapiro and Mike Eason; Producer: Sam Katzman; Screenwriters: Herbert Dalmas and George H. Plympton; Based on *The Last of the Mohicans* by James Fenimore Cooper; Vitacolor Cinematographers: Ray Fernstrom and Ira H. Morgan; Editor: James Sweeney; Art Director: Paul Palmentola; Set Decorator: Sidney Clifford; Music: Mischa Bakaleinikoff; Running Time: 78 minutes.

Cast—Jon Hall (*Major Duncan Heywood*); Michael O'Shea (*Hawk-Eye*); Evelyn Ankers (*Alice Munro*); Julie Bishop (*Cora Munro*); Buster Crabbe (*Magua*); Rick Vallin (*Uncas*); Buzz Henry (*Davy Munro*); Guy Hedlund (*General Alexander Munro*); Frederick Worlock (*General Webb*); Emmett Vogan (*Bob Wheelwright*).

James Fenimore Cooper's 1826 novel had previously reached the American screen in a 1920 silent picture starring Wallace Beery and Barbara

Last of the Redmen. BC, Buzz Henry, Julie Bishop, Evelyn Ankers and Jon Hall (Columbia Pictures, 1947).

Bedford, under the direction of Maurice Tourneur and Clarence Brown. A 1936 talkie version with Randolph Scott and Binnie Barnes was directed by George B. Seitz. This 1947 remake, with its classic title somewhat altered ("They wouldn't let us use the name," explained Buster in a 1960s interview), was guided by Westerns specialist George Sherman and shot in the Vitacolor process, a cost-saver whose results were always most effective with outdoor scenery, such as the California locations where much of *Last of the Redmen* was filmed.

It's set during the French and Indian War of 1757 in upstate New York, where the British stationed at Fort Edward and Fort William Henry steel themselves against an expected attack from French forces and their Iroquois Indian allies from Canada. The Iroquois scout Magua (Buster Crabbe), who serves the British, informs Fort Edward's commander General Webb (Frederick Worlock) that he has seen Iroquois approaching the Fort, not from the north but from the south. Webb fears for the welfare of three incoming visitors, the two daughters and young son of Fort Henry's commander, General Alexander Munro (Guy Hedlund), who are under the escort of Major Duncan Heywood (Jon Hall). Despite the ongoing threat of an Iroquois attack, Alice and Cora Munro (Evelyn Ankers and Julie Bishop) arrive safely with their brother Davy (Buzz Henry).

The white scout Hawk-Eye (Michael O'Shea) informs Webb that Magua isn't to be trusted, and lied about the threat of attacking Indian forces. But Webb disregards the warning, dispatching his men to the south to stave off any possible French-and-Indian attack. And he arranges to have the three younger Munros join their father to the north at Fort Henry. At the same time, General Munro attempts to advise Webb that the Iroquois are north of Fort Edward, but his Indian runner is ambushed and slain en route.

Traveling northward with the Munro siblings, Heywood is unaware of the danger ahead, while Hawk-Eye and the Mohican chief Uncas (Rick Vallin) find the dead messenger, and seek to warn Heywood. When the two groups meet, Hawk-Eye is charged with safe delivery of the Munros, while Magua reveals his treacherous nature by abandoning the others during an Iroquois attack.

Heywood goes one-on-one with Magua, but is pursued by the Iroquois until rescued by the sharp-shooting Hawk-Eye, who maps out a plan to trap the Indians by first permitting them to kidnap Alice, Cora and Davy, before tracking them to Magua's village. There, Uncas informs the chief that the Munros are really *his* captives, taken from him by Magua.

While Davy creates a diversion with firecrackers, Hawk-Eye rescues Alice and Cora, heading for Fort Henry. On the way, they encounter General Munro, whose fort has been overtaken by the Iroquois. It's a reunion observed by Magua and his followers. However, Hawk-Eye helps prepare the British for the expected Indian attack by circling their wagons. In the ensuing battle, Magua is killed in hand-to-hand combat with Uncas, and reinforcements arrive to dispatch the Iroquois. Alice and Uncas are casualties of the conflict.

Reviewing this movie in *The New York Times*, Thomas M. Pryor noted that the adaptation was a very liberal one, concluding: "And don't be too harsh on the actors—they are really nice people, trying hard to make a living." *Variety* credited Buster Crabbe's treacherous Indian as the picture's most convincing of the three male leads.

Cooper's classic novel would later inspire an eight-part BBC-TV series in 1971, a 1985 TV-movie starring Steve Forrest, and a popular 1992 theatrical feature with Daniel Day-Lewis.

The Sea Hound

A Columbia serial: 1947

Chapter Titles: 1—"Captain Silver Sails Again"; 2—"Spanish Gold"; 3—"The Mystery of the Map"; 4—"Menaced by Ryaks"; 5—"Captain Silver's Strategy"; 6—"The Sea Hound at Bay"; 7—"Rand's Treachery"; 8—"In the Admiral's Lair"; 9—"On the Water Wheel"; 10— "On the Treasure Trail"; 11—"Sea Hound Attacked"; 12—"Dangerous Waters"; 13—"The Panther's Prey"; 14—"The Fatal Doublecross"; 15—"Captain Silver's Last Stand."

Credits—Directors: Walter B. Eason, Mack V. Wright and (uncredited) Sam Newfield; Producer: Sam Katzman; Screenwriters: George H. Plympton, Lewis Clay and Arthur Hoerl; Based on the radio program and comic book; Cinematographer: Ira H. Morgan; Editor: Earl Turner; Art Director: Paul Palmentola; Set Decorator: Sydney Moore; Music: Paul Sawtell; Stunt Double: Wally West; Shown in 15 chapters running approximately 20 minutes each.

Cast—Buster Crabbe (*Captain Silver*); Jimmy Lloyd (*Tex*); Pamela Blake (*Ann Whitney*); Ralph Hodges (*Jerry*); Robert Barron (*The Admiral*); Hugh Prosser (*Stanley*

The Sea Hound. BC and Pamela Blake (Columbia Pictures, 1947).

Rand); Rick Vallin (*Manila*); Jack Ingram (*Murdock*); Spencer Chan (*Kukai*); Milton Kibbee (*John Whitney*); Al Baffert (*Lon*); Stanley Blystone (*Black Mike*); Robert Duncan (*Sloan*); Pierce Lyden (*Vardman*); Rusty Westcoatt (*Singapore*).

After seven years of feature films, Buster returned to the serial form with this 15-episode adventure yarn. It would be the first of three chapter plays he would star in for Columbia Pictures that would mark the end of his reign as a serials king.

This serial takes its title from the schooner manned by Buster's Captain Silver, whose crew encompasses Tex (Jimmy Lloyd), young Jerry (Ralph Hodges), the scientist Kukai (Spencer Chan) and their canine mascot Flecha. When the *Sea Hound* receives a distress signal from the *Esmeralda*, a yacht owned by wealthy Stanley Rand (Hugh Prosser), Silver sails to his aid. In Typhoon Cove, he finds Rand, his sidekick Vardman (Pierce Lyden) and guest Ann Whitney (Pamela Blake) cornered by pirates employed by a seagoing master crook known as the Admiral (Robert Barron). After routing the predators, Silver and his crew learn that Rand and Ann were on the island to join Ann's father, who claimed to know the location of buried Spanish gold.

With Rand's old map to guide them, Silver's party searches the area's waters for a legendary sunken galleon. Silver locates a portion of the wreck, and discovers an empty treasure chest before learning that the wreck has been looted by the Ryak natives.

In port, Silver and his group are menaced by bullies, but protected by the Admiral, under the guise of friendship. The Admiral invites them inland to his rubber plantation, as his guests. But the situation becomes less amicable when the Admiral learns that Rand and Vardman had stolen a secret treasure map from Ann's father, who had then been captured by the Ryaks. Silver and his friends now find themselves prisoners of the Admiral's gang but put up a fight and manage to escape.

The Admiral's men steal aboard the *Sea Hound* that night, removing a copy of the map revealing the location of the Spanish gold. Rand and Vardman now switch loyalties from Silver to the Admiral, but are soon betrayed when the latter imprisons them for concealing details about the treasure. The Ryaks wage an attack, seizing Rand and Vardman.

Silver discovers that John Whitney (Milton Kibbee) has been located, and is being held prisoner aboard the Admiral's ship, the *Albatross*. Waging a one-man rescue mission, Silver succeeds in retrieving Ann's father, but with the Admiral's henchmen in full pursuit. In the jungle, where the Whitneys are reunited, Silver, Tex and Jerry join them in fighting the enemy before Ann and her father are caught by Vardman and Rand. In exchange for their capture, the treacherous pair are to share the treasure with the Admiral.

Whitney escapes while the Ryaks attack, making prisoners of Tex, Jerry and the Admiral. When the Admiral tries bargaining with the natives to save himself, he's killed in retaliation by one of his own men, who then jeopardizes the Ryak chief by taking him hostage. Silver rescues the Ryak leader, the Admiral's murderer falls to his death, and the natives express their gratitude by freeing Jerry and Tex. Silver is rewarded with the Spanish gold, and he and his friends are free to sail away on the *Sea Hound.*

Caged Fury

A Pine-Thomas Production, released by Paramount Pictures: 1948

Credits—Director: William Berke; Assistant Director: Howard B. Pine; Executive Producers: William H. Pine and William C. Thomas; Screenwriter: David Lang; Cinematographer: Ellis W. Carter; Editor: Howard Smith; Art Director: Lewis H. Creber; Set Decorator: Alfred Kegerris; Music: Harry Lubin; Running Time: 61 minutes.

Cast—Richard Denning (*Blaney Lewis*); Sheila Ryan (*Kit Warren*); Buster Crabbe (*Smiley*); Mary Beth Hughes (*Lola Tremaine*); Frank Wilcox (*Dan Corey*); Lane Chandler, Jackie the Lion.

Buster continued to alternate playing good guys with bad guys, returning to the Pine-Thomas unit for *Caged Fury.* Billed third after hero Richard Denning and heroine Sheila Ryan, he had here one of his best villain roles as an evil-minded circus clown, perversely named Smiley. Speaking of this aspect of his career in an early–'60s interview, the actor said, "I think the best work I've done in the films in the last 25 or 30 years I've been around have been the heavy and not the leading man, so to speak. It's much more interesting work. You don't have to worry about what the audience's reaction to your performance is going to be. The nastier you are, the better it is."

Caged Fury packs a lot of melodramatic action into its modest 61-minute length. It's set amid the Corey and Murray Circus, where Blaney (Richard Denning) and Smiley perform with the lions, as does the latter's girlfriend Lola (Mary Beth Hughes). When Blaney's girl Kit (Sheila Ryan) expresses an interest in joining the act, Smiley—who harbors a secret desire for her—encourages her, deliberately stirring up Lola's jealousy. At the same time, the act's star lion Sultan begins to cause trouble and Blaney tries to talk circus boss Dan Corey (Frank Wilcox) into firing the difficult Lola.

Smiley begins secretly tormenting Sultan, causing Lola's death when she's unable to escape the cat's fury during her act. It turns out that Smiley deliberately prevented her escape from the cage with a bolt he removed before its discovery by the coroner. After Lola's death is ruled an accident, Smiley helps engineer Kit's replacing her with the lions. It's a move that

Caged Fury. Sheila Ryan and BC (Paramount Pictures, 1948).

damages her relationship with Blaney, for her ambition to succeed in the circus act now takes precedence over her relationship with him.

Their cooler personal status pleases Smiley, who hopes to replace Blaney in Kit's affections. At the conclusion of their winter training session, Kit's ready to perform on their upcoming tour. Meanwhile, unknown to the others, Smiley continues to stir up trouble by dressing in Blaney's circus uniform and mercilessly teasing Sultan to incur the animal's hostility toward Blaney. But a guard witnesses Smiley's subterfuge and reports his discovery to Blaney and Dan.

As expected, Sultan turns on Blaney during the act, but Smiley's machinations backfire, and it's *he* who is injured. Blaney, who has reconciled with Kit, tells her of his suspicions about Smiley. After his recovery, Smiley returns to the lion act, now attempting to cause Kit's demise as he earlier had Lola's. Dan catches him tampering with the cage's mechanism, and Smiley kills Dan in retaliation, escaping in a car which then crashes.

At the circus, the now-married Kit and Blaney maintain the lion act as partners. An unexpected reappearance by Smiley, who had jumped from the doomed auto, brings things to a turbulent conclusion when an intense fight with Blaney results in a conflagration in the big tent. The lions go free, and justice triumphs when the tormented Sultan meets his tormentor, killing Smiley, while the beast is shot down by a circus guard. Blaney and Kit plan to reopen with new tents and animals.

Variety's critic "Brog." called *Caged Fury* "among the best, if not the best, of the [Pine-Thomas] thrillers..."

Captive Girl (Jungle Jim and the Captive Girl)

A Columbia Picture: 1950

Credits—Director: William Berke; Assistant Director: Paul Donnelly; Producer: Sam Katzman; Screenwriter: Carroll Young; Based on the Alex Raymond comic strip *Jungle Jim*; Sepia Cinematographer: Ira H. Morgan; Editor: Henry Batista; Art Director: Paul Palmentola; Set Decorator: James Crowe; Music: Mischa Bakaleinikoff; Running Time: 74 minutes.

Cast—Johnny Weissmuller (*Jungle Jim*); Buster Crabbe (*Barton*); Anita Lhoest (*Joan Martindale*); Rick Vallin (*Mahala*); John Dehner (*Hakim*); Rusty Westcoatt (*Silva*); Nelson Leigh (*Missionary*).

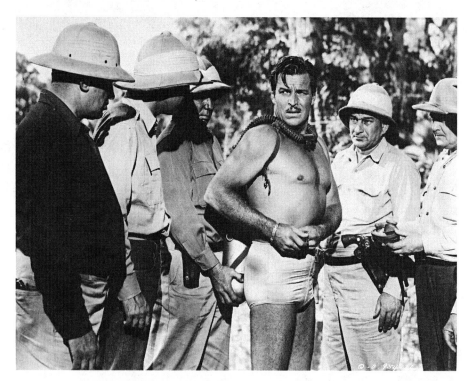

Captive Girl. BC as Barton (Columbia Pictures, 1950).

Columbia now had the bright idea of teaming Buster, their current serial star, with Johnny Weissmuller, their ongoing "Jungle Jim" series headliner. And to make it an aquatic trio, *Captive Girl*'s female lead went to a more recent champion swimmer, Anita Lhoest. And providing yet another degree of familiar separation, the *Jungle Jim* comic strip, like that of *Flash Gordon*, was the brainchild of artist Alex Raymond. Lest there be any doubt that *Captive Girl* was part of Weissmuller's series, the rest of the cast took supporting billing, Buster Crabbe included.

In a wild African setting, Jungle Jim (Weissmuller) is approached by Mahala (Rick Vallin), a tribal chief who had been studying abroad, to locate a white mystery woman reputed to live somewhere in the jungle with a tiger. She is said to have waged attacks on the tribe's medicine men, particularly Hakim (John Dehner), the head witch doctor. A missionary (Nelson Leigh) reasons that this woman could be the grown offspring of the Martindales, an archaeologist couple murdered years earlier while hunting for the legendary Lagoon of the Dead.

Hakim, who resents Mahala's return, had been subbing as the tribe's chief during his absence. It's no coincidence that, en route to the village, Mahala and Jim are unsuccessfully endangered by an avalanche caused by Hakim's men. At the village, Mahala is informed about the white woman, whom Hakim intends to track down and kill. Jim vows to find her before Hakim does.

While searching for the mystery woman, Jim meets the explorer Barton (Crabbe), who's intent on finding the Lagoon of the Dead and its jade and gold treasures. Jim also manages to evade several of Hakim's efforts to kill him, before he and Mahala track their quarry to a secret cave behind a waterfall. There they find old photos of the Martindales, proving the mystery woman to be their surviving daughter Joan, as well as evidence that it was Hakim who murdered them.

With Barton, Jim and Mahala locate a hidden passage linking the cave to the lagoon, where Barton and his men dive for treasured sacrificial relics. Meanwhile, Jim locates Joan (Anita Lhoest), saving her from death by quicksand. Hakim now consorts with Barton in a plot to massacre Jim, Mahala and Joan, who had witnessed her parents' killing.

Hakim attacks Jim, leaving him for dead as he prepares to sacrifice the captured Joan and Mahala to the gods of the lagoon. But a recovered Jim rallies the assistance of his animal friends, leading an attack in which Hakim and Barton are killed. Now in possession of the lagoon's treasure, Mahala plans to use it for the good of his village.

This was Buster's second and last screen-teaming with fellow swim champ—and movie Tarzan—Weissmuller.

Pirates of the High Seas

A Columbia serial: 1950

Chapter Titles: 1—"Mystery Mission"; 2—"Attacked by Pirates"; 3—"Dangerous Depths"; 4—"Blasted to Atoms"; 5—"The Missing Mate"; 6—"Secret of the Ivory Case"; 7—"Captured by Savages"; 8—"The Vanishing Music Box"; 9—"Booby Trap"; 10—"A Savage Snare"; 11—"Sinister Cavern"; 12—"Blast from the Depths"; 13—"Cave In"; 14—"Secret of the Music Box"; 15—"Diamonds from the Sea"

Credits—Directors: Spencer Gordon Bennet and Thomas Carr; Producer: Sam Katzman; Screenwriters: Joseph F. Poland, David Mathews, George H. Plympton and Charles R. Condon; Cinematographer: Ira H. Morgan; Editor: Earl Turner; Art Director: Paul Palmentola; Set Decorator: Sidney Clifford; Musical Director: Mischa Bakaleinikoff; Shown in 15 chapters running approximately 20 minutes each.

Cast—Buster Crabbe (*Jeff Drake*); Lois Hall (*Carol Walsh*); Tommy Farrell (*Kelly Walsh*); Gene Roth (*Frederick Whitlock*); Tristram Coffin (*Castell*); Neyle Morrow (*Kalana*); Stanley Price (*Lamar*); Hugh Prosser (*Roper*); Symona Boniface (*Lotus Lady*); William Fawcett (*Wharton*); Terry Frost (*Carter*); Lee Roberts (*Barker*); Rusty Westcoatt (*Adams*); Pierce Lyden (*Durk*); I. Stanford Jolley (*Turner*); Marshall Reed (*Shark*).

Pirates of the High Seas. Tristram Coffin, BC and Tommy Farrell (Columbia Pictures, 1950).

In his second of three serials for Columbia, Buster's once again the skipper of a ship, the *Viking*, sailing Pacific waters.

On the island of Taluha, Captain Jeff Drake rallies to the aid of Kelly Walsh (Tommy Farrell), a former Navy pal whose freighter has become the target of a pirate cruiser. Jeff's partners in seaboard adventure include Kelly's sister Carol (Lois Hall), Taluha's owner Frederick Whitlock (Gene Roth) and Castell (Tristram Coffin), who's tracking war criminals.

But nothing on Taluha is quite what it initially appears to be, and there follows a fast-mounting succession of unusual occurrences. Whitlock, it turns out, is a criminal mastermind and the man responsible for that pirate ship. On the other hand, Castell is himself a fugitive war criminal, hunting for a lost cache of sunken diamonds.

It takes some doing, amid 15 episodes of melodramatic escapades, but eventually Jeff, Carol and Kelly uncover the mystery surrounding the pirate ship, unmask the villains and retrieve the diamond treasure.

Marking the passage of time required to shoot a 300-minute serial, Buster's weight appears to fluctuate accordingly. In fact, he sometimes looks rather hefty here in his tight T-shirt.

King of the Congo (The Mighty Thunda)

A Columbia serial: 1952

Chapter Titles: 1—"Mission of Menace"; 2—"Red Shadows in the Jungle"; 3—"Into the Valley of Mist"; 4—"Thunda Meets His Match"; 5—"Thunda Turns the Tables"; 6—"Thunda's Desperate Chance"; 7—"Thunda Trapped"; 8—"Mission of Evil"; 9—"Menace of the Magnetic Rocks"; 10—"Lair of the Leopard"; 11—"An Ally from the Sky"; 12—"Riding Wild"; 13—"Savage Vengeance"; 14—"Judgment of the Jungle"

Credits—Directors: Spencer Gordon Bennet and Wallace A. Grissell; Assistant Director: Charles S. Gould; Producer: Sam Katzman; Screenwriters: George H. Plympton, Royal K. Cole and Arthur Hoerl; Based on the comic book *Thunda*; Cinematographer: William P. Whitley; Editor: Earl Turner; Music: Mischa Bakaleinikoff; Shown in 14 chapters running approximately 20 minutes each.

Cast—Buster Crabbe (*Thunda/Roger Drum*); Gloria Dea (*Pha*); Leonard Penn (*Boris*); Jack Ingram (*Clark*); Rusty Westcoatt (*Kor*); Nick Stuart (*Degar*); Rick Vallin (*Andreov*); Neyle Morrow (*Nahee*); Bart Davidson (*Alexis*); Alex Montoya (*Lipah*); Bernie Gozier (*Zahlia*); William Fawcett (*High Priest*); Lee Roberts (*Blake*); Frank Ellis (*Ivan*).

King of the Congo not only brought Buster Crabbe's illustrious serial-star career to a close, but made him the record-holder—with nine chapter-plays to his credit—of any sound-era male headliner in that field.

Here, Buster trades his customary sea captain's cap and T-shirt for a

King of the Congo. Gloria Dea and BC (Columbia Pictures, 1952).

jungle loincloth to portray Roger Drum, a U.S. Air Force captain who intercepts a mystery plane delivering secret microfilm to a subversive organization in Africa. Shooting down the aircraft, Drum takes on the dead pilot's identity, proceeding to the Dark Continent, where he crashlands in the jungle.

He's rescued from the wreckage by the Rock People and their leader, an exotic beauty named Pha (Gloria Dea), who are impressed by Drum's strength and dub him "Thunda, King of the Congo." The subversives, led by a man named Boris (Leonard Penn), attack the Rock People, under the impression that Thunda is their missing flier. Pursuant to his original mission, Thunda pretends to be their man, delivering the microfilm while thus incurring the hatred of Pha and the Rock People.

Placed in an awkward position, Thunda feigns allegiance to Boris and his group, while simultaneously rescuing Pha and her followers from the subversives' plot against them. Matters become even more involved when an aggressive tribe called the Cave Men come up against not only the Rock People, but also Boris's men.

Thunda learns that Boris is working to find a mineral deposit more powerful than uranium, and he's exposed as an impostor by a spy named

Alexis (Bart Davidson), who knows that Thunda wasn't the original micro-film messenger. Boris announces his intent to kill Thunda, but the pretender escapes, rejoining the Rock People.

From here on, it's a cliffhanging succession of challenging obstacles for Thunda, among them explosions, rockslides and predatory jungle beasts, to say nothing of the belligerent Cave Men. Eventually, the arrival of another Air Force officer, Lieutenant Blake (Lee Roberts), helps Thunda and the Rock People defeat the subversives. Fleeing for their lives, Alexis and Boris are killed by wild jungle denizens. Finally, Thunda and Pha witness a reconciliation between the Rock People and the Cave Men.

This last of Crabbe's nine serials foreshadowed the end of the chapterplay format altogether. Four years later, Columbia would mark the death of serials with a pair of inauspicious and now nearly forgotten 1956 entries, *Perils of the Wilderness* and *Blazing the Overland Trail*.

Gun Brothers

A Grand Production, released by United Artists: 1956

Credits—Director: Sidney Salkow; Screenwriters: Gerald Drayson Adams and Richard Schayer; Cinematographer: Kenneth Peach; Editor: Arthur Hilton; Art Director: Arthur Lonergan; Set Decorator: Herman N. Schoenbrun; Costumes: Einar Bourman; Music: Irving Gertz; Running Time: 79 minutes.

Cast—Buster Crabbe (*Chad Santee*); Neville Brand (*Jubal Santee*); Ann Robinson (*Rose Fargo*); James Seay (*Blackjack Silk*); Michael Ansara (*Shawnee Jack*); Walter Sande (*Yellowstone Kelly*); Lita Milan (*Meeteetse*); Roy Barcroft (*Sheriff Jorgen*); Slim Pickens (*Moose MacLain*); Dorothy Ford (*Molly MacLain*).

This Cain and Abel oater is set in 1877 in Wyoming's Jackson Hole territory, where a fellow named Chad Santee (Buster Crabbe) returns home after serving in the U.S. Cavalry, with plans to join his brother Jubal (Neville Brand), whom he believes to be a successful rancher. In reality, Jubal has become a stagecoach robber and cattle rustler, and bosses a tough gang of saddle tramps, led by a fellow called Shawnee Jack (Michael Ansara).

Sibling enmity soon arises when Jubal mistakenly assumes that brother Chad has informed the local sheriff (Roy Barcroft) about his lawless activities. However, it's when Shawnee Jack betrays Jubal to form his own gang that the brothers unite against him, fighting side by side until Jubal is killed in a gun battle. Chad is consoled by Rose Fargo (Ann Robinson), the dance hall singer with whom he's become romantically involved.

Variety praised Sidney Salkow's well-paced direction, opining that "Buster Crabbe and Neville Brand carry off the good and bad brother characters with all-around good performances."

Gun Brothers. BC and Ann Robinson (United Artists Pictures, 1956).

The Lawless Eighties

A Ventura Production, released by Republic Pictures: 1957

Credits—Director: Joseph Kane; Assistant Director: Virgil Hart; Producer: Rudy Ralston; Screenwriter: Kenneth Gamet; Based on the novel *Brother Van* by Alson Jesse Smith; Naturama Cinematographer: Jack Marta; Editor: Joseph Harrison; Art Director: Ralph Oberg; Set Decorator: John McCarthy, Jr.; Costumes: Alexis David-off; Music: Gerald Roberts; Running Time: 70 minutes.

Cast—Buster Crabbe (*Linc Prescott*); John Smith (*William Wesley Van Orsdel*, aka *"Brother Van"*); Marilyn Saris (*Lynn Sutter*); Ted de Corsia (*Grat Bandas*); Anthony Caruso (*Wolf*); John Doucette (*Art "Pig" Corbin*); Frank Ferguson (*Owen Sutter*); Sheila Bromley (*Myra Sutter*); Walter Reed (*Capt. Ellis North*); Robert "Buzz" Henry (*Little Wolf*); Will J. White (*Lieutenant Reed*); Bob Swan (*Loman*).

The initial focus here is on the awkwardly named William Wesley Van Orsdel (John Smith), a Bible-toting, circuit-riding missionary better known as "Brother Van," who arrives in the Deadwood Territory, where store-keeper Grat Bandas (Ted de Corsia) is plotting to start an Indian war. After Bandas' menacing henchman Corbin (John Doucette) nearly immolates

The Lawless Eighties. John Smith and BC (Republic Pictures, 1957).

captive Indian Little Wolf (Robert "Buzz" Henry), Brother Van rescues the Native American and is shot for his efforts. But he's aided by traveling gunslinger Linc Prescott (Buster Crabbe), who brings Van to the Sutter ranch, where his wounded arm is attended to by the rancher's daughter Lynn (Marilyn Saris).

Lynn takes a shine to Prescott, but is discouraged by his subsequent alliance to Bandas, who hires the unsuspecting loner for his dead-on marksmanship. Later, Prescott discovers the truth about Bandas' operations and attempts to leave his employ, only to tangle with his deadly henchmen.

Eventually, Prescott is wounded, but manages to elude the Bandas gang, which nearly lynches Indian chief Wolf (Anthony Caruso) before they're brought to justice by Prescott, Brother Van and the local cavalry. At the film's conclusion, Bandas and Corbin are killed, and Prescott appears ready to settle down with Lynn. As for Brother Van, he seems to have found a new ministry in Deadwood.

The Lawless Eighties, variously termed an "average oater" and an "okay action Western," is best appreciated today for its crisp, well-lit black-and white cinematography by Jack Marta.

Badman's Country

A Peerless Picture, released by Warner Bros.: 1958.

Credits—Director: Fred F. Sears; Assistant Director: Horace Hough; Producer: Robert E. Kent; Screenwriter: Orville H. Hampton; Cinematographer: Benjamin H. Kline; Editor: Grant Whytock; Special Effects: Henry Adams; Art Director: Gene Kelly; Set Decorator: Herman Schoenbrun; Music: Irving Gertz; Title Song: Robert E. Kent, sung by The Mellowmen; Wardrobe: Jack Masters; Running Time: 68 minutes.

Cast—George Montgomery (*Pat Garrett*); Neville Brand (*Butch Cassidy*); Buster Crabbe (*Wyatt Earp*); Karin Booth (*Lorna Farrell*); Gregory Walcott (*Bat Masterson*); Malcolm Atterbury (*Buffalo Bill Cody*); Russell Johnson (*Sundance*); Richard Devon (*Harvey Logan*); Morris Ankrum (*Mayor Coleman*); Dan Riss (*Marshall McAfee*); Lewis Martin, Steve Drexel, Fred Graham, John Harmon, Al Wyatt, Fred Krone, William Bryant, Jack Kenny, Tim Sullivan, Jack Carol, Leroy Johnson.

A standard Western programmer designed for the bottom half of a Warner Bros. double-bill, *Badman's Country*'s main focus of interest may well have been the celebrated historic names depicted by George Montgomery (Pat Garrett), Neville Brand (Butch Cassidy), Buster Crabbe (Wyatt Earp), Gregory Walcott (Bat Masterson), Malcolm Atterbury (Buffalo Bill Cody) and Russell Johnson (the Sundance Kid). And, if the onscreen exploits of this septet are of dubious historic accuracy here, then at least there's plenty to entertain the action-oriented Saturday-matinee crowd.

Orville H. Hampton's screenplay may initially sound derivative to fans of the Oscar-winning *High Noon*: Kansas lawman Garrett is about to retire his badge and settle down with his bride Lorna (Karin Booth) to a life of ranching. Little does he know that, outside of town, Butch Cassidy and his outlaw gang are about to stage a bank robbery that could net them half a million dollars. As in the Gary Cooper Western classic, our hero has problems winning the support of his townsmen, because of fear. Learning of the holdup plans, Garrett succeeds in getting support from legendary badge-wearers Earp, Masterson and Cody.

Following a ferocious shootout, Cassidy and his surviving gunmen surrender their weapons to the four law-keepers. Garrett's now free to face a new future with his bride in California.

Of the few trade papers that covered this one, *The Film Daily* called it "a satisfactory entry in its classification," while *Variety* noted, "The cast has been capably directed by the late Fred F. Sears."

Gunfighters of Abilene

A Vogue Picture, released by United Artists: 1960

Credits—Director: Edward L. Cahn; Producer: Robert E. Kent; Screenwriter: Orville H. Hampton; Cinematographer: Maury Gertsman; Editor: Edward Mann; Art Director: William Glasgow; Music: Paul Dunlap; Running Time: 67 minutes.

Gunfighters of Abilene. Judith Ames, BC and Barton MacLane (United Artists Pictures, 1960).

Cast—Buster Crabbe (*Kip Tanner*); Barton MacLane (*Seth Hainline*); Judith Ames (*Alice Hainline*); Arthur Space (*Rigley*); Eugenia Paul (*Raquel*); Russell Thorson (*Marshal Wilkinson*); Kenneth MacDonald (*Harker*); Richard Cutting (*Hendricks*); Richard Devon (*Marty Ruger*); Lee Farr (*Jud Hainline*); Jan Arvan (*Miguel*); Hank Patterson (*Andy Ferris*); Reed Howes (*Durwood*); Boyd "Red" Morgan (*Gene Tanner*).

Buster's last picture to feature his name atop the cast in a leading role was this routine B-Western, an unimportant United Artists release at the beginning of 1960. Courtesy of Orville H. Hampton, the screenwriter of the actor's previous feature (1958's *Badman's Country*), we're again in the setting of a Kansas town.

Buster's a professional gunslinger named Kip Tanner, who's summoned to Abilene by his brother Gene. But Gene seems to have disappeared from sight, and Kip learns that his missing sibling is also a prime suspect in the theft of $68,000 from area landowners. Seeking the truth of the situation, Kip comes up against Seth Hainline (Barton MacLane), a wealthy rancher whose daughter Alice (Judith Ames) had been about to marry Gene— against her father's wishes.

In time, Kip discovers that Gene was killed by Seth, both to prevent the marriage and to grab Gene's land for himself. In an effort to trap Kip, Seth mistakenly kills his own son Jud (Lee Farr). A climactic gunfight ends in Seth's demise, leaving Kip to claim his brother's ranch, as well as the beautiful Alice.

Variety's critic observed that "Buster Crabbe proves he has vim and vigor yet."

The Bounty Killer

A Premiere Production, released by Embassy Pictures: 1965

Credits—Director: Spencer Gordon Bennet; Assistant Director: Clark Paylow; Executive Producer: Pat B. Rooney; Producer: Alex Gordon; Screenwriters: Ruth Alexander and Leo Gordon; Technicolor-Techniscope Cinematographer: Frederick E. West; Editor: Ronald Sinclair; Art Director: Don Ament; Music: Ronald Stein; Running Time: 92 minutes.

Cast—Dan Duryea (*Willie Duggan*); Audrey Dalton (*Carole Ridgeway*); Fuzzy Knight (*Luther*); Rod Cameron (*Johnny Liam*); Richard Arlen (*Ridgeway*); Buster Crabbe (*Mike Clayman*); Johnny Mack Brown (*Sheriff Green*); Bob Steele (*Red*); Bronco Billy Anderson (*Man in Cantina*); Peter Duryea (*Young Bounty Hunter*); Grady Sutton (*Preacher*); John Reach (*Jeb*); Eddie Quillan (*Pianist*); Norman Willis (*Hank*); Edmund Cobb (*Townsman*); Duane Ament (*Ben Liam*); Emory Parnell (*Sam*); Daniel J. White (*Marshal Davis*); I. Stanford Jolley (*Sheriff Jones*); Red Morgan (*Seddon*); Dolores Domasin (*Waitress*); Dudley Ross (*Indian*); Ronn Delanor (*Joe*); Tom Kennedy (*Waiter*).

Like the 1960s Westerns economically produced by Paramount's A. C. Lyles, this outdoor programmer offers an array of sagebrush-associated actors whose careers had seen better days in earlier decades.

In the leading role, Dan Duryea plays Willie Duggan, a mild-mannered tenderfoot from the East who has gone West seeking his fortune. But Willie learns some fast lessons when he tries to save saloon girl Carole Ridgeway (Audrey Dalton) from the pawings of a drunken miner. It's an act that draws the attention of gunslinger Johnny Liam (Rod Cameron), who informs him about the local law of the gun.

Employed as a payroll guard, Willie's forced to kill an outlaw when he and his partner Luther (Fuzzy Knight) are ambushed. After collecting the bounty on that outlaw's head, Willie and Luther determine to become professional bounty hunters, although idealistic Willie wants only to capture them alive. Their first catch: a notorious outlaw named Mike Clayman (Buster Crabbe), who gets rescued by a colleague and kills Luther.

Abandoned to die in the desert, Willie is saved by Carole's father (Richard Arlen) and nursed back to health at the Ridgeway ranch. Willie, embittered by his pal's death, sets out to track Clayman with a sawed-off shotgun, earning himself a new reputation as a ruthless bounty hunter. Both Liam and Clayman are among his victims.

Willie accidentally kills an innocent churchgoer, and finds himself a hunted man with a price on his head. En route to the border with Carole, he's shot down by a younger bounty hunter (uncredited Peter Duryea, the star's son).

Leonard Maltin's Movie Guide (2006) records this one's chief interest being its "cast of old timers from Hollywood Westerns," citing it as "Interesting on all counts" for being "adult, low key and minus a happy ending."

Arizona Raiders

An Admiral Picture, released by Columbia Pictures; 1965

Credits—Director: William Witney; Assistant Director: Jack Lacey; Producer: Grant Whytock; Screenwriters: Alex Gottlieb, Mary Willingham and Willard Willingham; Story: Frank Gruber and Richard Schayer; Eastmancolor-Techniscope Cinematographer: Jacques Marquette; Editor: Grant Whytock; Art Director: Paul Sylos, Jr.; Set Decorator: Harry Reif; Music: Richard La Salle; Costumes: Joseph Dimmitt; Running Time: 88 minutes.

Cast—Audie Murphy (*Clint Bonner*); Michael Dante (*Brady*); Ben Cooper (*Willie Martin*); Buster Crabbe (*Captain Andrews*); Gloria Talbott (*Martina*); Ray Stricklyn (*Danny Bonner*); George Keymas (*Montana*); Fred Krone (*Matt Edwards*); Willard Willingham (*Eddie*); Red Morgan (*Tex*); Fred Graham (*Quantrill*).

Arizona Raiders. **Audie Murphy and BC (Columbia Pictures, 1965).**

For his second 1965 Western feature, Buster now rose to fourth billing in this Audie Murphy vehicle for Columbia Pictures. Murphy plays a Confederate Army hero named Clint Bonner who has turned guerilla and joined Quantrill's Raiders when his folks are killed by carpetbaggers. After the death of Quantrill (Fred Graham), Clint and his buddy Willie Martin (Ben Cooper) are captured by Union soldiers under the command of Captain Andrews (Buster Crabbe), and are sentenced to 20 years at hard labor. Andrews is later named to head the newly formed Arizona Rangers in tracking down a band of former Quantrill killers, who attacked a peaceful Yaqui Indian village and kidnapped the chief's daughter Martina (Gloria Talbott).

Andrews arranges for the "escape" of Clint and Willie, with a promise of unconditional pardon, if they'll help him round up the outlaws. Because he wants revenge on Montana (George Keymas), an old enemy who now commands the Raiders, Clint agrees. Tracking Montana to the Indian village, Clint kills him, but decides to abandon plans for a border-crossing escape when he learns that the bandits have killed both his younger brother Danny (Ray Stricklyn) and Willie.

Clint returns to join forces with Captain Andrews and a number of

Yaqui braves to rescue Martina and destroy what remains of the outlaw gang. He can now look forward to a career with the Arizona Rangers.

Critics found this a competently made Audie Murphy Western, well-paced by the veteran serial director William Witney (*Spy Smasher, Perils of Nyoka*). *Variety* tabbed Buster's performance "convincing."

The Comeback Trail

A Dynamite Entertainment–Rearguard Production: 1982 (Completed in 1971)

Credits—Director-Producer-Screenwriter-Editor: Harry Hurwitz; Executive Producer: Max J. Rosenberg; Story: Roy Frumkes, Robert J. Winston and Hurwitz; Additional Material: Chuck McCann, Robert Staats, Irwin Corey and Henny Youngman; Deluxe Color Cinematographers: Victor Petrashevitz and Joao Fernandes; Music: Igo Kantor; Production Coordinator: David Wolfson; Running Time: 80 minutes.

Cast—Chuck McCann (*Enrico Kodak*); Buster Crabbe (*Duke Montana*); Robert Staats (*E. Eddie Eastman*); Ina Balin (*Julie Thomas*); Jara Kahout (*German Director*); Henny Youngman, Prof. Irwin Corey, Hugh Hefner, Joe Franklin, Monti Rock III, Lenny Schultz, Mike Gentry.

The Comeback Trail. BC as Duke Montana (Rearguard Productions, 1971/1986).

Somewhat reminiscent of Mel Brooks' classic 1968 screen comedy *The Producers*, this improvisational feature focuses on a low-budget, exploitation-type moviemaker with the bizarre name of Enrico Kodak (Chuck McCann), who endeavors to rescue his Adequate Studios by producing a surefire flop. Buster plays an over-the-hill cowboy star, Duke Montana, whom they cast in the movie's strenuous leading role, with the hope that he'll succumb on the job, thus rewarding their efforts with a big insurance claim.

But, of course, nothing goes as planned: The has-been star reports to work looking fitter than ever, moving co-producers Kodak and Eastman (Robert Staats) to embark on a series of fruitless murder attempts to reach their dark-hearted goal. *The Comeback Trail* ends with Montana's career completely resuscitated, while Eastman and Kodak now work as the star's household help.

Following on the heels of producer-director-writer Harry Hurwitz's 1971 nostalgic comedy *The Projectionist*, this improvisational screen farce began shooting in Santa Fe in late 1970, before moving on to New York, where part of the episodic plot involves an attempt to film a Western in Central Park. In a 1977 interview with John C. Tibbetts, Buster spoke about *The Comeback Trail* with fondness: "Usually I don't like myself much on the screen. But this film was different."

In June of 1982, *The Comeback Trail* enjoyed a belated but brief engagement at New York's Thalia theatre; *Variety*'s critic wrote, "Final product is a series of disjointed episodes, with internal evidence of off-and-on tinkering reflecting a troubled shooting history." Speaking of Buster, he said, "One quickly begins to feel sorry for him, having been involved in such a tacky comeback."

In *The New York Times*, critic Janet Maslin wrote: "The best thing in *The Comeback Trail* is the swimming star Buster Crabbe, who looks trim, dives gracefully and speaks in a mellifluous voice not unlike President Reagan's. He's not on screen for long, though, and the rest of the movie is all wet."

The Alien Dead (It Fell from the Sky)

A Firebird Pictures Production, released on video: 1985 (Filmed in 1980)

Credits—Director: Fred Olen Ray; Executive Producer: Henry Kaplan; Producers: Fred Olen Ray and Chuck Sumner; Associate Producer: Shelley Youngren; Screenwriters: Martin Alan Nicholas and Fred Olen Ray; Color Cinematographers: Gary Singer, Peter Gamba and Fred Olen Ray; Editor: Mark Barrett; Music: Franklin Sledge and Chuck Sumner; Running Time: 73 minutes.

Cast—Buster Crabbe (*Sheriff Kowalski*); Ray Roberts (*Tom Corman*); Linda Lewis (*Shawn Michaels*); George Kelsey (*Emmett Michaels*); Mike Bonavia (*Miller Haze*); Dennis Underwood (*Deputy Campbell*); Martin Alan Nicholas, Norman Riggins, Edi Stroup, John Leirier, Rich Vogan, Shelley Youngren, Fred Olen Ray, Elena Contello, Nancy Karnz.

It took five years for this Florida-made 1980 quickie to be seen—when it finally went directly to video. Filmed when he was 70, this final Buster Crabbe feature paid the actor a mere $2,000, a third less than his salary for 1945's PRC Western *Prairie Rustlers*. And it does afford him top billing over a "no names" cast, thanks to longtime Crabbe fan Fred Olen Ray, who directed and co-produced before moving on to Hollywood—and somewhat bigger budgets.

Perhaps inspired by the surprising success of the Pittsburgh-made cult favorite *Night of the Living Dead*, this lurid little thriller centers on a group of young people who become bloodthirsty monsters after their boat is struck by a meteorite. Their subsequent murderous attacks on Florida swamp dwellers is at first attributed by Sheriff Kowalski (Crabbe) to an alligator. A reward is announced for the apprehension of such a beast, which attracts an offbeat assortment of would-be bounty hunters. But it takes the combined efforts of game warden Miller Haze (Mike Bonavia) and newspaper reporter Tom Corman (Ray Roberts) to ferret out the real source of the problem and contend with the creatures.

Reviewing the video cassette, *Variety*'s critic dubbed it "an amateurish monster film."

Swim Team

A Filmtel Ltd. Production, released on video by Prism Entertainment: 1987 (Filmed in 1979)

Credits—Director-Producer-Screenwriter: James Polakof; Executive Producer: Beverley Johnson; Color Cinematographer: Don Cirillo; Editor: Richard Chase; Music: Bogas and Munsen Productions; Running Time: 81 minutes.

Cast—James Daughton (*Danny*); Stephen "Flounder" Furst (*Bear*); Richard Young (*Johnny*); Jenny Neumann (*Erin*); Kim Day (*Debbie*); Buster Crabbe (*Rock Sands*); Elise-Anne (*Bobbie*); Stan Taff (*Shawn*); Gunilla Hutton (*Suzanne*); Pam Demarche (*Samantha*); Mickey Newbury (*Deputy Webb*); Jim Yallaly (*Chris*); Guy Fitch (*Mr. Ouch*); Joey Bartholomew (*Dirty Harry*).

It's not difficult to understand why *Swim Team* failed to find a theatrical release at the time of its production in 1979. Had it been more intelligently written and produced, this episodic story of a group of privileged, party-loving Florida teens realizing a more productive, goal-related lifestyle under the guidance of a taskmaster swimming coach, could have qualified as a Disney film. But not with this one's four-letter language and sexually suggestive situations.

In fact, there's little to sustain viewer interest in *Swim Team*'s plotless development, with leading characters and limp narrative elements occasionally hinting at relationships that ultimately go nowhere.

"Special guest star" Buster Crabbe's brief, completely gratuitous, eleventh-hour appearance as a visiting celebrity named "Rock Sands"— barely recognizable behind a mustache and dark glasses—adds no luster to the movie whatsoever, and only raises the question, "What was *that* all about?"

Eight years after completing the yet-to-be-released *Comeback Trail*, Buster made an inauspicious token return in this little-known pseudo-comedy. Shot prior to his final movie, *The Alien Dead*, it would nevertheless become the last Crabbe picture to reach the public when Prism Entertainment finally brought it out on video in 1987.

Bibliography

Barbour, Alan G. *Cliffhanger*. New York: A&W Publishers, 1977.
_____. *Days of Thrills and Adventure*. New York: Macmillan, 1970.
Cline, William C. *In the Nick of Time: Motion Picture Sound Serials*. Jefferson, NC: McFarland, 1984.
Cutter, Robert Arthur. "Flash Gordon Lives, But Up in Rye?" *After Dark*, February 1972.
Dixon, Wheeler. *Producers Releasing Corporation*. Jefferson, NC: McFarland, 1986.
Donati, William. *Ida Lupino: A Biography*. Lexington: The University Press of Kentucky, 1996.
Fetrow, Alan G. *Feature Films, 1950–1959*. Jefferson, NC: McFarland, 1999.
Frumkes, Roy. "Vivid Memories of Buster." *Films in Review*, July/August 1996.
Hanson, Patricia King (executive editor). *The American Film Institute Catalog: Feature Films, 1931–1940*. Berkeley: University of California Press, 1993.
_____ (executive editor). *The American Film Institute Catalog: Feature Films, 1941–1950*. Berkeley: University of California Press, 1999.
Hardy, Phil. *The Overlook Film Encyclopedia: The Gangster Film*. Woodstock, NY: The Overlook Press, 1998.
_____. *The Overlook Film Encyclopedia: Science Fiction*. Woodstock, NY: The Overlook Press, 1995.
_____. *The Overlook Film Encyclopedia: The Western*. Woodstock, NY: The Overlook Press, 1995.
Kinnard, Roy. *Science Fiction Serials*. Jefferson, NC: McFarland, 1998.
Lamparski, Richard. *Whatever Became of... (8th Edition)*. New York: Crown, 1982.
Lentz, Harris M., III. *Feature Films, 1960–1969*. Jefferson, NC: McFarland, 2001.
Maltin, Leonard (editor). *Leonard Maltin's Movie Encyclopedia*. New York: Penguin Group, 1994.
_____ (editor). *Leonard Maltin's Movie Guide (2006 Edition)*. New York: Penguin Group, 2005.
Miller, Don. *"B" Movies: An Informal Survey of the American Low-Budget Film, 1933–1945*. New York: Curtis Books, 1973.
_____. *Hollywood Corral*. New York: Popular Library, 1976.
Munden, Kenneth W. (executive editor). *The American Film Institute Catalog: Feature Films 1921–1930*. New York: R. R. Bowker, 1971.
Novak, Ralph. "Buster Crabbe, Conqueror of Ming the Merciless and Sundry Other Villains, Challenges Father Time." *People*, August 2, 1976.

Quinlan, David. *Quinlan's Film Stars (5th Edition)*. Washington, D.C.: Brassey's, 2000.

Schutz, Wayne. *The Motion Picture Serial: An Annotated Bibliography*. Metuchen, NJ: Scarecrow Press, 1992.

Shay, Don, and Ray Cabana, Jr. "*Kaleidoscope* Interviews Buster Crabbe." *Kaleidoscope* Vol. 2, No. 2, 1966.

Stedman, Raymond William. *The Serials*. Norman: University of Oklahoma Press, 1971.

Tibbetts, John C. "Man in Motion: An Interview with Buster Crabbe." *Films in Review*, July/August 1996.

Weiss, Ken, and Ed Goodgold. *To Be Continued...* New York: Crown, 1972.

Whitezel, Karl. *Buster Crabbe: A Self Portrait*. Tukwilla, WA: Karl Whitezel, 1997.

Index

Numbers in *bold italics* refer to pages with photographs.

195